This book is part of the Allyn and Bacon Series in Creative Teaching. The books in this series are:

I

Setting Conditions for Creative Teaching in the Elementary School
James A. Smith

II

*Creative Teaching of the Language Arts
in the Elementary School*
James A. Smith

III

*Creative Teaching of Reading and Literature
in the Elementary School*
James A. Smith

IV

*Creative Teaching of the Creative Arts
in the Elementary School*
James A. Smith

V

*Creative Teaching of the Social Studies
in the Elementary School*
James A. Smith

VI

*Creative Teaching of Mathematics
in the Elementary School*
Alvin M. Westcott and James A. Smith

VII

*Creative Teaching of Science
in the Elementary School*
Albert Piltz and Robert Sund

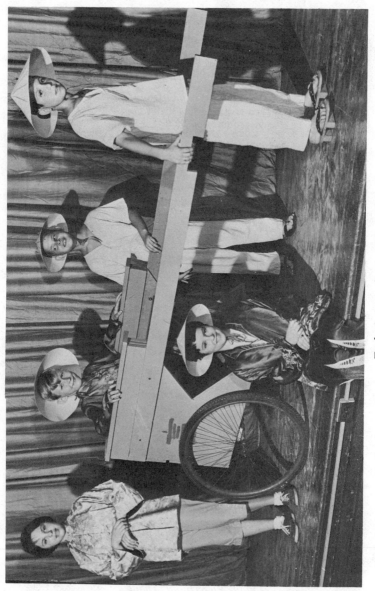

. . . To be is to understand. . . .

Creative Teaching of the Social Studies

in the Elementary School

James A. Smith
State University of New York at Oswego

foreword by E. Paul Torrance
University of Georgia

ALLYN AND BACON, INC.
BOSTON, LONDON, SYDNEY, TORONTO

Library of Congress Catalog Card Number: 67-11937

PRINTED IN THE UNITED STATES OF AMERICA

ISBN: 0-205-00089-4

Fourteenth printing . . . December, 1976

to Susan

Foreword

Many exciting, potentially powerful, and valid educational ideas have gone unused or have been forgotten altogether because no one has translated them into practical methods, instructional materials, textbooks, and the like. The idea of creative teaching has been among them. Creativity has been a persistent and recurrent issue throughout the history of education. Actually, the idea of creative ways of teaching has never had a very good chance to prove its worth. Teachers and educational leaders have continually struggled to understand the nature of creative functioning, the conditions that facilitate and inhibit creative growth, and the means of rewarding creative achievement. Bit by bit, advances have been made, and in recent years efforts to add to this kind of knowledge through research and experimentation have been accelerated. We need to know a great deal more than we do, but in my opinion we have made enough advances to make possible a more creative kind of education than has been known up to now. This is why imaginative, informed, and hard-working translators and creative synthesizers like Professor James A. Smith and his associates, who have created this series of books on setting the conditions for creative teaching and learning, are such a welcome asset to the educational enterprise.

The task of retooling—inventing and testing methods, creating tests and instructional materials, devising evaluation procedures and creating textbooks and methods of teacher education—for any new educational idea is enormous. It takes tremendous energy, creativity, courage, commitment, and willingness to risk on the part of many people. The inauguration of this series of books on creative teaching is a major venture for Professor Smith, his associates, and Allyn and Bacon. In the past, the adoption of new and improved educational ideas has been retarded by two powerful forces—teacher education institutions and textbook publishers. The case of Braille writing for the blind is an excellent example. Even after Louis Braille had perfected the method of writing that bears his name and had tested it successfully for five years, it was not adopted by schools for the blind. Opposition came from the training institutions because teachers would have to master this new way of writing and from textbook publishers because they would lose their investments in the enormous embossed books then used by the blind. It was not until many years after Braille's death that his method of writing for the blind was adopted.

Innovations in education are usually hailed as "fads" that will soon be forgotten. This is a common expression of resistance to change. Rarely, however, are valid and worthwhile innovations really forgotten, if they are translated into tested methods and materials. Braille had created an alphabet, a way of writing, that had been taught successfully to blind children. The idea of Braille writing could be rejected but it could not be forgotten. Similar statements might be made about the educational innovations of people like Socrates, Froebel, Montessori, and others. They created and tested methods and materials that have been rejected for a time, but the world has not been able to forget them. Many people have said that the idea of a more creative education is a fad that will pass and soon be forgotten. It *is* possible that creative ways of teaching may be rejected, but they will not be forgotten. Professor Smith and his co-authors in this seven-volume series have in a variety of ways expressed the definition, the spirit, and the truths of creative teaching in a way that will be difficult to forget.

The format of each book of this seven-volume series illustrates concretely many of the most important principles of creative teaching. Through the format and structure of these books, the author and publisher recognize the reader as self-acting and stimulus-seeking. The reader is provided both the guidance and the freedom necessary for creative growth. These books are a rich source of ideas, but this is not their greatest value. The reader who uses them for rapid reading or for occasional reference will miss an important opportunity for personal growth and professional development in creative directions. The "great ideas" quoted at the beginning of chapters are provocative. The suggested activities preceding most chapters provide worthwhile explorations in creativity. The content of the chapters provides a wealth of information that translates research findings into classroom methods and instructional materials. The exercises and questions at the end of each chapter will help the reader to make a creative synthesis of these experiences.

The authors offer themselves as models of creative teaching.

They bring to their task the fresh aroma of first-hand experiences in creative teaching in the college and university classroom and in elementary schools. They also offer the reader a variety of other models of creative teaching, making him feel almost as though "he were there." Participation in the experiences of the authors and the teachers they have observed, however, is not enough. The authors have added to this the kind of guidance that helps the reader identify, understand, and generalize the important principles at work in these experiences. This should increase the chances that the reader will develop useful skills and be able to transform his own classroom behavior.

Each of the seven books has its own unique contribution, along with a consistent philosophy. Book I is a creative synthesis of Professor Smith's rich experience in teaching children and teachers of children, a vast amount of research concerning creativity and classroom learning, and his theories of education. It is far more than this, however. The author has gone beyond all of these and, building onto the contributions of others, added his own innovations. He has distilled a great deal of the essence of the creativity of children. Book II, *Creative Teaching of the Language Arts in the Elementary School,* is a comprehensive, well-organized, and rich source of ideas. Book III, *Creative Teaching of Reading and Literature in the Elementary School,* is perhaps my own favorite. It is interesting and exciting and assumes a positive and consistent position on important issues in teaching reading. It will be difficult for the reader to resist becoming a creative reader. The way in which the author heightens expectations and challenges the reader to do things with what he reads is quite compelling. The books on social studies, science, the arts, and mathematics have their own unique features and should be valuable in courses on teaching methods in these areas and to teachers in service who want to become more skilled in setting the conditions for creative learning.

It is my own hope that your creative use of this series of books will help you realize more fully your own dream of helping your pupils live more creatively. This is the challenge of our day. In the past, we have been able to survive with static goals and concepts. This is no longer true. Things are changing so rapidly that our civilization can no longer survive if we insist on thinking and living in static terms and returning to the "old ways."

E. PAUL TORRANCE
University of Georgia

Preface

The greatest problem in the world today is man's inability to live with man in peace and harmony. The technological revolution has catapulted us to the threshold of the Space Age more quickly than we are able to cope with the problems that same technology has forced upon us. One thing is certain: Nuclear warfare would mean the total destruction of the human race. Consequently, man *must* learn to live with his fellowman. Never before in history has there been a mandate so strong or so compulsive.

The problems created by our advances in science cannot be solved as they were in the past. History provides only a portion of the answers, because we are facing problems today which never existed before. New solutions are needed to meet them. In every aspect of human culture, these problems exist—in politics, education, economics, sociology, psychology, industry, medicine, science.

The solution lies in the creative minds of men. But creativity has become a precious commodity, and throughout the world there is competition for the minds that possess it. Therefore, the development of the creative powers of our youth is essential. Since the area of the social studies is that part of the curriculum which attempts to teach children the problems of man and his relation to other men (the skills of living together, the methods of identifying, refining, and solving problems, the skills of research, scientific investigation, and a scientific attitude toward life problems), the elementary school must play a vital part in developing the creativity of each child and in helping children find creative ways of living together. Through the social studies program children learn most directly how to take their places as participating, contributing citizens in a democratic society. And in a democratic society individuals and their individuality count!

This is the fifth book in a series on creative teaching. Like the other books in the series, it attempts to cull from the mass of research in the area of creativity those basic principles which pertain uniquely to the social studies. It tries to translate them into creative teaching acts so that children will not only learn the knowledge, skills, values, understandings, concepts, and attitudes needed to take their effective place in society, but will also become self-realized through the development of the greatest of all human assets—their creativity.

Book I of this series, *Setting Conditions for Creative Teaching in the Elementary School,* should be combined with this volume so that the reader will understand fully the author's intent and purposes. This book follows through on the basic principles for developing creative powers in children and creative teaching in teachers as established in that book. Like Book I, it is written with two groups of teachers in mind: the pre-service and the in-service.

The author is indebted to many people for the materials in this manuscript. Among them are the many children with whom he worked, the creative teacher-colleagues he observed, his college students (especially his student teachers who dared to be creative in their teaching), and those special individuals who believe, as he does, that the fate of any nation lies in its youth. The latter include: Mrs. Helen Cleveland, teacher and principal in Alliance, Ohio, who is a creative teacher; and Helen Arens, a creative student teacher.

He gives special acknowledgment to his daughter Susan, a teacher and an inspiration for his work. To her he dedicates this book.

JAMES A. SMITH
Oswego, New York

Contents

Part One: The Nature of the Social Studies   1

I   Principles Basic to Creative Teaching   3

Introduction   3
A Definition   8
Principles of Creative Teaching as They Relate to the
     Social Studies   8
Basic Principles of Creativity   16
Summary   17

II   Purposes and Objectives   22

Introduction   22
Definitions   23
What Are the Objectives in Social Living?   24
Summary   29

III   The Social-Emotional Nature of Creativity   34

Introduction   34
Summary   40

Part Two: The Nurture of Creativity Through the Social Studies   45

IV   Creative Social Living   47

Introduction   47
The Appropriate Physical Environment   48
The Social-Emotional Conditions   53

Psychological Conditions   54
Intellectual Conditions   55
Summary   56

V Organizational Skills   **61**

Introduction   61
Pupil Teacher Planning   62
Summary   76

VI Unit Teaching   **80**

Introduction   80
Unit Teaching: Outcomes   80
Teaching a Unit   82
The Scientific Method as Creative Social Learning   100
Selecting Unit Content   101
Summary   103

VII Creativity Is Individualism   **108**

Introduction   108
Grouping for Individual and Creative Development   112
Summary   120

VIII Using the Textbook to Develop Creativity   **125**

Introduction   125
The Textbook as a Resource Material   127
Summary   156

IX Values and Character Development   **159**

Introduction   159
Dramatization   160
Role-playing and Role-reversal   163
The Sociodrama   166
The Structured Dramatization   167
Puppets   175

The Open-ended Story 176
The Problem Story 178
The Problem Picture 180
Bibliotherapy 185
Filmstrip Situations 186
Film Problems 186
Activities 186
Summary 190

X The Creative Teaching of Study Skills 194

Introduction 194
Developing Study Skills 196
Primary Grades 197
The Intermediate Grades 198
Summary 215

XI Using Audio-visual Materials to Develop Creativity 220

Introduction 220
Creative Uses of Audio-visual Materials 224
Summary 227

XII The Skills of Group Living 230

Introduction 230
The Class Discussion 233
The Panel Discussion 240
Buzz Groups 241
Brainstorming 242
Developing Evaluation Skills 244
Deferred Evaluation 264
Creative Evaluation 265
Summary 266

XII Conclusion 271

Summary 271

Index 275

Part One

The Nature of the Social Studies

I

Principles Basic to Creative Teaching

Creativity is the encounter of the intensively conscious human being with his world.[1]

ROLLO MAY

TO THE READER

This chapter presents a review of the material in Book I of this series. If you have already read that book, you will need only to skim this material to relate the basic concepts of creative teaching to the area of the social studies. If you have not read Book I, it would be to your advantage to do so, for the author has designed that book and this volume as companion texts.

Introduction

One day last fall I visited a student teacher in a second-grade classroom. Her name is Helen Arens, and she is one of the most capable and creative people I know. If there is such a thing as a natural born teacher, Helen is it.

Helen Arens had come to seminar many evenings disturbed about the hostility, the aggressiveness, and the lack of a working rapport among the students as well as between some teachers and students in her practice school. She had developed a missionary spirit toward creating good human relationships among the children in her classroom. Her cooperating teacher, equally concerned, came with her to seminar to discuss ways they might develop such relationships.

We had decided that the prescribed curriculum paid too little attention to this important facet of their work, and we sought creative ways to develop human relationships among the children. We reviewed the material on creativity which we had studied before Helen's

[1] Rollo May, "The Nature of Creativity," in *Creativity and Its Cultivation*, ed. Harold H. Anderson (New York: Harper and Brothers, Publishers, 1959), p. 68.

student teaching experience to help the two teachers plan creative ways to approach their problem.

On this particular fall day, Helen was using the *structured dramatization* as a technique to accomplish her objectives. She had been concerned about the fact that the children in her room showed little respect for each other's work. She had seen children lay heavy objects on newly moulded clay forms, squashing them. Some children borrowed things from neighbors without returning them. Once or twice she had even seen a child deliberately deface the work of another.

Her basic problem was *to help the children build respect for each other's work and for all work in general.* Miss Arens wrote a simple drama, ran it off on the ditto machine, and had her best readers read it to the rest of the class for a reading lesson. Though Miss Arens did not write her play about children destroying other children's clay objects, she did write one around the generalized concept, "A Lack of Respect for Someone's Work."

After the dramatization a discussion was held, and from it emerged certain values and appreciations. Following is a copy of Miss Arens' drama and excerpts from the discussion that followed.

WORK OR PLAY?

Characters
MR. SMITH, a carpenter
JIMMY SMITH, his son
MARY JONES, a neighbor
Scene: Mr. Smith's porch
Time: After school

(*Jimmy Smith and Mary Jones have just jumped off the school bus. They are coming up on the porch. Mr. Smith is on the porch. He is sawing some boards.*)

JIMMY:	Hi, Dad!
MR. SMITH:	Hi, Jimmy. Home from school already?
JIMMY:	Gee, yes, Dad. It's four o'clock.
MR. SMITH:	So it is. How time flies! Who's your friend, Jimmy?
JIMMY:	This is Mary Jones, Dad.
MR. SMITH:	Hello, Mary.
MARY:	Hello, Mr. Smith.
JIMMY:	Mary's come to play with me. Her father's going to pick her up at five.
MR. SMITH:	That's nice. What does your father do, Mary?
MARY:	He's a carpenter. I guess you're a carpenter too.
MR. SMITH:	No, Mary. I'm a farmer.

MARY:	You're sawing boards.
MR. SMITH:	I'm making Mrs. Smith a bookcase. Sawing is my hobby.
JIMMY:	I like to saw, too.
MR. SMITH:	He sure does. Say, it *is* getting late. I guess I'll have to leave you two. I have some work to do in my garden. Bye, Mary. Come again.
MARY:	Bye, Mr. Smith. I will. (*He goes off the porch.*)
MARY:	Jimmy, how does your father make money if he doesn't saw and nail all the time?
JIMMY:	He farms.
MARY:	What do you mean—he farms?
JIMMY:	Why, he raises cows and has a big garden. . . .
MARY:	Do you mean that keeping a big garden is his work?
JIMMY:	Why, yes.
MARY:	(*laughs*) Gee, your father doesn't work very hard, does he?
JIMMY:	He does so! He works real hard. Why he gets up early in the morning and works hard all day.
MARY:	I don't see how keeping a garden could be much work! Why, my father works all day building houses. When he comes home he works in the garden. He thinks that's fun. He calls garden work his hobby.
JIMMY:	Well, my father earns money by selling the things he raises in our big garden. And when he comes in at night, he saws and does carpentry work. He thinks carpentry work is fun. He says building things is his hobby!
MARY:	That's funny. My father gets tired of his work sometimes but he never gets tired of his garden.
JIMMY:	Yeah, my father gets tired of his garden sometimes but he *never* gets tired of building things.
MARY:	That's awfully funny, Jimmy. How can some things be work for some people and fun for others?
JIMMY:	Gee, I don't know. Say, that *is* funny!

END

Discussion

MISS ARENS:	Well, you read that real well, boys and girls. Shall we show how much we liked it, children? (*the children clap hands*). Now, I'd like to talk to you about the play. What did Jimmy and Mary think was funny?
SALLY:	They thought it was funny because Mary's father was a carpenter and Jimmy's father thought that being a carpenter was just fun.
MISS ARENS:	Was that all?
BILLY:	They thought it was funny because Jimmy's father was a farmer and Mary's father thought farming was fun.

MISS ARENS:	Do *you* think it was funny that one man's work was another man's fun?
MANY CHILDREN:	Yes!
MISS ARENS:	What *is* fun?
ARNIE:	It's what you *do* for fun.
MISS ARENS:	Yes, but what does it mean to have fun?
JACKIE:	It means play. Play is fun.
MISS ARENS:	Yes, play is fun. What makes play?
BILL:	Oh, games and cowboys and making things.
MISS ARENS:	Yes. When you make things do you sometimes saw and nail and work hard at it?
BILL:	Yes.
MISS ARENS:	I remember the airplane you made yesterday, Bill. You worked real hard on it.
BILL:	Yes, but it was fun!
MISS ARENS:	Can work sometimes be fun?
MANY CHILDREN:	Yes!
MISS ARENS:	I guess we could say that sometimes play is fun and sometimes work is fun, and that sometimes they are both hard, too, couldn't we?
MANY CHILDREN:	Yes!
MARSHA:	Sometimes I help my mother with the dishes and I think it's fun.
MISS ARENS:	Does your mother like to do dishes, Marsha?
MARSHA:	No, she hates to do the dishes!
MISS ARENS:	Marsha's mother doesn't like to do the dishes but Marsha thinks it's fun—just like Mr. Smith and Mr. Jones.
HARRY:	I like to make things but I don't like to do dishes.
MISS ARENS:	We all like to do some things and we don't like to do some things. Could we say that the things that give us pleasure are the things that are fun!
MARY:	Yes, but sometimes I don't like to do something; then when it's done, I'm happy.
MISS ARENS:	Like what, Mary?
MARY:	Like dumping the trash for my mother.
MISS ARENS:	Mary is saying that we get pleasure from work *and* play. Almost everything that we do gives us pleasure if we do it well, I guess. Now, tell me, what do you think that we learned from the play?
HARRY:	That work and play are both fun.
MARY:	That both work and play give us pleasure.
JOEL:	What one person thinks is work another person thinks is play.
NICK:	What some people do is work and to another person it is play.
MISS ARENS:	Those are all good ideas. I'd like to ask one more question: When we see someone doing a job, how can we tell if he's working or playing?

JACKIE:	We can't always. Maybe he plays at home and works in the office.
MISS ARENS:	In either case, the person is probably getting pleasure just as we do when we work and play.
BILL:	Yes.
MISS ARENS:	Everybody's work helps someone else and his play is mostly for himself, don't you think?
ARNIE:	Sometimes.
MISS ARENS:	In any case, which is more important, work or play?
BILL:	Work, I think, because it gets you money and it is generally something you do for other people.
MARY:	I think play is more important.
MISS ARENS:	Does anyone think they *both* are?
SEVERAL CHILDREN:	Yes!
MISS ARENS:	We would not be very happy if we had *all* work or *all* play. Both are good for us, don't you think?

*   *   *

The creative approach to problem solving in the above illustration was proven successful to some degree by the fact that the next day Arnie suggested that the children clear off a shelf on which to place clay objects so that they could dry safely. Later in the week Joel suggested that a rope on which the children could hang their paintings to dry be stretched across the front of the room.

Helen Arens could have lectured the children in her classroom. She could have moralized about their lack of consideration and cooperation, but she used a more creative approach. She motivated the children with a fresh technique—she involved them all in the process of developing values and understandings without imposing her own.

Helen Arens, student teacher, is a creative teacher!

What makes a creative teacher? In order to understand the concept of creative teaching, one must understand the emerging concepts of creativity.

In Book I of this series[2] both of these two questions are explored; that volume should be read as a companion to this one so that the work on the following pages may be more thoroughly understood. In each of the succeeding books of the series, the basic principles of creativity and creative teaching are reviewed in the first chapter. The author presumes that the reader is already familiar with these principles and will review them in this chapter simply as a memory-refresher. In the chapters that follow, these principles will be

---

[2] James A. Smith, *Setting Conditions for Creative Teaching in the Elementary School* (Boston: Allyn and Bacon, Inc., 1966).

developed, through illustrations, as they relate to the teaching of social studies and social living in the elementary classroom.

A Definition

Creativity is defined in this series as the ability to tap one's experiences and to come up with something new. This new product need not be new to the world, but it *must* be new to the individual. This simple definition explains the kind of creativity most commonly shown by children. Because there are degrees of creativity, a higher degree of it would mean that the creator would produce something new to the world—a new math formula, a new technique for painting, a way to reach the moon. Because creativity is a process *and* a product, attention must be paid to the process if it is to be developed in children. The illustration presented above shows the creative process at work. The product was a concept. Miss Arens developed creative thinking simply by asking open-ended questions, by reflecting and clarifying the children's thinking, by obtaining complete involvement through the presentation of the social drama, and by encouraging the children to work through the problem to a solution. All comments of the children were accepted and explored, and divergent thinking processes were developed.

Principles of Creative Teaching as They Relate to the Social Studies

In the past the basis for accepted behavior has been rooted in the Judeo-Christian concepts of morality prevalent throughout this country. The teaching of these concepts has been through moralizing to children. While the values on which our present culture is built are evidence that this sort of teaching must have been successful to some degree, the decline of morality and the decay of many of man's values indicate that this type of teaching has not been as successful as we might hope.

Obviously, there must be change in values as new knowledges are revealed, just as there are changes in everything else. But no culture can survive without a basic set of values from which the members of a particular society design their mode of behavior. These basic values must be identified, and they must be incorporated in the social studies program as goals for teachers. Respect for work, as well as respect for one another's work, is one such value, as Miss Arens well knows.

Moralizing is verbalizing, and young children learn more from what they see, feel, and experience than from what they hear. One of the reasons for a deterioration of basic values in a culture is that children do not see what they hear. Children are taught on the verbal level to love one another, but they are exposed to violence, hate, greed, jealousy, and dishonesty continually through television, moving pictures, picture magazines, newspapers and even in so-called comic books.

Moralizing doesn't always work; there must be better ways. Miss Arens used a better way. She tried to build values of living together in her class by helping them to feel, to experience, and to identify with a situation. The result was that children could *understand* the value of respecting each other's work as a sensible means of living together.

The approach to *all* social studies teaching has all too often been verbal in nature. By using creative approaches, and by thoroughly understanding the purpose of social studies teaching in the elementary school, we stand a better chance of attaining our goals.

All teachers can be creative. Research in the area of creativity has provided us with a basic set of principles within the range of all teachers' abilities. I have identified eighteen such principles as a basis for creative teaching in this series. They are summarized below.

1. *In creative teaching, something new, different or unique results.* This implies that the process or product of the creative teaching art must be new. In the social studies it may be a new way to solve a problem, arriving at a new concept, developing a new skill or concept, or producing a new instrument.

2. *In creative teaching, divergent thinking processes are stressed.* Divergent thinking processes are not concerned with an absolute or correct answer. In divergent thinking, knowledge, facts, concepts, understandings, and skills learned through convergent thinking processes are put to new uses, and new answers, rather than an absolute or correct answer, result. Divergent thinking develops such qualities as flexibility, fluency of ideas, spontaneity, uniqueness, and these processes are the basis for creative thinking.

Training in divergent thinking processes results in other rewards besides the ability to think creatively. Sensing and identifying problems is often as important as solving them, and teaching for creative thinking helps children to sense problems and difficulties. Creative thinkers tend to sense gaps in information or disharmonies among facts. Teaching for divergent products helps to develop these important skills in children.

Up to now the training of the divergent thinking processes in the elementary schools has been neglected, in spite of its importance, because little has been known about it and its relation to creativity. In teaching the social studies, the teacher is given many opportunities to develop both convergent and divergent thinking processes. To be creative, children need more knowledge than ever before; and this knowledge will be obtained largely through convergent processes working toward one correct answer. To be creative, children must put this knowledge to new uses; and this quality will be developed largely through divergent thinking processes—working for many answers. Examples of both types of teaching will be given throughout this book.

3. *In creative teaching, motivational tensions are a prerequisite to the creative process. The process serves as a tension relieving agent.* Miss Arens attained this strong tension involvement through her little drama. Tension was relieved through the discussion that followed, in which all the children said what they wished to say. While motivation is essential to all learning, a strong involvement in any lesson that hopes to develop creativity must be felt by all children.

4. *In creative teaching, open-ended situations are utilized.* After Miss Arens provided a strong motivation for the children, she kept them motivated by the type of question she asked. Once the dramatization was complete, the situation was open-ended. There was no *one* solution to the problem. True, Miss Arens guided the discussion until the children came up with *some* solutions and established *some* values, but she had no definite preconceived idea as to whether or not the drama would "take," or how the children would react. Notice that she accepted *all* ideas.

Open-endedness in teaching means that children are presented with situations where they put their knowledges, understandings, facts, and skills to work. In teaching the social studies, the teacher can develop creative critical thinking through the use of open-ended situations, as we shall see on the following pages (see pp. 159–190).

5. *In creative teaching, there comes a time when the teacher withdraws and children face the unknown themselves.* In the illustra-

tion presented above, Miss Arens prepared the drama, began the discussion and then gradually changed her role from that of motivator and leader to that of guide in clarifying the children's thinking and reflecting their feelings.

The teaching of creativity and the development of divergent thinking processes differ from the development of convergent thinking processes mainly in this one manner. In teaching the capitals of the states, for instance, the teacher can predict the outcome of her lesson as well as the learnings the children will acquire. But in the lesson above Miss Arens could not follow the lesson through to this type of closure before it was presented. She made certain that she had built highly motivating tensions in the children, and then she let them release these tensions in individual ways through discussion. In creative teaching the children produce the answers.

6. *In creative teaching the outcomes are unpredictable.* In developing creativity through the social studies, there are many instances where the outcomes cannot be specifically predicted. Miss Arens knew her plan would lead to some general outcomes, but she did not know exactly where the discussion would go. Such procedures call for skill in leading discussions.

7. *In creative teaching, conditions are set which make possible preconscious thinking.* All the experiences of children are stored in the vast reservoir of the brain, either in the conscious, where it is readily used, or in the subconscious, where it is rarely used. Creativity cannot be taught; we can only set conditions for it. By rewarding it when it comes to the surface, we reinforce it and reassure its further appearance. Chapter III of this book deals with the conditions necessary to help creativity appear so that we can get at it and work with it. Creative people are those who can sink taps into the subconscious, as well as the conscious, to find knowledges and skills previously learned which they use in solving current problems. A permissive atmosphere and certain psychological securities must be present in the classroom if children are to be free to explore their subconscious as well as their conscious minds and use their backlog of experiences in new ways.

8. *Creative teaching means encouraging children to generate and develop their own ideas.* In Miss Arens' situation, her ability at leading a discussion proved to be a key factor in helping the children express their ideas.

The social studies curriculum affords many opportunities for children to express their ideas, as, for instance, when they discuss current controversial issues, prepare exhibits, plan displays, create maps, make murals, design dioramas, or write reports.

9. *In creative teaching, differences, uniqueness, individuality, and originality are stressed and rewarded.* In teaching the social studies, the development of individuals is essential. See Chapter III for a detailed development of this theme.

10. *In creative teaching, the process is as important as the product.* In Miss Arens' lesson the *process* of thinking through the problem at hand was creative. The steps of creative production have been defined by Marksberry in her book, *Foundation of Creativity*,[3] as follows: (1) a period of preparation when the creator becomes involved with and identifies with the problem at hand; (2) a period of incubation when the creator lives with and is even tormented by the problem; (3) a period of insight when all parts of the problem seem to be clear; (4) a period of illumination or inspiration when the ideas or answers seem to come (this may be a moment of discovery); and (5) a period of verification, elaboration, perfecting, and evaluation when the product is tested for its worth. The tension built during the problem solving situation is relieved at this point.

The social studies offer many situations where the total creative process may be practiced. We have seen one such instance in Miss Arens' lesson above. It can also be developed in presenting creative reports, making murals, writing plays, comparing data to use in problem solving, and discussing controversial issues. Many illustrations of creative teaching to develop creative processes in the social studies appear in the following chapters.

11. *In creative teaching, certain conditions must be set to permit creativity to appear.* So important is this principle to creative development that it is discussed in detail in Chapter IV of this book, p. 47.

12. *Creative teaching is success- rather than failure-oriented.* In Miss Arens' lesson, no child failed in the sense that his contribution was rejected, ridiculed, or ignored. Children will fail at times through not knowing or understanding certain skills and knowledge in the social studies. But there is a difference between failure and failure experiences. Failure experiences help children understand the true conditions of life and help build character, but repeated failure can only result in psychological damage to personalities. When failure

[3] Mary Lee Marksberry, *Foundation of Creativity* (New York: Harper & Row, 1963).

experiences are used as learning situations, they are resolved and eventually become successes. Failure, excessive criticism, rejection, and negative approaches to child control may result in withdrawal and lack of fluency and spontaneity in a child. Since these qualities appear to be necessary for creative development, they cannot be negated through excessive failure or negativism.

13. *In creative teaching, provision is made for learning many knowledges and skills, but provision is also made to apply these knowledges and skills in new situations.* In a sixth-grade class the need for a three-dimensional map arose, and Mr. Arnold, the teacher, said he would show the class how to make one. Without bothering to find out what the children knew about making such a map, he showed them how to make one of salt and flour.

Mr. Endres, on the other hand, had the children list all the materials they had ever experienced which could be used three-dimensionally. From these they chose those which best fitted their criteria for use of the map. They decided on salt and flour because it held its shape, it could be painted, it was light, it could be transported easily about the room, it could be hung, and it was easy to work with. All these children were using many divergent answers to problems. They were evaluating, passing judgment, and developing the affiliated skills of creative production. The open-ended learning situation previously explained is an integral part of this concept.

14. *In creative teaching, self-initiated learning is encouraged.* The area of the social studies offers unique opportunities to develop self-initiated learning. The skills of research, outlining, summarization, reporting, and reference greatly assist in helping children gain techniques to acquire the necessary information to solve problems by themselves. Chapters VIII, X and XII of this book are devoted to illustrations of creative ways these skills may be acquired and applied to develop self-initiated learning.

15. *In creative teaching, skills of constructive criticism and evaluation are developed.* Constructive criticism encourages creativity. Learning how to offer constructive criticism effectively is a skill required of people living together closely. In developing creativity results are more fruitful when criticism and evaluation are deferred until all possible ideas are presented. The area of the social studies offers many opportunities for teaching and practicing techniques of constructive criticism. One indirect approach to developing this skill is shown in the illustration of Miss Arens' lesson.

Ability to evaluate, make decisions, pass judgment, weigh evidence, do research, outline, synthesize, and draw conclusions are all part of the evaluation process and are necessary to both creative and critical thinking. A large portion of Chapters VIII and X of this book is devoted to the development of these skills in the social studies program. Deferred judgment and deferred evaluation tend to increase creative ideation. Prestated standards often inhibit the child in expressing his ideas.

16. *In creative teaching, ideas and objects are manipulated and explored.* Current research studies in the area of creativity indicate that there is a high correlation between creative output and the opportunity to explore, experiment, and manipulate. Since the social studies, such as geography, economics, history, political science, sociology, and psychology, encompass those disciplines, and since these are all disciplines which contain records of man's ideas, the teaching of the social studies is uniquely suited to the exploration and manipulation of ideas and objects. Many illustrations of the development of this concept will be presented in Chapter III and in Part II of this book.

17. *Creative teaching employs democratic processes.* The basic goal of the social studies program is to develop the democratic citizen for the democratic society. The social studies are often called "citizenship education." The function and contribution of the individual as a citizen in his society must be stressed as a part of the social studies program. To learn about democratic processes, children must live under a democratic regime. In the small society of the classroom and community, each child prepares for this place in the larger society. The development of his own individuality is important both for the contribution he will make to his culture and for his own self-realization. In a democratically structured classroom, children not only learn how democracy works, they are also free to participate in planning. They are free to express their ideas, to enter into evaluation techniques, to explore, experiment, and manipulate objects, words, and ideas, and to become individuals, all of which is necessary to develop the creative personality. Where autocracy implies conformity to rules set by a leader, democracy implies conformity to decisions made by the population, with plenty of opportunity for nonconformity within these conformity limits. Rigid conformity has been declared an enemy to creative development.

18. *In creative teaching, methods are used which are unique to the development of creativity.* The social studies curriculum can be

planned to employ these unique methods throughout the daily program. These methods have been identified by Alex Osborn[4] and Sidney Parnes[5] in their courses in Creative Problem Solving with adults at the University of Buffalo. The author has found them to be very successful with children.[6] Among these methods is the application of the principle of *deferred judgment* mentioned above. Dr. Osborn suggests that creative thinking powers may be stretched through the process of *creative ideation,* in which the products of creativity are subjected to the following thought processes: To what new uses can I put it? How can I adapt it, modify it, magnify it, minify it, substitute something for it, rearrange it, reverse it, combine it with something else?

Other unique methods of creative ideation have been described in other books in this series. The social studies curriculum lends itself well to the employment of these techniques for creative ideation. Miss Arens, in her skillful use of discussion, stretched creative ideation through many of these techniques. These special techniques can be employed in the social studies program in such instances as building dioramas and models, making classroom films, planning interesting reports, holding debates, producing dramatizations, and fostering discussions.

Among the attributes identified with creative people is that they are more sensitive to problems. Dr. Parnes hopes to build in students, as a result of his course, an attitude of constructive discontent. This, he feels, should help them become more sensitive to the problems around them. He identifies three types of questions: fact-finding questions, decision or judgment questions, and creative questions. The first two types call for facts or judgments: the third type calls for ideas. Such a question as, "Why are the roofs of houses in the Norwegian countries built with steep roofs?" falls into the first two categories, while a question such as, "How can I make American History more interesting to my students?" comes under category three.

Other authors also have used classifications that will aid the

[4] Alex F. Osborn, *Applied Imagination: Principles and Procedures of Creative Thinking* (New York: Charles Scribner's Sons, 1957).

[5] Sidney J. Parnes, *Instructor's Manual for Semester Courses in Creative Problem-Solving,* rev. ed. (Buffalo: Creative Education Foundation, 1963).

[6] See Books II, III and IV of this series, James A. Smith, *Creative Teaching of the Language Arts in the Elementary School, Creative Teaching of Reading and Literature in the Elementary School,* and *Creative Teaching of the Creative Arts in the Elementary School* (Boston: Allyn and Bacon, Inc., 1967).

teacher in developing schemes for the types of questions to be used in developing creative responses.[7]

Another aid to creative thinking is a careful definition of the problem or a redefinition of any given problem. This defining and redefining of a problem helps the individual to visualize more than one mode of attack on the problem. A new viewpoint may often open the way to a solution to the problem.

Narrowing a broad problem into specific problems or subproblems helps the individual focus on creative ways of attacking the subproblems, which, in turn, will bring a creative solution to the whole problem. A problem such as, "How can we raise money for our senior trip to Washington?" may be broken down into many subproblems, such as, "What can we make to sell at a profit?" "What affairs can we give for *entertainment* which will provide us with a profit?" "What services can we provide that will realize a profit?" Brainstorming each of the subproblems eventually leads to the solution of the large problem. Unit teaching as described in Chapter VI of this book is a demonstration of the practical application of this.

The incubation of a concept problem generally leads to greater creative production. This means that, once the pertinent facts on a specific problem have been gathered and the problem has been well defined, the individual allows the problem to incubate—he allows himself to collect ideas twenty-four hours a day by permitting the subconscious as well as the conscious mind to work.

All of these methods have implications for developing creative output through the utilization of problems selected from social studies content.

Basic Principles of Creativity

Now that the basic principles of creative teaching have been discussed, one more thought must be added: creative teachers must be aware of the knowledge being accumulated in the area of creativity to have a full understanding of its development. A large portion of Book I of this series was devoted to a discussion of this knowledge. The basic principles presented in that volume are summarized here:

---

[7] See the following sources: Norris M. Sanders, *Classroom Questions: What Kinds?* (New York: Harper & Row, 1966); B. S. Bloom *et al., Taxonomy of Educational Objectives* (New York: Longmans, Green, 1956); and J. P. Guilford, "Three Faces of Intellect," *American Psychologist,* 1959, 496–79.

1. All children are born creative.
2. There is a relationship between creativity and intelligence; highly creative people are always highly intelligent although highly intelligent people are not always creative. However, all children can create to some degree.
3. Creativity is a form of giftedness that is not measured by current intelligence tests.
4. All areas of the curriculum may be used to develop creativity.
5. Creativity is a process and a product.
6. Creativity is developed by focusing on those processes of the intellect which fall into the general area of divergent thinking. This area of the intellect has been greatly neglected in our teaching up to this point.
7. All creative processes cannot always be developed at one time or in one lesson. Lessons must be planned to focus on each process.
8. Creativity cannot be taught; we can only set conditions for it to happen and insure its reappearance through reinforcement.
9. More knowledge, more skills, and more facts than ever before are required in order for creativity to be developed.
10. The theories of creative development lead us to believe that children must be able to tap all of life's experiences in order to become truly creative—unnecessary rules and actions may force much of their experience into the preconscious or subconscious, where it cannot be readily used.
11. Excessive and/or compulsive conformity and rigidity are true enemies of creativity. The creative person is neither compulsively conforming nor compulsively nonconforming. He is free to conform or not conform in terms of what he believes to be true, right, effective, or best for the situation.
12. Children go through definite steps in the creative process.
13. Creative teaching and creative learning can be more effective than other types of teaching and learning. They are especially effective for certain kinds of children, among them those who do not seem to learn well by other methods.
14. Children who have lost much of their creativity may be helped to regain it by special methods of teaching.

Summary

Creative teaching is a special method of teaching. Although creative teaching employs the principles of all good teaching, its attainment is possible only when teachers understand those factors which make it different from other methods of teaching. The social studies content of the elementary school curriculum is uniquely suited to the development of creative powers because the objectives and content relate so closely to the daily living of the child and to the role he must play as an adult in a democratic society. All teachers can develop their own creative powers through the application of the basic principles mentioned in this chapter to their own teaching. Creative teaching places children in unique, unusual, clever problem-solving situations so that their own creative powers develop. Creative teaching also means that teachers work specifically on developing those components of the intellect which contribute to the development of the total creative process. The teaching of the social studies can be a creative process for developing creative people.

TO THE COLLEGE STUDENT

1. Send for the film, *The Face of Lincoln* (University of Southern California at Los Angeles). After you have seen the film, brainstorm ways you might use it as a motivational device for developing a social studies lesson for any chosen grade which will develop creativity in the children.

2. In your class, brainstorm other ways Helen Arens might have handled the problem posed at the beginning of this chapter in a creative fashion. For instance, how might she have used puppets or role-playing (see page 175)?

3. Identify ten of the most important values that seem necessary in order for people to live comfortably together. Then list as many creative ways as possible to develop these values in children.

4. Keep a bulletin board in your classroom entitled "Creativity in the News." Collect newspaper and magazine articles for it. After you have done this for a few weeks decide whether creativity is becoming a popular news item. Note the type of papers and magazines publishing these articles. Would you say that research and news about creativity is reaching the lay public? What effect do you feel this will have on the school's part in the development of creativity?

5. Make a list of indications of change in our values as they have occurred in your lifetime. Examine them; are the changes for the good of society? If not, how do you suggest values are changed? Is there such a thing as a spoken value system and a behavioral value system? Are they different?

TO THE CLASSROOM TEACHER

1. Can any of the values of living together be taught through the use of divergent thinking processes? What about respect for property, freedom of speech and the press, contributing to the welfare of others? Plan some lessons using divergent thinking processes which will help children develop these values and others.

2. Can certain skills of living together be developed through divergent thinking processes? What about skills relating to research, map reading, making decisions, and passing judgments? Plan some creative lessons that will help to develop these skills.

3. Examine your own program and note the instances throughout the day when you organize your class or plan your lessons so that individual differences are considered. Do you tend to *meet* individual differences or *develop* them? Is there a difference? Do you develop them in any of the instances you have noted? Can you think of ways you could develop valuable differences that exist in your students?

4. Observe the bulletin boards in your classrooms. Do they reflect the creative ideas of your students or are they filled with your own ideas? Think of ways you might develop creativity in your children through the use of bulletin boards.

TO THE COLLEGE STUDENT AND THE CLASSROOM TEACHER

1. Following is a lesson in social studies observed in a fourth-grade classroom. Using the principles of creative teaching as they are defined in this chapter, replan the lesson in such a fashion that divergent thinking processes will be employed and a creative lesson will result.

*   *   *

Miss Dee, a fourth-grade teacher, has been teaching about foods. Here is a list of questions she has been asking for years:

1. Where is the corn belt?
2. What states are included in the corn belt?
3. Why do we call this area the corn belt?
4. What is the climate like in the corn belt?

5. How is the corn planted on a large farm?
6. How does it grow? How is it harvested?
7. What products do we get from corn?
8. Where is the corn sent?
9. How does the United States rank with the rest of the world in corn production?
10. How does this compare with other countries, in quality as well as amount?

Obviously, Miss Dee teaches from the textbook. Her method is as follows: She puts the questions on the board. Under them she puts the page references where they can be found in the social studies text. The children are given a period of time to read. Then a signal is given, books are closed, and the class goes through the list of questions and answers each one by raising hands if the answer is known.

Your problem: Using the principles of open-ended, divergent, and creative learning, redesign Miss Dee's lesson as follows:

1. Plan a *method* of teaching based on principles of creativity.
2. Using the same ideas, replan *each* question so it provokes critical thinking.

*   *   *

2. Read Chapter V in Mary Lee Marksberry's book, *Foundation of Creativity,* pages 151–167, for a review of the concepts that may be developed in the creative teaching of the social studies.

3. Using Osborn's lists to develop creative ideation, think through the following problems and note how one creative idea, often built on another, has proven to be profitable to the creator. For example:

    a. *Object:* a bar of soap; *technique:* how to put it in other forms. *Answer:* (divergent thinking processes) soap flakes, soap chips, powdered detergent, liquid soap, cream soap, etc.

    b. *Object:* unsafe highway; *technique:* how to broaden it. *Answer:* wider highways with malls or cement rises in the middle make safer turnpike roads.

    c. Now try *object:* a coke bottle; *technique:* new uses.

    d. *Object:* a discarded antique butter churn; *technique:* adapt to new uses.

    e. *Object:* a picture on the wall; *technique:* substitute some decoration for it.

    f. *Object:* table for a Halloween party; *technique:* magnify it.

SELECTED BIBLIOGRAPHY

ANDERSON, H. E. (ed.). *Creativity and Its Cultivation.* New York: Harper and Brothers, 1959.

ANDERSON, H. H. "Creativity and Education," *AHE College and University Bulletin,* XIII, No. 14 (May 1, 1961).

CARPENTER, R. "Creativity: Its Nature and Nurture," *Educational Leadership,* LXXXII (1962), 391–95.

GETZELS, JACOB W. and PHILIP W. JACKSON. *Creativity and Intelligence.* New York: John Wiley & Sons, Inc., 1962.

GUILFORD, J. P. "The Structure of Intellect," *Psychological Bulletin,* LIII (1956), 275–95.

————. "Three Faces of Intellect," *American Psychologist,* XIV (1959), 469–79.

MASLOW, A. H. "Cognition of Being in the Peak-Experiences," *Journal of Genetic Psychology,* XCIV (March, 1959), 43–46.

————. *Motivation and Personality.* New York: Harper and Brothers, 1954.

MEARNS, HUGHES. *Creative Power: The Education of Youth in the Creative Arts,* rev. ed. New York: Dover Publications, 1929.

MURPHY, GARDNER. *Human Potentialities.* New York: Basic Books Inc., 1958.

OSBORN, ALEX F. *Applied Imagination,* rev. ed. New York: Charles Scribner's Sons, 1965.

————. *The Creative Education Movement.* Buffalo: The Creative Education Foundation.

RUGG, HAROLD. *Imagination: An Inquiry Into the Sources and Conditions that Stimulate Creativity.* New York: Harper & Row, 1963.

SMITH, JAMES A. *Creativity: Its Nature and Nurture.* Syracuse: School of Education, Syracuse University, 1964.

TAYLOR, CALVIN W. *Creativity: Progress and Potential.* New York: McGraw-Hill, 1964.

TAYLOR, CALVIN W. and FRANK BARRON. *Scientific Creativity: Its Recognition and Development.* New York: John Wiley & Sons, Inc., 1963.

TORRANCE, E. PAUL (ed.). *Creativity.* Minneapolis: University of Minnesota, Center for Continuation Study of the General Extension Division, 1959.

————. *Guiding Creative Talent.* Englewood Cliffs: Prentice-Hall, Inc., 1965.

————. *Rewarding Creative Behavior.* Englewood Cliffs: Prentice-Hall, Inc., 1965.

WERTHEIMER, M. *Productive Thinking.* New York: Harper and Brothers, 1945, 1959.

ZIRBES, LAURA. *Spurs to Creative Thinking.* New York: G. P. Putnam's Sons, 1959.

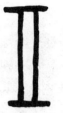

Purposes and Objectives

The Social Studies make rich contributions to the growth and development of children because the central function of the Social Studies is identified with the central purposes of education—the development of democratic citizenship.[1]

JOHN MICHAELIS

TO THE READER

Before you read this chapter, make lists of all those qualities and characteristics that people must have in order to be effective, functioning members of a democratic society. Classify your statements. Then discuss these problems with your colleagues: How are these qualities and characteristics developed in people? Which of the problems on your list are the jobs of the school? Which will be developed by knowledge and which by the techniques of teaching? Compare your list with those of the experts by skimming this chapter.

Introduction

Learning to live together does not just happen with the act of growing up. We have come to realize more and more that training is needed to develop in men those qualities and skills essential to successful life in a democratic society. Children must *practice* the act of sharing ideas without acting emotionally; they must *practice* critical and creative thinking; they must *learn* to listen to other people's viewpoints; they must *learn* to use democratic processes and group dynamics; they must *develop* empathy and understanding of people who are different from them.

Our schools were founded to perpetuate our political ideology. The primary reason for the establishment of the American public school was to take care of all those needs in the functioning of a democratic society which could not be left to chance. One of the first

[1] John Michaelis, *Social Studies for Children in a Democracy,* rev. ed. (Englewood Cliffs, N.J.: Prentice-Hall, Inc., 1956), p. 3.

needs was literacy; today one need is learning to live together in peace and harmony. We are committed to developing these skills in children so that each child may function as an individual in a democratic country. In a democracy, and in a democracy alone, individuals count; their rights and freedoms are respected. Creativity functions best in a free society of free thinkers. Our social studies program should be the core for developing the creative thinkers of our republic.

Definitions

Because the terms "social studies" and "social sciences" have become clouded with a variety of meanings in their development, the following terms will be used in this book.

The *social sciences* are those bodies of knowledge which man has accumulated from his studies of economics, sociology, political science, history, geography, civics, and anthropology.

The *social studies* are the facts selected from this reservoir of truths to be used for instructional purposes. The term *citizenship education* has often been substituted for *social studies,* especially when it is thought of in terms of social living.

Social living is the translation of the social studies into action in the classroom. Social living is concerned with the practice of necessary skills and the utilization of knowledge for effective patterns of living together. Social living is concerned with the building of sound, creative human relationships.

The teaching of social studies in the Space Age must incorporate the concept of social living. Children must learn diverse and complicated skills of living together and developing sound human relationships. Relationships may well be defined as the fourth *R* in the school curriculum. Conditions may be set in the classroom to provide children with opportunities to develop creative and aesthetic living.

The skills of living together are not learned from a textbook. Textbook teaching never has fulfilled the destiny of the social studies program. It was never meant to. In the future it will be even less effective. It has already been demonstrated in recent years that knowledge is accumulating so fast that many textbooks are outdated before they leave the press.

In today's social studies program the textbook plays a different role than it has in the past. This new role is defined in Chapter VIII of this book (see page 125).

Though education alone cannot take full responsibility, the world today reflects a type of teaching that failed to show people how to live together. In pioneer societies much of the social development was naturally provided for in small home groups and family gatherings. Families in themselves were large enough to provide companionship, status, and purpose for each child on varying age levels. The families lived far apart and the need to know how to meet, to work with, and to play with large groups was not as necessary as it now is. Today people must learn to live next door to each other and to accept their neighbors' ideas and eccentricities.

Teaching the social studies is concerned with teaching children techniques, attitudes, values, understandings, concepts, and skills, as well as factual matter. School becomes a place where children come to learn *how* to learn. The modern concepts of social studies teaching are directed as much at the development or change of behavior in individuals as at the accumulation of factual knowledge. The school attempts to help each child develop techniques for solving the problems he will face daily by giving him practice in solving these problems on his own age level. The content of the social studies curriculum as it has developed through the social functions approach is concerned with the problems man has faced in all his civilizations —those of food, clothing, shelter, pleasure, science, health, safety, transportation, communication, education, government, and organization. Children face these problems of their culture at an early age, and the school can utilize them as the core of the subject-matter it teaches. Each area is one that has been accentuated by the process of grouping for better social living, and each is one that must, therefore, be resolved by a group rather than an individual. The school must encourage groups to solve such problems through the sound techniques of a scientific method.

What Are the Objectives in Social Living?

Many professional groups have organized definite objectives for education in social living. Chief among them is the Educational Policies Commission, which has set up these goals for the educated person:

THE OBJECTIVES OF SELF-REALIZATION

The educated person:
Has an appetite for learning.
Can speak the mother tongue clearly.
Writes the mother tongue effectively.
Solves his problems of counting and calculating.
Is skilled in listening and observing.
Understands the basic facts concerning health and disease.
Protects his own health and that of his dependents.
Works to improve the health of the community.
Is participant and spectator in many sports and other pastimes.
Has mental resources for the use of leisure.
Appreciates beauty.
Gives responsible direction to his own life.

THE OBJECTIVES OF HUMAN RELATIONSHIPS

The educated person:
Puts human relationships first.
Enjoys a rich, sincere, and varied social life.
Can work and play with others.
Observes the amenities of social behavior.
Appreciates the family as a social institution.
Conserves family ideals.
Is skilled in homemaking.
Maintains democratic family relationships.

THE OBJECTIVES OF ECONOMIC EFFICIENCY

The educated person:
Knows the satisfaction of good workmanship.
Understands the requirements and opportunities for various jobs.
Has selected his occupation.
Succeeds in his chosen vocation.
Maintains and improves his efficiency.
Appreciates the social value of his work.

The educated consumer:
Plans the economics of his own life.
Develops standards for guiding his expenditures.
Is an informed and skillful buyer.
Takes appropriate measures to safeguard his interests.

THE OBJECTIVES OF CIVIC RESPONSIBILITY

The educated citizen:
Is sensitive to the disparities of human circumstances.
Acts to correct unsatisfactory conditions.
Seeks to understand social structures and social processes.
Has defenses against propaganda.
Respects honest differences of opinion.
Has a regard for the nation's resources.
Measures scientific advance by its contribution to the general welfare.

Respects the law.
Is economically literate.
Accepts his civic duties.
Acts upon an unswerving loyalty to democratic ideals.[2]

These objectives are all directed toward creating change in the behavior of the individual. A good social studies program develops within each child self-discipline and understanding of the world and the problems of the world. It attempts to prepare the individual for living in his present world and to foster an appreciation of the viewpoints and beliefs of other people. It teaches him to understand and appreciate other cultures in the light of the knowledge he has of his own. It gives him a historical perspective necessary for appreciation and interpretation of his own mode of life. It teaches him to use and appreciate the natural resources of his community. It helps him understand modern living and shows him ways he can adapt his environment to meet his own needs. It equips him with the skills for discovering and learning by himself. It shows him constructive ways to spend his leisure time and fosters wise and economic living. It gives him the ability to think critically, to develop many skills, to maintain good mental and physical health, to have a sense of security in his neighborhood, to have poise and status in his peer groups. It fosters in him good social attitudes, his own special aptitudes, and democratic ideals.

Specifically, a modern program of social living helps the child to become a democratic citizen by cultivating skills and techniques unique to living in a democracy. He develops the ability to take part in a group discussion, the responsibility for group planning and caring for group liberties, the ability to recognize the other fellow's worth— the tolerance to accept others' ideas and ways, the ability to reflect and act on pressing social problems, the ability to make wise decisions, the understanding of group processes in meeting social processes, open-mindedness in dealing with others, a sense of cooperation, independent action and self-direction, and a faith in himself and his own creative abilities.

This places much of the emphasis of attaining goals on method or technique. Only through method of teaching can many values be built and attitudes be developed. When these techniques of teaching are creative and exciting to children the objectives can be fulfilled.

[2] Educational Policies Commission, *The Purposes of Education in American Democracy* (Washington, D.C.: The National Education Association, 1938).

Recently a group of teachers in a large school system met to set up their goals and objectives for teaching the social studies. With the above overall principles as their guide, these teachers defined their objectives for teaching social studies as follows:

Our Objectives: to build certain characteristics, traits, values, knowledges, skills, abilities, understandings, concepts, appreciations and attitudes in each child in order to develop an effective citizen for a democratic society. . . .

1. *Attitudes* to be developed in our children:
                    Open-mindedness.
                    Concern for others.
                    Cooperation.
                    Courtesy.
                    Respect for individuals and property.
                    Integrity.
                    Tolerance.
                    Honesty.
                    Civic responsibility.
                    Conservation.
                    Self-worth, self-development.
                    Love for learning.
                    Concern for general welfare.
                    Consent of governed.
                    Freedom of inquiry.

2. *Skills* we want to develop in our children:
            Skills at problem solving.
            Self evaluation and group evaluation.
            Critical thinking.
            Communication skills (listening, etc.).
            Map and chart skills.
            Study skills: the ability to do research.
                    the ability to outline.
                    the ability to use original sources.
                    the ability to summarize.
                    the ability to record data.
                    the ability to take notes.
                    the ability to select main ideas.
                    the ability to read for details.
                    the ability to make oral and written reports.
                    the ability to plan.
                    the ability to read and use maps.
                    the ability to read and use charts, graphs and cartoons.

3. *Values* to be developed in our children:
                    Value of democratic principles.
                    Moral values.

Aesthetic values.
Spiritual values.
Conservation.
Equality of opportunity.
Guarantee of civil liberties.
Pursuit of happiness.

4. *Knowledge* to be developed in our children:
Democracy.
Culture—heritage.
Other cultures.
World problems.
Races.
Creeds.
Economic factors.
Citizenship.
Family life.
Other families.
Conservation.

5. *Abilities* to be developed:
Creativeness.
Self-control.
To work in groups.
To communicate with others—and peers.
Critical thinking.
Creative thinking.
To make decisions.
To pass judgments.
To apply knowledge and learnings.
Sharing each other's viewpoints.
Ability to plan.
To organize.

6. *Appreciations* to be developed:
Of environment.
Aesthetic sense—fine things.
Respect for work.
Enjoyment of a rich, full life.

7. *Characteristics* to be developed:
Self-direction.
Self-realization (creativeness).
Physical fitness.
Resourcefulness.
Initiative.
Cooperation.
Open-mindedness.
Appreciation (culture, heritage, etc.).

8. *Traits* to be developed:
>Insight.
>Understanding.
>Responsibility.
>Honesty.
>Sincerity.
>Sense of humor.

Once the specific objectives for teaching the social studies content and providing for social living have been set, a school staff must translate them into action. This is done by choosing from the reservoir of social science concepts those which will be taught and determining the *method* or technique to be employed. In the *method* lies the opportunity for the teacher to be creative in her teaching. From the *method* comes the creative social experiences of the children. If the creative approach to teaching is employed, creative powers in children can be developed.

Summary

The social studies program is not simply a combination of geography, history, and civics, as some schools propose. Nor is it a series of lessons in reading comprehension—a study of the accumulation of man's experiences with man in the past with the intent of utilizing this knowledge to solve the problems of the present. It is more than that; it means providing the opportunity for children to learn and practice the necessary knowledge and skills needed for them to take their place as effective individuals in their society—both as children and as adults. The problems of the Space Age are new to the world and cannot always be solved in terms of the experiences of the past. creative thinkers are needed more than ever before. Therefore the new social studies program must assume the responsibility of developing citizens who can meet inevitable change with the ability to solve creatively the problems introduced by that change.

TO THE COLLEGE STUDENT

1. Read *The Big Red Schoolhouse* by Fred M. Hechinger (see bibliography). Discuss this book in class. What would you say are the major objectives for Russia's educational system? Does the author

present a clear and unbiased picture of both the Russian and American school systems?

2. Make a list of all the ways an autocratic classroom interferes with creative development.

3. Write a theme on the following topic: "Those Things I Would Be Willing To Die For." Share this in class and discuss those values young adults hold precious.

4. If you have not seen the following films, any one of them will give you the basis for a good discussion on values and understandings.

The Toymaker (16 min., black and white, Athena Films)
The House I Live In (10 min., black and white, Young America Films)
Brotherhood of Man (10 min., color, Brandon)
Boundary Lines (10 min., color, McGraw-Hill)

5. Discuss the following questions as objectively as possible:
Is there prejudice on your college campus? Where?
Is there religious prejudice?
Is there racial intolerance?
Is there unfair discrimination?

6. Here is a chance to do some creative thinking, and to see how many ideas you can use to prove your point. After discussing the above questions, discuss this one: Are prejudice and intolerance founded in any truth, and if so, what?

TO THE CLASSROOM TEACHER

1. Evaluate your social studies program and ask yourself what you are doing to develop traits, characteristics, values, and appreciations mentioned in this chapter. What can you do to develop them or to improve them if you are already working with them? The following chapters in the book will help you.

2. Education is the process that changes human behavior. Observe your children over a week's period and try to note in each child a behavior change which you have brought about through something you have taught him or something you have done for him.

3. Examine your present social studies textbook, especially the section on Africa, and note the so-called facts recorded there which have lost their validity since the book was published. Think of ways teachers can keep real facts before the children. How should textbooks of this nature be used?

TO THE COLLEGE STUDENT AND THE CLASSROOM TEACHER

1. Almost always, when a dictator rises to power, the first thing he does is to confiscate the school system. Discuss the reasons for this. Refer to page 22 and decide whether or not the motivation for doing this is the same as that behind the public schools of America.

2. The aims of education as set up by the Educational Policies Commission and the aims of teaching the social studies as outlined in this chapter are similar in many ways. Study both lists and decide how they are alike. Then consider this statement: The goals of all education are best met through the social studies program. How do you feel about this?

3. Make a list of all the things you can think of that cannot be left to chance if democracy is to survive. Is the school taking care of all of these functions? Should it?

4. The Educational Policies Commission recently published five purposes of the American public school today. Find these purposes and discuss them. Notice that the latest to be added is: To develop the creative role.

5. The author remembers one of his elementary school teachers making the following statements:

"Man's occupations are largely determined by the climate in which he lives."
"Nevada is a desert state and will always be sparsely settled."
"The south is agricultural, the north is largely industrial."
"The shortest route from New York to Tokyo is through the Panama Canal."

All these statements are now false, while a few years ago they were taught as fact. What is wrong with teaching that allows no room for change in facts or change in concepts? Discuss the circumstances which brought about the change in these one-time "facts." When children grow up with such misconceptions, often they operate for years in ignorance. How, in a good social studies program, can this sort of thing be avoided?

6. It is the constitutional right of all citizens in a democracy to have equal opportunity. Read *Elmtown's Youth* by A. B. Hollingshead (New York: John Wiley) and decide whether or not this equality of opportunity really exists. Read Vance Packard's *The Status Seekers* (see bibliography) and note whether or not the condition has changed any since *Elmtown's Youth*. Is a structured class society part of the democratic dream? Does a structured class society provide equal opportunity for the *creative* development of all its members?

SELECTED BIBLIOGRAPHY

ADAMS, WESLEY. *Teaching Social Studies in the Elementary Schools.* Boston: D. C. Heath and Company, 1952.

AMBROSE, EDNA and ALICE MIEL. *Children's Social Learning.* Washington, D.C.: The Association for Supervision and Curriculum Development of the National Education Association, 1958.

CLEMENTS, H. M., W. R. FIEDLER, and B. R. TABACHNICK. *Social Study: Inquiry in Elementary Classrooms.* Indianapolis: Bobbs-Merrill Company, Inc., 1966.

HILL, WILHELMINA (ed.). *Social Studies in the Elementary School Program.* Washington, D.C.: United States Department of Health, Education and Welfare, 1960.

HECHINGER, FRED. *The Big Red Schoolhouse.* New York: Doubleday and Company, 1959.

HOLLINGSHEAD, A. *Elmtown's Youth.* New York: John Wiley & Sons, Inc., 1949.

HORATIO, HENRY V. *New Social Studies Methodology.* Minneapolis, Minn.: Burgess Publishing Company, 1958.

HUNNICUTT, L. (ed.). *Social Studies for the Middle Grades: Yearbook of the National Council for Social Studies.* Washington, D.C.: The National Education Association, 1960.

JAROLIMEK, JOHN. *Social Studies in Elementary Education.* New York: The Macmillan Company, 1959.

JOHNSON, EARL. *Theory and Practice in the Social Studies.* New York: The Macmillan Company, 1958.

MERRITT, EDITH. *Working With Children in the Social Studies.* San Francisco: Wadsworth Publishing Company, 1961.

MICHAELIS, JOHN. *Social Studies for Children in a Democracy.* Englewood Cliffs, N.J.: Prentice-Hall, Inc., 1959.

MIEL, ALICE and PEGGY BROGAN. *More Than Social Studies*. Englewood Cliffs, N.J.: Prentice-Hall, Inc., 1957.

MOFFATT, MAURICE. *Social Studies Instruction*. Englewood Cliffs, N.J.: Prentice-Hall, Inc., 1950.

OTTO, HENRY J. *Social Education in Elementary Schools*. New York: Holt, Rinehart and Winston, Inc., 1956.

PACKARD, VANCE. *The Status Seekers*. New York: David McKay Company, Inc., 1959.

PRESTON, RALPH. *Teaching Social Studies in the Elementary School*. New York: Rinehart and Company, 1957.

TIEGS, ERNEST W. and FAY ADAMS. *Teaching the Social Studies*. New York: Ginn and Company, 1959.

The Social-Emotional Nature of Creativity

. . . We are interested in the constructive side of creativeness, and I wonder if it cannot be reduced to just one word—*care*. I believe that any fine thing must above all else reflect human care, and when this care is uninhibited by conformity and is really profound, it is creative.

. . . So we might say that, if we are going to be creative, all we need is a deep sense of care. First, however, we must have a purpose or a way of life that is commensurate with human needs.
. . . human life has no boundaries provided it recognizes the wonderful and beautiful potentialities of the individual human being.[1]

ALAN DOW

TO THE READER

Try to define those qualities which make for gracious and creative living. Do you feel our present social structure and our current school programs devote enough attention to this aspect of man's development? Do children have enough practice in the art of gracious living in their schools today? Read this chapter with the intent of noting any conflicts between your ideas of gracious living and the known qualities of creative children. After you finish reading this chapter, try to resolve any differences among these conflicts.

Introduction

Creative people have often been categorized as eccentric or "different" from other people. Research in recent years has indicated that creative children do exhibit certain traits and characteristics that noncreative children do not show. Chapter V of Book I of this series[2] presents a detailed report of this research. Inasmuch as the major objectives of the social studies are concerned with social develop-

---

[1] Alan Dow, "An Architect's View on Creativity," in *Creativity and Its Cultivation,* ed. Harold H. Anderson (New York: Harper and Brothers, Publishers, 1959), pp. 42–43.

[2] James A. Smith, *Setting Conditions for Creative Teaching in the Elementary School* (Boston: Allyn and Bacon, Inc., 1966), pp. 65–81.

ment, the social-emotional behavior of creative individuals must be understood. Often their behavior has not been accepted in the ordinary classroom as worthy. School personnel may need to reevaluate their feelings about this behavior and reassess their modes of dealing with it to make certain that creative behavior is rewarded rather than punished. Certain aspects of the social behavior of creative individuals may exist because of their nonacceptance by their peers, but other aspects of it may be *necessary* for creative development. Because research is not yet conclusive in this matter, one of the immediate jobs of the teacher will be to explore creative behavior in respect to these two differences.

A review of this type of behavior appears to be a necessary base for setting conditions for the teaching of the social studies. Creative people generally are not poorly adjusted nor necessarily eccentric, as some people believe. Although *all* the behavior reviewed below is not found in each creative person, it is more often found in creative individuals than in noncreative ones, and a thread of consistency seems to prevail.

In Torrance's research on the socialization abilities of creative people, he found some interesting factors. Creative children, for instance, tend to remain individualistic when subjected to group pressures. They are not easily persuaded to change their point of view until they have evidence to prove they are wrong. Most children learn to renounce, suppress, or redirect the drives and impulses which differ from accepted social standards and to conform with the norms and expectations of society. They learn to restrain their thoughts and actions to retain their status with the total group. In this process, individuality, to a large degree, is lost. The creative child tends to hold on to his individuality.[3]

Torrance also found that creative people often cause tensions within a group because their unusual ideas present a threat to the group. Striving for autonomy and searching for solutions, the creative person attempts to work his way around blocks erected by other members of the group and to overcome restrictions and organizational controls. Often he is not given credit for his ideas even when the group uses them in the final solution to a problem.

In the personality development of the highly creative child, three characteristics stand out. First, there is a tendency for them to gain a

---

[3] E. Paul Torrance, *Guiding Creative Talent* (Englewood Cliffs, N.J.: Prentice-Hall, Inc., 1962), pp. 50–51.

reputation for having wild and silly ideas. Second, their work is characterized by high productivity of ideas "off the beaten track." Third, their work is characterized by humor or playfulness. These characteristics would appear to be of considerable importance to the teacher and counselor in assisting the highly creative child to adjust without sacrificing his creativity.[4]

Torrance feels that we may expect decrements in creative thinking ability and in creative production at about the ages of five, nine, and twelve, and that these are all transitional periods in educational careers in our society.[5]

Dr. Torrance and others have also been interested in the effect of grouping on creativity.[6] They conclude that we may expect greater disruptive social stress when we divide classroom groups heterogeneously than when we divide them homogeneously for creative activities. Creative thinking is likely to be stimulated by increasing social stress; but when stress mounts beyond a certain point, thinking is disrupted and productivity diminishes.

Viewed from the understandings wrought by this research, it is questionable that creative children can be labeled socially different in the sense of eccentricity or weakness. The ability to remain individualistic under such circumstances demonstrates character and strength, especially when the end result may be to alienate themselves from their peers, and their teacher as well. Often the creative ideas of these people are considered silly and are ignored or ridiculed by their teachers. In fact, research shows that creative children are often treated along punitive lines,[7] which often forces the creative child to choose between social acceptance or his own personal intellectual convictions. If he chooses to follow his convictions, he may alienate himself, or, determined to follow through on an idea, he may appear to be different.

There are other qualities that identify the creative child. He likes to work at challenging, difficult, and dangerous tasks. Creative children are also challenged by disorder; they seek to bring order from

---

[4] E. Paul Torrance, *Sex-Role Identification and Creative Thinking* (Minneapolis: Bureau of Educational Research, University of Minnesota, 1959).

[5] E. Paul Torrance, *Guiding Creative Talent* (Englewood Cliffs, N.J.: Prentice-Hall, Inc., 1962), p. 103.

[6] E. Paul Torrance, F. B. Baker, and J. E. Bowers, *Explorations in Creative Thinking in the Early School Years* (Minneapolis: Bureau of Educational Research, University of Minnesota, 1954).

[7] E. Paul Torrance, "Current Research on the Nature of Creative Talent," *Journal of Counseling Psychology*, VI, No. 4 (1959), pp. 309–16.

disorder—although they do not find it difficult to live with disorder in their own environment. They are more concerned with seeking for a purpose than for environmental order. Because of their willingness to cope with the unsolved and the unusual, they may become psychologically estranged from other children.

Driven by the desire to arrive at purposes and ideas, the creative child may appear to be in the trance-like state described by Rugg[8] in his studies of imagination. Rugg implies that in this state the child's mind is in what he labels the "transliminal chamber," where it is free to draw from both his conscious and his subconscious. If the teacher or children interpret this period of absorption as daydreaming or inattention, the child may be punished or ridiculed, and this necessary stage in creative production may be discouraged.

Creative children often exhibit other types of behavior which are not readily accepted by the traditional teacher. Among them is low sociability. Because creative children are more open to life experiences, creative boys may show stronger feminine interests than noncreative boys. Creative children tend to be more introverted, although they are often bolder and more self-assertive than noncreative children.

Other qualities which the researchers have attributed to creative children are: a certain amount of ego-centeredness, playfulness, an occasional lack of cooperation, a certain amount of Bohemianism, nonconformity, radical outlook, lack of adherence to conventions (courtesy included), excessive questioning, a certain amount of stubbornness, some timidity, some emotionalism, self-satisfaction, temperament and a resistance to teacher-domination. Creative children do, however, also display behavior which can be considered acceptable according to current concepts of worthy behavior. They are enthusiastic and show the ability to become highly motivated. Creative children possess a sensitivity to problems and the ability to define and identify them. They are flexible in their thinking, possess verbal and ideational fluency, are able to abstract and analyze, and will stick to a goal until disproven. They possess an ability to redefine and rearrange, to evaluate and synthesize, and they are highly independent.

Creative children have keen intuition and possess strong retention ability. They have an excellent sense of humor. They are

[8] Harold Rugg, *Imagination: An Inquiry into the Sources and Conditions that Stimulate Creativity* (New York: Harper & Row, 1963).

interested in the less conventional and are more receptive to the ideas of others. Creative children are more resourceful than noncreative children; they are more accepting of self, more mature emotionally, and more capable of dealing with emotional and social problems.

Highly creative children are also highly intelligent, although this type of giftedness is not measured by the current intelligence test, which measures intellectual but not creative giftedness. They achieve as well as noncreative children.

Creative children have a higher reaction to experience in terms of feeling and thought. They are more sensitive to beauty and take more from an experience than other children do. They are self-sufficient, willing to tackle difficult jobs, determined to excel, industrious, persistent, and versatile. They possess the courage to stick to their conscientious convictions. The creative child is a self-starter and is rarely bored. He is willing to take risks and possesses a certain sense of destiny. Creative children are more capable of self-realization than other individuals are.

In the research of Getzels and Jackson, other social differences between the creative and the noncreative child were brought to light.[9] It was found that creative children came from different homes and from parents with a different orientation toward themselves and their children. These parents were different in education, in their careers, and in the home intellectual environment they provided. They were also different in their attitudes toward their children, their children's education, and the qualities they would like their children to have. This implies that the creative character has its formulative beginnings in the home. In the high-I.Q. families, individual divergences were limited and risks minimized, while in the high-creative families, individual divergence was admitted and risks accepted.

Getzels and Jackson[10] also studied the differences in the teacher's attitude toward intellectually gifted and creatively gifted children. They found that the teacher tends to want the "gifted" child (as she defines him) in the classroom, but that parents do not tend to want the "gifted" child (as they define him) in the family. (They saw other qualities as being more important than those used to define giftedness.)

These men also found that the qualities the teacher held to be most characteristic of the gifted child were not related to those she

[9] Jacob W. Getzels and Philip W. Jackson, *Creativity and Intelligence: Explorations with Gifted Students* (New York: John Wiley & Sons, Inc., 1962), p. 74.

[10] *Ibid.*, p. 119.

believed most likely to make for success when the child became an adult. She ranked I.Q., good marks, and creativity highest in defining giftedness as against these qualities for adult success: getting along with others, goal-directedness, and emotional stability. Parents defined the gifted child as possessing the following: creativeness, high I.Q., and goal-directedness. The qualities they felt necessary for success in adult life were: getting along with others, goal-directedness, and emotional stability. Neither teachers nor parents included intelligence or creativity within the first three qualities making for adult success.

Getzels and Jackson also found that high-I.Q. children and high-creative children agreed on those qualities which make for success in adulthood and on the qualities teachers preferred in their students, but they disagreed greatly on the qualities which they wanted for themselves. The high-I.Q. students rated the qualities they value for themselves and those they believe to lead to success as adults quite closely. The high-creativity students showed almost no correlation in rating the qualities they value for themselves and those they believe to lead to success.[11]

High-I.Q. students showed a close relationship between the qualities they would like for themselves and the qualities they believe teachers like in students, which suggests that high-I.Q. students may be highly teacher-oriented. On the other hand, for the highly creative students, the comparison showed little or no relationship, suggesting that this group is not highly teacher-oriented.

Studies of children identified as creative indicate that they have a strong sense of honesty. The creative child is in search of truth. He is trying to "be" rather than just appear to be. This honesty and drive for truth may lead to a frankness that is often interpreted as rudeness. Other values commonly implemented by the church, the school, and the family may appear to be violated by the creative child because of his honesty and search for truth. Among them are forms of courtesy, appearing to be considerate of others, being visibly industrious, sharing, and cooperating.

Torrance has devised a provocative "Ideal Child Checklist" and an instrument titled "What Kind of a Person Are You?" which will help the teacher identify those qualities in children which aid or hinder their creative development.[12]

---

[11] *Ibid.*, pp. 35–36.

[12] E. Paul Torrance, *Preliminary Manual for the What Kind of a Person Are You Test* (Minneapolis: University Studies of Creative Behavior, Department of Educational Psychology, University of Minnesota, 1966).

Summary

That these differences in personality, parent attitude, teacher attitude, and self-attitude exist in the ordinary classroom poses some challenging problems for school personnel in planning for the conscientious development of creative power in children. It implies that certain conditions, different from the commonly accepted ones, must be set within the classroom in order to include: (1) the development of creativity and (2) the development of the art of living together.

TO THE COLLEGE STUDENT

1. There are many causes for behavior. Behavior may be genuine or affected. Some people play a role in order to impress others; often in so behaving they are attempting to cover up those qualities in themselves which they do not want others to discover. Have you known people who play the role of the artist, motion-picture star, poet, actor, or author but who really are none of these? How do they affect the role? Notice their clothes, manner of dress, living conditions, their mannerisms, and their activities. They are often imitating the stereotyped conception of a person they admire. Can you differentiate between the true character and the affected one? How? Discuss this problem in class.

2. How are stereotypes derived? From the lives of famous people that you have read about or seen depicted on the motion-picture screen, make a list of the people in each of the following fields who represent the stereotyped conception and those who do not: art, music, literature, science, law, journalism, army intelligence.

3. What comes to mind—that is, what words do you associate with each of the following words: Italian, Irishman, Copper, sleuth, conductor, actor, actress, poet, inventor? Analyze your list. How many represent stereotypes? Is there any justification for stereotypes? Discuss this.

4. Do some reading on the following statement, and then hold a discussion on it: Children (ages three to eight) have stereotyped conceptions of races.

5. Work out an organizational plan for a self-contained class-room on any grade level that is as ideal as possible for developing creative production in the children.

TO THE CLASSROOM TEACHER

1. In light of the research reported in this chapter, examine your plan of organization for the school day and consider this question: At what times during the school day does your plan best allow for creative development?

2. Educators have often been accused of negating one objective of education in attempting to accomplish another. If the development of creative thinking is to be an objective of the elementary school, what current accepted practices will need to be changed so that it will not be negated by current practices of teaching and organization within the classroom?

3. Look among your students for some of the characteristics described in this chapter. Observe over a period of several days the children who possess them. Note their creative output. After reading this chapter can you be more tolerant of this behavior? Think of ways you can channel this behavior into constructive production.

4. A few years ago the ridiculous phrase "the over-achiever" crept into the jargon of the educator. The over-achiever was the child who seemed always to achieve higher than his intelligence quotient would warrant. In terms of what you have read so far in this book, explain the over-achiever. What would be a more realistic name for such a child?

5. From the work of Getzels and Jackson, who studied the home environment of highly creative and highly intelligent children, would you say that conditions set at home have much to do with the creative development of children before and after they reach school age?

6. It is fairly certain that, if creative thinking is an objective of education, parents will need to understand this new concept. Plan an educational program for the parents of your school which will help them to understand the concepts of creativity and the manner in which you are attempting to implement these concepts. Do not

overlook the use of popular current modes of communication, such as the P.T.A., Mothers' Clubs, the school visiting night, report cards, etc.

7. Does your school have a place on the report card which indicates the child's creative growth? Should it have? How would you measure the creative growth of children? How would you report it?

TO THE COLLEGE STUDENT AND THE CLASSROOM TEACHER

1. All of the following people were considered to be eccentric or foolish at one time in their lives. Were they? If not, how do you explain people's attitude toward them? Review material in Chapters I, II, and III for your answers.

> Robert Fulton (Fulton's Folly)
> De Witt Clinton (Clinton's Ditch)
> The Wright Brothers
> Alexander Graham Bell
> Sir Isaac Newton
> Christopher Columbus

2. How does each of the beliefs of the above people demonstrate one or more principles of the creative process? *Example:* The concept that water does not run uphill is a sample of the idea of functional fixedness and prevented many people from understanding Clinton's concept of the lock that could raise boats to higher levels.

3. Make a list of all the characteristics of creative people that are mentioned in this chapter and check those which we would like to see developed in all children because they are essential to creative and aesthetic living in a democratic society.

4. Torrance states that decrements in creative thinking and creative production may be expected at about ages five, nine, and twelve, times when there are transitional periods in educational careers. What happens to children at these ages which may contribute to a slump in creative production? Discuss this question in class.

5. Discuss Torrance's conclusion that heterogeneous grouping is likely to stimulate creative thinking in terms of currently popular organizational plans such as: ability grouping, the nongraded school,

the multigraded school, departmentalization, team-teaching, the Joplin Plan, the self-contained classroom, and others.

6. Maslow states that the status need comes before the creative need and that highly creative acts are performed generally by people who are comfortable with their status. Torrance states that creative children often cause tension within groups. Could it be that their creative ideas serve as a threat to other group members? Discuss this with your classmates.

SELECTED BIBLIOGRAPHY

BLOOM, B. S. "Some Effects of Cultural, Social and Educational Conditions on Creativity," in *The Second University of Utah Conference on the Identification of Creative Scientific Talent.* Salt Lake City: University of Utah Press, 1958.

CARLSON, RUTH K. "Emergence of Creative Personality." *Childhood Education,* XXXVI (1960), 402–04.

FLESCHER, IRWIN. "Anxiety and Achievement of Intellectually Gifted and Creatively Gifted Children," *Journal of Psychology,* 56 (1963), 251–68.

GETZELS, JACOB W. and PHILIP W. JACKSON. *Creativity and Intelligence.* New York: John Wiley & Sons, Inc., 1962.

HAMMER, E. T. "Emotional Stability and Creativity," *Percept Skills,* XII (1961), 102.

LASSWELL, H. D. "The Social Setting of Creativity," in H. Anderson, ed., *Creativity and Its Cultivation.* New York: Harper and Brothers, 1959.

LEHNER, GEORGE, T. J. and ELLA KUBE. *The Dynamics of Personal Adjustment.* Englewood Cliffs, N.J.: Prentice-Hall, Inc., 1955.

MEER, B. "Measures of Intelligence and Creativity," *Journal of Psychology,* XXXIX (1955), 117–26.

MEER, B. and M. L. STERN. "Measures of Intelligence and Creativity," *Creativity and the Individual.* Glencoe, Illinois: The Free Press, 1960.

RUGG, HAROLD. *Imagination: An Inquiry into the Sources and Conditions that Stimulate Creativity.* New York: Harper & Row, 1963.

STEIN, MORRIS I. and SHIRLEY HEINZE. *Creativity and the Individual.* Glencoe, Illinois: The Free Press, 1960.

TAYLOR, CALVIN W. and JOHN L. HOLLAND. "Development and Application of Tests of Creativity," *Review of Educational Research,* XXXIII (February, 1962), 91–102.

TORRANCE, E. PAUL. *Guiding Creative Talent.* Englewood Cliffs, N.J.: Prentice-Hall, Inc., 1962.

———. *Highly Intelligent and Highly Creative Children in a Laboratory School.* Minneapolis: Bureau of Educational Research, University of Minnesota, 1959.

————. *Rewarding Creative Behavior*. Englewood Cliffs, N. J.: Prentice-Hall, Inc., 1965.

TORRANCE, E. PAUL, FRANK B. BAKER, and JOHN E. BOWERS. "Exploration in Creative Thinking in the Early School Year," *Research Memoranda*. Minneapolis: Bureau of Educational Research, University of Minnesota, 1960.

Part Two

The Nurture of
Creativity Through
the Social Studies

Creative
Social
Living

. . . To be creative means to consider the whole process of life as a process of birth, and not to take any state of life as the final stage. Most people die before they are fully born. Creativeness means to be born before one dies.

*   *   *

. . . Without courage and faith, creativity is impossible, and hence the understanding and cultivation of courage and faith are indispensable conditions for the development of the creative attitude.[1]

ERICH FROMM

TO THE READER

Creative teaching can be fulfilled to a great degree by new ideas in school construction which make possible the moving of walls and the enclosure of space for different patterns of grouping in a variety of learning situations. Make simple floor plans or models of an ideal school situation for carrying out: (1) an ungraded school, (2) a multigraded school, (3) a self-contained classroom. Plan for such concepts as team-teaching, television teaching, and flexible use of materials. Check to see if you included most necessary details by reading this chapter. The author would like to see some of your plans.

Introduction

Creativity cannot be taught as such: we can only set conditions for it to happen. In Book I of this series the basic conditions for creating a classroom laboratory were described. Other conditions need to be considered as they apply to the teaching of the social studies.[2]

[1] Erich Fromm, "The Creative Attitude," in *Creativity and Its Cultivation*, ed. Harold H. Anderson (New York: Harper and Brothers, Publishers, 1959), pp. 53–54.

[2] James A. Smith, *Setting Conditions for Creative Teaching in the Elementary School* (Boston: Allyn and Bacon, Inc., 1966), Chapter VIII.

The Appropriate Physical Environment

Early advocates of the Progressive Education movement were among the first educators to recommend that the classroom, to be truly a learning laboratory, must be a workroom. Many of the ideas of the past seem applicable to the present as ways to develop creativity and should be preserved, and this is one of them. Many of these ideas, it is true, provided for creative development on an "accidental" basis, although this cannot be said of this particular premise. Recent research in the area of creativity would indicate that the progressives were on the right track. Their concepts regarding a special environment to accomplish specific goals have been verified by recent research, and a fresh look must be taken at the concept of the classroom as a laboratory for developing creativity and other social skills.

One of the plans involved in designing a classroom laboratory which now makes sense in terms of developing creativity was the idea of classroom centers. The schoolroom was divided into working spaces where the materials for various areas of the curriculum were kept in such a manner that they were easily accessible to children. This arrangement provided for grouping children for various activities so that they could use the materials and yet be somewhat isolated from other children. In such a classroom the tools children used in their work were readily available and the floor space was utilized economically, with opportunity for rearrangement of furniture to create large work and play areas. Materials could be easily manipulated and explored.

Movable furniture is necessary in such a situation, for if the children are to work in groups (both large and small), the furniture arrangement will vary from day to day, even from period to period. The children themselves should have a part in planning their room.

Some teachers prefer to have their children enter a bare schoolroom on the first day of school and begin from scratch to build a workable, functional, attractive classroom. Others feel they miss the opportunity to study their children and discover their interests, needs, and individual differences by having them enter such a classroom; they plan a first-day program with definite objectives in mind, with the understanding that the classroom will be changed by the children as they have the experience of replanning it.

Considering that creative children are challenged to bring order out of disorder, the planning of the classroom as a working laboratory may well be one of the first planned experiences which teachers utilize to develop creative qualities in the children. The arrangement of the classroom will undergird the pattern of social living which is to take place in the class.

In one fourth-grade classroom, the teacher planned the physical setting with the children by making a floor plan on the chalkboard. Such decisions as to where the reading center should be with respect to light, where the art center should be with respect to the location of the sink, and what changes in arrangement should be made were roughed in on the floor plan. A list of the centers of interest was then made and the material the class needed in each center was discussed. Articles that were not available in the school were underlined, and the children offered to find them outside of school and bring them for temporary or permanent use. Some articles, such as exhibit shelves, they planned to make. These lists looked something like this:

Our Science Center:

fishbowls
dry cells
magnet
bulletin board
science books
mayonnaise jars
coffee cans
screen for cages
cages
terrarium
aquarium
rock collections for other exhibits
science leaflets and magazines
show table
exhibit shelves

Our Social Studies Center:

encyclopedias
reference books
dictionary
Information Please
storybooks
a classroom file
a globe
maps
magazines

books
pamphlets
radio or TV set
bookcase
exhibit shelves

Our Art and Music Center:

instruments
music books
piano

victrola
records
cupboards

easel
colored construction paper
water paint
enamel paint
pans
hot plate
crayons
art books
bulletin boards
scissors

drawing paper
manila paper
easel paper
brushes
clay
box scrap cloth
box scrap paper
material for arrangements
cupboards

Our Shop Center:

workbench
hammers
saw
bit and brace
screw driver
tool holder
bulletin board

scrap wood
pliers
coping saws
box of nails
magazines
vise

Our Reading Center:

reading books
story books
book jackets
magazines
bulletin boards

pamphlets
bookcases
reading table
chairs
SRA materials
reading machine

Other Parts of Our Room:

beauty center
vocabulary chart
planning center around board
isolation spot behind screen (table, chairs, and typewriter)
bookshelves or cupboards for texts and aids:
    arithmetic aids
    spelling aids
    language texts
    workbooks
audio-visual materials

After the arrangement of the room was determined and the materials listed, the aesthetic qualities of the room were discussed. Holding colored construction paper against the walls, the children chose color schemes. A survey of the material available led to a listing of furniture that could be painted and that which could not. Children agreed to bring bricks and planks for the centers where there were no bookcases. These could be painted to carry the color scheme around the room. The class decided to cover the bulletin boards with butcher's paper and paint them over with water paint which harmonized with the room color scheme to make soft, pleasant backgrounds for mounting pictures and children's work. The possibility of making drapes for the windows and frames for the children's pictures was discussed. Next the class decided which jobs should be done at once and by whom, a list of necessary materials was made, and they formed committees to go to work the next day.

From such a first day's experience the children were well launched on the type of program that can lead them to respect other's abilities, to tolerance and appreciation of each other's ideas, to

FIGURE 4–1. *A planning and report center for the sevens and eights.*

FIGURE 4–2. *A shop center for the sixes.*

acceptance of responsibility, to acquisition of working skills and new knowledge, to new organization techniques, and to creating a pleasant working atmosphere. Creative children will thrive under such arrangements, and other children will learn skills that contribute to their creative development.

In such an environment children are given independence as soon as they can accept it. Committees are formed to care for the various centers and perform housekeeping and administrative duties. A permissive atmosphere, where children are free to make mistakes without developing guilt feelings, is developed. Teachers and children plan together, and together they solve the problems that arise. In this atmosphere, true democratic living is promoted, and the skills the child practices are those he will need for rich and intelligent living in adulthood. The physical environment is important, but the social-emotional environment is even more important.

The Social-Emotional Conditions[3]

The most important and necessary condition to be considered in the social-emotional structure of the classroom is that the teacher recognize the qualities and characteristics of the creative child as they were presented in Chapter III and accept them. This may mean that she will observe and interpret some behavior differently than she has previously, and may be more accepting of the type of behavior that appears to develop creativity. At the same time she must be concerned about social growth and development and must find ways to build acceptance among the members of the total group for each child in the group.

Creative behavior may be encouraged by the following practices:

1. Reward various kinds and varying degrees of creative achievement among children and encourage individuality, uniqueness, originality, and independence.
2. Develop an atmosphere in the classroom which is permissive and "expectant" to the extent that children feel free to manipulate, experiment with, and explore ideas and objects, and are not threatened with making mistakes or experiencing failure.
3. Help children recognize the value of their own and each other's creative powers and, in so doing, encourage all children to accept the creative child more fully, thus diminishing his anxieties and fears.
4. Stress *both* convergent *and* divergent thinking processes by teaching knowledges that can be used for creative problem-solving; but place emphasis frequently on open-ended situations and develop creative acceptance of realistic limitations in a problem situation.
5. Plan high motivational procedures so that children become involved in their own learnings, and then employ the best techniques of discussion, questioning, and flexible thinking so that they are provided with the opportunity to talk about their ideas.
6. Teach directly for creative development by fostering those skills closely affiliated with it: outlining, summarizing, evaluating, synthesizing, critical thinking, making decisions, passing judgment, visual acuity, and retention ability.
7. Help the children to set reasonable goals that (because they are defined together) are recognized by the teacher, and then help the children arrive at basic principles rather than memorize excessive numbers of facts.[4]

[3] *Ibid.*, Chapter V, pp. 65–81.
[4] *Ibid.*, Chapter VIII, pp. 117–148.

8. Make the curriculum experience-centered and utilize *all* areas of the curriculum to foster creative development.
9. Avoid the equation of divergency with mental illness and delinquency.
10. Avoid the fine-line definition of work and play, and modify the misplaced emphasis (in both work and play) on sex roles.
11. Avoid unnecessary and excessive conformity.
12. Develop an appreciation of creativity in the classroom.

Psychological Conditions

For creative social growth, certain psychological conditions must be set in the classroom. Reviewed from Chapter III, Book I of this series,[5] they are as follows. Certain securities must exist to make the child feel safe to venture forth into creative exploration. In addition to those mentioned under social-emotional conditions are the following:

1. An absence of threat to self.
2. Acceptance of each individual within the group.
3. Confidence that one has the necessary background and ability to face the problem ahead.
4. Self-awareness, the ability to keep in touch with one's feelings.
5. The willingness to be different because of lack of social threat.
6. An ability to accept the ideas of others.
7. The ability to meet failure experiences in social as well as intellectual relations.
8. A permissive atmosphere where experimentation and exploration is accepted.
9. A great deal of practice in creative thinking.
10. A knowledgeable and accepting attitude on the part of parents and teachers toward creativity.
11. An understanding that excessive obedience tends to destroy creative drive.
12. Using democratic practices in the classroom.
13. Understanding the developmental characteristics of children at each age level as well as each child's potential ability so that the teacher will know what to expect from each child at each age level.

Some illustrations of the effectiveness of these conditions are presented in Part II of this book.[6]

---

[5] *Ibid.*, Chapter III, pp. 25–45.
[6] See page 159.

Intellectual Conditions

Chapter IV of Book I of this series, *Setting Conditions for Creative Teaching in the Elementary School,* deals with the necessary intellectual conditions which must be set for developing creativity. While all of these conditions apply to all teaching, a comment about the intellectual conditions for creative development through the social studies is in order.

A great deal of emphasis has been placed throughout this series on divergent thinking processes to develop creativity. Teaching the social studies has long been regarded as helping children to understand the problems of mankind through the problem-solving approach. This approach has been largely constructed of techniques that develop convergent thinking processes, collecting facts already known, and arriving at a solution to a problem that has already been solved by someone else. When we add the development of divergent processes to the convergent thinking processes, we add a new dimension. Social studies teaching will not be considered the teaching of facts and knowledge of the social sciences, but will present facts and knowledges to children with the intent of their applying them to possible solutions to current problems. This calls for skill on the part of the teacher in handling discussion, in phrasing questions, and in developing group abilities and group dynamics. Many of the older methods of teaching, such as the unit method (see Chapter VI of this book), are especially adaptable to this plan and may be renewed with vigor because of their proven worth and their adaptiveness to the development of creativity.

In the creative teaching of the social studies it must be remembered that creativity cannot be identified by the current intelligence test, yet creativity is a kind of giftedness. Many children will be able to create sound ideas for good human relationships within the classroom. The teacher has no instrument at this writing which will help her predict this. She can only make certain that she searches for these creative children by listening to them and watching their behavior. She must also be aware that all children are capable of creative production to some degree. The best way to identify creative talent is to look for originality in thought, ability to redefine, flexibility of thinking, associational fluency, ability to verbalize fluently, ideational fluency, and the ability to elaborate and evaluate. Children who seem to possess these qualities are probably more creative than other children.

These abilities may be developed in children through carefully planned lessons. They are all components of the creative act and can be developed separately. Setting the proper intellectual conditions for developing creative power means that teachers work at each of these abilities and that they make sure they are frequently utilized in creative problem-solving.

Another factor required for creative production is an understanding of the creative process as described in Chapter I of this book or more explicitly in Chapter VI, Book I of this series. When teachers know how creative problem-solving takes place, they will not be tempted to force creativity. This knowledge can help the teacher understand the child who is in the process of creating, and will make a decided difference in the type of homework and school assignments which she gives. It will influence her methodology in the classroom. Creative problem-solving requires a different set of skills than other types of problem-solving; it requires the whole of the individual—his experience, his knowledge, his skills, his intellect, his convergent thinking abilities, his flexibility, his personality, and a complete absorption in the problem.

In creative problem-solving the solution offers tremendous satisfaction—not only because a problem has been solved and a job completed, but because the product has aesthetic qualities and both the process and the product have been satisfying to the creator, who has given of himself to the project. Something of himself has emerged in a form that he recognizes (and which others recognize) as his own unique contribution to the solution.

Summary

Creativity, as we have defined it, cannot really be taught. Certain component parts of the creative thought process, such as those mentioned above, can be taught. Basically, in one sense we can only set conditions for it to happen and to encourage its reappearance through reinforcement.

Certain conditions may be set in the classroom to bring creativity into the open where it can be utilized. These conditions center around the physical conditions in the environment, the social-emotional climate of the classroom, the psychological conditions established by school personnel, and the kind of intellectual stimulus planned by the teacher.

The key to the development of creative problem-solving and creative endeavor, however, lies almost entirely in the teacher's responsiveness to the child's creative efforts. Teachers can teach for creative development by engaging children in a sequence of experiences that give them practice in many of the skills of creative thinking, as later chapters in this book will demonstrate. In this sense the teacher can guide, direct, and hope to develop creative effort. But because the answers to the problems are not known at the onset of a lesson (indeed, the problems themselves may not all be known), the guidance and direction set by the teacher will result in behavior or processes or products which are not predetermined. In this sense they are not taught because they are discovered as the process develops.

Setting the proper conditions will draw out creativeness, and acceptance and praise of the resulting creative process or product will encourage its appearance again and again.

TO THE COLLEGE STUDENT

1. Read the quotations from Erich Fromm at the beginning of this chapter. Discuss the second quote as a necessary condition for creative living in the classroom.

2. Frank Lloyd Wright once said, "A house is space enclosed for a purpose." Might this definition also be applied to a school? If so, what modifications in the plans of the traditional schoolroom would you advocate as a necessary change for the development of creativity?

3. Consider the conditions described in this chapter and use them as an evaluation of your college classrooms. Are some of your college classrooms better set up to develop creativity than others? Would you say that most college administrators consider the development of creativity to be one of their major objectives?

4. Plan a self-contained college classroom that will not only accomplish the objectives of perpetuating knowledge in the subject-matter area for which it is intended, but will develop creativity as well. Be sure to consider equipment, seating arrangement, facilities, etc.

5. Make a list of objectives you would have as a teacher for any grade level on the first day of school. Plan a classroom setup that will make it possible for you to accomplish these objectives.

TO THE CLASSROOM TEACHER

1. Make a check list of factors necessary for the development of creative thinking and creative production as described in this chapter and use it to evaluate your own classroom. If you can recognize the deficiencies in current existing conditions, make plans to remedy them. Is your classroom really a working laboratory?

2. Look at the list of social-emotional conditions necessary for creative production in the classroom as described on page 53. With this list in mind, consider the following questions:

a. Can you as a teacher overpraise a child's art work? What dangers are inherent in this?

b. Is it possible for children to be creative under certain restrictions and pressures? When is this condition acceptable or even necessary?

c. What parts of your school program are already devoted to developing many of the components of creativity, such as audio acuity, visual acuity, outlining, summarizing, and other areas mentioned under point 6, page 53?

d. In one given situation a group of children were allowed to use any materials they chose from a large supply to design a poster. In another situation they were asked to construct a poster with only four basic materials. Which situation set the best conditions to challenge creative thinking and creative production?

e. Do reading groups called before the teacher for the purpose of teaching from the basic manual set conditions for much creative development? How could reading group lessons be made more creative?

3. Set up a beauty center in your classroom; perhaps you could place a small table where everyone could see it. On it set a frame that has been salvaged from an old picture or made from cardboard. Choose groups of children to make some sort of still life arrangement within this frame each day. Suggest themes and ideas but encourage the children to create their arrangements by themselves. Note how this one activity increases their ability to create and to stretch their

imagination. The beauty center can become a springboard for art, music, and creative writing activities.

TO THE COLLEGE STUDENT AND
THE CLASSROOM TEACHER

1. Teachers can provoke creativity in many ways. One is the manner by which they ask questions. For instance, when a teacher says, "What is that supposed to be?" when she views a child's painting, she is practically demanding that the child answer with a definite label. "Tell me about your painting," allows the child to describe in his own creative way his creative product. Below is a list of questions your author recently heard in various classrooms. Reword them so they are more likely to evoke creative responses in the children:

"What is the first step we go through in solving arithmetic problems?"
"I have placed on the chalkboard a list of the inventions which re-sulted from Edison's invention of the electric light. Why is Thomas Edison an important man to remember?"
"The fireman is a community helper. In what ways does the fireman help us?"
"Read the next chapter in your science book and tell me how seeds are spread by nature?"
"What color do I get when I mix yellow and red?"
"What part of speech is *walk?*"

2. Which of the following projects, suggested by various text-books, set conditions for creative activity, and which are simply busy work?

"Draw a plan of a medieval castle as it is described in this chapter." (Grade 5)
"Make three houses like this. Color one red, one blue, and one yellow." (Grade 1)
"Make a list of the states and opposite each write its capital." (Grade 6)
"Visit a supermarket and list all the ways you see foods being pre-served today. Try to find out at what time on your time-line each way of preserving food was introduced." (Grades 4–6)
"If you live near a library, visit it and ask to see some real old newspapers. Then look at the advertisements. Notice the differences in tools, clothes, materials, and services for sale. Notice, too, the difference in prices. What brought about all these changes?" (Grades 4–6)
"Find a copy of a constitution to see just what it is that people are fighting for. The Constitution of the United States would be a good one for this purpose." (Grade 5)

"Look at home to see if you have some articles made in the Lowland Countries. Do you perhaps have some Delft china, or a Belgian rug, or some Dutch tulips? Make a list of all the things you can find that members of your class have from the Lowlands of Europe." (Grade 6)

"After you have found some children to whom to write in England, make a tape-recording of your British program and mail it to them. Ask them if their teacher will send one to you for you to play in your class." (Grade 6)

"List three causes of the War Between the States." (Grade 6)

SELECTED BIBLIOGRAPHY

ASSOCIATION FOR CHILDHOOD EDUCATION INTERNATIONAL. *Children Can Work Independently.* Washington, D.C.: The Association, 1952.

———. *Space Arrangement, Beauty in School.* Washington, D.C.: The Association, 1958.

ASSOCIATION FOR SUPERVISION AND CURRICULUM DEVELOPMENT. *Creating a Good Environment for Learning.* Washington, D. C.: National Education Association, 1954.

BEAUCHAMP, C. *Basic Dimensions of Elementary Method.* Boston: Allyn and Bacon, Inc., 1959.

DUNKEL, H. B. "Creativity and Education," *Educational Theory,* XI (October, 1961), 209–16.

GUILFORD, J. P. "Factors That Aid and Hinder Creativity," *Teachers College Record,* LXII (February, 1962), 380–92.

HACK, LOUISE E. "Using Committees in the Classroom," *Rinehart Education Pamphlets.* New York: Rinehart and Company, Inc., 1958.

HARAP, HENRY. *Social Living in the Curriculum.* Nashville, Tennessee: George Peabody College for Teachers, 1952.

LEVINGER, LEAH. "The Teacher's Role in Creativity: Discussion," *American Journal Orthopsychiatry,* XXIX (1959), 291–97.

MIEL, ALICE (ed.). *Creativity in Teaching: Invitations and Instances.* Belmont, California: Wadsworth Publishing Co., Inc., 1961.

MYERS, R. E. and E. PAUL TORRANCE. "Can Teachers Encourage Creative Thinking?" *Educational Leadership,* XIX (1961), 156–59.

STEPHENS, ADAM D. *Toward the Development of Creativity in Early Childhood.* University of Toledo: College of Education, 1963.

TAYLOR, CALVIN. "Clues to Creative Teaching" (a series of ten articles), *The Instructor* (September–June, 1963–64).

——— (ed.). *Widening Horizons in Creativity.* New York: John Wiley & Sons, 1965.

TORRANCE, E. PAUL. *Creativity: What Research Says to the Teacher.* Washington, D.C.: National Education Association, 1963.

WILT, MARION E. *Creativity in the Elementary School.* New York: Appleton-Century-Crofts, Inc., 1959.

WOLFSON, B. J. "Creativity in the Classroom," *Elementary English,* XXXVII (November, 1961), 523–24.

V
Organizational Skills

Throughout the development of civilization, man has been, above all, an orderer. Throughout time and in all places of the earth he has transformed wild hillsides into gardens of ordered beauty. Working his will upon the chaotic watershed of the Tennessee, he organized that huge area into a cultivated valley of farms and towns, with channels for production and distribution, transportation, communication, and markets. In the recurring episodes of Western history, creative men have transformed political anarchy into order, rebuilt disrupted economic systems, and stated the mood and the mind of the people in poems, songs, plays, paintings, dances. The creative task is always the same, whether it be in art, science or invention: that of reducing miscellany to order. This is the principle of form, variously called "Heaven's first law," the "first principle of the universe," "modern science's final explanation," and "the foundation of all art." It is the basis of the sciences and arts of man. Its synonyms are organization, organism, the unity of the whole.[1]

HAROLD RUGG

TO THE READER
Think of all the organizational skills required of you in your daily living. Many of these skills are automatic in your way of life. If all art and creativity grow from man's ability to organize his experiences into new acts, think of all the ways you can to make the skills necessary for living and creating automatic in children. Then read this chapter. Did you list skills not dealt with in the following pages?

Introduction

Creative children are challenged by disorder; they enjoy creating order, seeing relationships, and setting goals. They thrive on independence and the ability to express themselves.

Teaching the skills of organization and complete involvement contributes to the development of creative powers. There is no better way to do this than through the involvement of children in their own

[1] Harold Rugg, *Imagination: An Inquiry Into the Sources and Conditions that Stimulate Creativity* (New York: Harper & Row, Publishers, 1963), pp. 124–125.

learning through pupil-teacher planning. This idea, popular a few years ago, has fallen into disuse in many schools because of new organizational plans set up by administrators and imposed on children. As an aid to creative development, pupil-teacher planning needs reevaluating.

Berger, Guilford, and Christensen[2] contend that planning must be broadly conceived as a term covering a number of classes of activities and entailing a number of separate abilities. Their research with planning enabled them to isolate and define the following abilities as those involved in planning: verbal comprehension, numerical facility, visualization, general reasoning, logical evaluation, ideational fluency, education of conceptual relations, judgment, originality, and adaptive flexibility. Four new abilities were labeled by the researchers: ordering, elaboration, perceptual foresight, and conceptual foresight.

Pupil Teacher Planning

If we check those qualities which contribute to the development of creativity as mentioned by Guilford and others (see Book I of this series)[3] we will note that many are developed in the planning process. In this sense the development of planning abilities contributes extensively to the development of creativity.

Aside from its contribution to the development of creative powers, pupil-teacher planning is important for many reasons. First, one learns to plan by having the experience of planning. Many adults do not know how to organize and plan because they have never learned. College students often must take courses in which they learn how to study and how to plan a school day because they waste hours of time in aimless activity and poor study techniques. This results in failing grades in spite of a high intelligence. Children should plan to learn how to organize with ease and skill.

Second, children should know the purpose behind the work they do. When children themselves have a part in planning, they are better motivated to their tasks and the work is meaningful to them. Research tells us that learning is more effective when the learners par-

[2] R. M. Berger, J. P. Guilford, and P. R. Christensen, "A Factor-Analytic Study of Planning Abilities," *Psychological Monographs,* LXXI, No. 6 (1957).

[3] James A. Smith, *Setting Conditions for Creative Teaching in the Elementary School* (Boston: Allyn and Bacon, Inc., 1966).

ticipate in the planning of the learning act and in the carrying out of those plans.

Last, creativity is a way of living. The elements necessary in developing creative people are being promoted in helping children organize, in seeing relationships, in making decisions, passing judgments, in preplanning, and in using their imaginations. Careful planning does not mean overly-structured classrooms—in fact, it is only when the teacher and children have set goals together that they can fully take advantage of incidental learnings that arise and utilize them to accomplish predetermined objectives.

Pupil-teacher planning places responsibility on the child. Each child has the opportunity to develop his day to some extent. He has a great deal of independence and develops self-discipline, which is true discipline. He thinks critically and helps make important decisions. He becomes more self-directing.

Children who, under the guidance of teachers, help plan their own work soon learn the value of the communication of ideas. They see that ideas from many people are often better than ideas from one person. They experience group dynamics and true democratic processes. And their free time is used in fulfilling the work they have set out to accomplish as a group or as individuals. Goals become clearer to the child.

A fourth-grade teacher was once helping a student with his reading. Paul was a word-reader, and the teacher was attempting to develop his eyespan. Day after day she put him through flash-card drills, phrase games, and workbook exercises, but Paul made little progress. Daily he went cooperatively through the routine she had set up for him, but finally one day, after a particularly fruitless drill period, Paul looked up in a troubled fashion and said, "Miss Martin, what the heck are you trying to do to me?" Progress, in this case, was lacking because Paul did not understand his problem or the process the teacher was using to remedy it.

Pupil-teacher planning begins with the abilities of the children, anywhere, at any time. Many children come to kindergarten with a fine sense of organization and an ability to plan. These children have helped parents plan picnics, they have planned how to spend their allowance, they have had a share in planning their own parties and their holiday fun. They can plan with the teacher in the kindergarten. Generally, such planning takes place in several periods throughout the day, for the attention span is short, and the plans, if recorded on the board, are not read by children at this age.

Careful and beneficial pupil-teacher planning cannot be carried out unless the teacher herself is a master at planning and organizing. She must make careful long-term plans to guide her. These plans are not fulfilled to the letter—to follow them rigidly would hinder creativity. They are often modified or changed, but they guide the group to goals and aims that give purposeful direction. Most of all in her organization, she must include plans on *how to plan with the students*.

Often teachers formulate adequate plans for step-by-step planning but fail to provide plans for a physical setup to carry them out. If the teacher is breaking the class up into committees after a general discussion, it is well to give some children the responsibility of arranging the desks and chairs in groups before the general group disperses. When they are ready to go into committees, the teacher can say, "Let's let Bill's committee meet at this table, Anne's will meet here, and Joe's group will meet here." A set of placards with numbers is sometimes used as an economical way of keeping things moving. A placard is placed on each table or in each center, and Bill's group uses Table 1, and so forth.

The physical arrangement for each period must be anticipated if the daily program is to function smoothly and children are to keep out of each other's way. Room centers can help in determining physical organization. Children working on art projects will use the art center; those doing research will use the reading center. If the teacher can keep a visual image of the children at work in her mind as she plans the day's work, she can make provision for a variety of grouping with a minimum of furniture moving and time consumption.

An interplay of ideas is necessary if creativity is to be developed, and careful plans for various kinds of grouping make such interplay possible. Anticipating difficulty or hitches in *new* organizational patterns to be used with children often gives the teacher the foresight to deal with any problems that might arise. A country school teacher, for example, who was taking a group to a moving-picture theater for the first time, helped the children dramatize these situations over and over: buying the tickets, entering the dark theater, finding seats with the aid of an usher, watching the new medium they would see. This type of planning through role-playing gave the children security and helped to make the trip a successful one.

Procedures in planning, as in all good teaching, should be varied. The children's ideas should be utilized and are often as effective as those of the teacher. Skill in planning is developmental; the goal is to lead each child toward independence and to give each self-direction. Following are some excerpts showing creative ways teachers have helped children to gain self-direction and independence through planning.

Planning in the Kindergarten

Miss Morris is the teacher of a kindergarten group in the suburb of Eastwood. She has a master plan in mind for each day's work; here is her plan for one day.

As soon as the children arrived, Miss Morris turned on the lights, and they all came to the front of the room for a planning period. Miss Morris had worked out a plan to help these children plan. She had collected pictures of children engaged in various kindergarten activities and mounted them on heavy colored poster paper. There were pictures of children singing, eating, going for a walk, and listening to a story. After a discussion of the pictures Miss Morris suggested they all decide what they were going to do for the whole morning and put the pictures on the chalk tray in that order. First they were going to work, so a picture of children engaged in various activities was put up. Next came a picture of the children singing, then the story, the midmorning lunch, and so on. Children soon learned to run to the picture to "see what they were going to do next." Through this technique, they also learned eventually to plan a day by themselves.

Later in the year, after some children had learned numbers, Miss Morris numbered the pictures. A few of the older children would be ready to read. For them she would place a symbolic representation above the picture on the chalkboard, such as "We read," "We sing," and "We eat." Still later she would put these phrases in chart form away from the pictures, and the advanced children in the class would learn to read the plans directly from the chart. By the time this group reached the first grade they would be veterans at helping the teacher plan a daily schedule.

On this particular day, after the first period (which was the planning period), the children shared their contributions for the day and learned about the new things in the room. Then they decided what each child would do during the next period—the work period. During the work period Miss Morris went to each child to help him plan another job if he finished the one assigned during the planning period.

The children tidied the room at the end of the work period. Then they met in a group around Miss Morris for a talking (reporting) and singing period. Following this, the children had a snack and rest time. Later, when rest time was finished, Miss Morris brought the children together to plan a morning walk to the grocery store at the corner where they purchased juice for the week. Back in their room from the walk they planned a dramatization of *Peter Rabbit,* which Miss Morris had read on the previous day.

Notice these important things about the way Miss Morris planned for her kindergarten.

1. She planned only one or two periods at a time because five-year-olds grow restless if they are kept at one thing too long. Their attention span is not yet developed for long "listening" periods and generally cannot be relied on for too long. Also, their memories are short, and they cannot remember for long what they are to do. At the same time she planned for the day so that advanced children could develop their skills in planning.
2. Miss Morris planned a few new activities around some common fixed activities. She planned a work period first because the children came from home well-rested and wanting a great deal of activity (five-year-olds work off their energy by spurts of movement). She planned some activities at the *same time* of day she always planned them since five-year-olds receive a great deal of security from fixed and routine periods during their day. Often they denote time from a familiar or fixed part of the day, such as, "I'll do that after my nap," or, "We took a walk to the grocery store after our juice." Fixed periods in a five-year-old's day give him a base from which to operate. Between these fixed periods there can be a great deal of flexibility and creativeness in planning.
3. She planned for many short, changing activities. In so doing she met the physical, social, and emotional needs of the five-year-olds.
4. Within her master plan there was a great deal of flexibility and allowance for children's ideas to be used in the planning of the short periods.
5. Her planning was concerned with the actions of people. She was child-oriented rather than things-oriented. All the children's ideas were used. She helped them to plan a balanced day.

Planning at the First Grade Level

Miss Stell is the first-grade teacher in Westvale, another suburban community. She knows "sixes" well. From her knowledge of them, she, too, is able to make master plans within which the children develop plans of their own. She plans for the total group and is acquainted with the plan of each individual within it. Here are some sample pages from her plan book:

PLANS FOR WEDNESDAY

8:45

All have something to do but Bill, Michael, Patty, and Eileen.

Ideas: Start Bill on stocking the terrarium.
Mike can begin rock exhibit.
Patty—poster for animal show.
Eileen—begin chart of farm animals; use catalogue for pictures.

9:00   *We Plan*

Check all activities from day before. Help children choose new activities from chart.

We Work

Job 1: *Allen, Jimmy, Paula*—help them start charts to give report; help plan reports.
2: *Dennis*—begin chart on farm machinery.
3: *Mary*—wants to build a model of farm; use sandtable.
4: *Marsha and Irene*—begin experiment on types of soil; plant seeds in four Dixie cups of different soil.
5: *Irene* cups of different soil.
6: *Pete, Richie, Mark*—finish incubator. Put in eggs and set temperature.
7: *Gladys, Cheryl, David*—turn at easel.
8: *Bill*—paint milk truck.
9: *Esther*—wants to make farmer puppets.
10: *Michael*—persuade him to paint puppet stage, perhaps. If not, select job from Job Chart.
11: *Lucy, Al, Isabel, Patty*—finish mural.
12: *Eileen, Margie*—want to do montages.
13: *Ellen*—will make milk order chart.

10:00

Lunch: Play records—"Farmer in the Dell."
Play game when lunch is over.

10:25

Talk time: 1. Reports from all; evaluate jobs.
2. Special reports:
a. Allen, Jimmy, Paula.
b. Marsha—experiment with soil.
c. Pete, Richie, Mark—the incubator.
d. Lucy, Al, Isabel, Patty—report on mural.
3. Talk; get ready for Mr. Henry's visit this afternoon.

10:45

Compose, on a chart, letter of thanks to Mr. Henry for farm visit. Have advanced group read it. Put in envelope and mail.

11:00

Music—farm songs.
New song—"Little Red Wagon." Dramatize.
Animal sounds with drums, violins; children take turns.

11:15

Mr. Henry is coming. Gladys will introduce him. Pictures taken of children while visiting his farm. Discuss—good chance to review vocabulary and introduce new words. Watch especially for silo, ensilage, combine, tractor, bale, etc.

Miss Stell's plans resulted from a day which ran as follows:

8:45

The children arrived and hung up their wraps. She greeted each one and helped each find an unfinished job from the day before or some other activity to pursue.

9:00   *We Plan*

Miss Stell flicked the lights and the children brought their chairs to the front of the room in a semicircle facing the empty pocket charts. On the chart the children planned the day, putting pictures and strips of cardboard in the pocket chart to show the sequence of events.

9:20   *We Work*

The children were working on a farm unit. Allen, Jimmy, and Paula (who were excellent readers) were looking up the answers to some questions the children had asked since their return from the farm.

There were four easels in the room, so Dennis, Mary, Irene and Marsha were to have their turn at painting pictures of their trip to the farm.

Pete, Richie and Mark had been fascinated by the incubator, so Miss Stell had obtained materials for them to construct a simple incubator.

Gladys, Cheryl, David, and Esther chose block play for their work period. They wanted to construct a barn with stanchions for the cows.

Bill went to the construction center, where he worked at making a milk truck.

Esther and Michael modeled clay cows, milk stools, and farm equipment to go in the barn.

Lucy, Al, Isabel, and Patty painted a mural.

Some of the children had obb jobs to do.

Miss Stell remembered that many children finished the jobs they had planned to do. At this point, they did one of two things: they came to her to have her read the chart of other things to do, or they chose something they wanted to do themselves. Some read books, some painted, three children fingerpainted, some worked puzzles, others played house in the housekeeping center. Those who wanted other group work set up by the class chose such jobs as: making a scissors holder, making a scrapbook cover for pictures collected on the farm, writing their names, pasting pictures on chart paper for Miss Stell for the afternoon reading group.

9:50	*We Eat*	Miss Stell played a recording softly while they ate and talked.

10:15   *We Talk*   At 10:15 the tables were cleared, and Miss Stell and the children talked about the work period.

Allen, Jimmy, and Paula gave the answers to some of the questions they had read about.

Dennis, Mary, Irene, and Marsha told about their pictures.

Gladys, Cheryl, David, and Esther dramatized a farm story with the clay cows and props made by Esther and Michael for their block barn.

All the children evaluated the mural and decided it would take another day to finish it.

Those who finished their jobs chose other ones for the next day.

10:40   *We Dance*   Today the children had worked out rhythms of farm animals. The climax of the period had been the barnyard song they created, put to music and danced.

11:00   *We Sing*   Miss Stell then taught the children a few new farm songs.

P.M.

1:00   *We Read*   After the children returned from lunch and a noon-hour rest, Miss Stell had a short planning period and then broke them up into five reading groups. For each group Miss Stell had different objectives. All the children were on different levels of reading ability. Miss Stell grouped them at least once each day so she could help them with their reading progress.

One group of five were her superior readers. For this group, Miss Stell had found advanced books. She had printed questions on cards and slipped the cards in the books in places where the answers could be found.

Group 2 consisted of four children who were reading well in a first-grade reader. They were far enough along so Miss Stell could work with them on word analysis and word construction.

There were nine children in Group 3. These were children who were reading at about the average reading level for this particular time of year.

When Miss Stell joined the group they checked the work they had done, then put it away. They brought their chairs to the corner of the room where their chart holder was located. Miss Stell introduced a picture, pasted on the top of a sheet of chart paper, of a farmer having trouble with his tractor.

The children made up a delightful story called "The Stubborn Tractor." Miss Stell printed it on a chart with a flo pen as they dictated it. Then the children read it to each other. While they were doing this Miss Stell printed the story once more on strips of paper. The children then matched these strips to the original story. Then they cut the strips into phrases and words and matched them to the original story or had fun making mixed-up stories.

Then Miss Stell moved on to the next group, composed of children who were in the readiness stage of reading. They were just beginning to read words. She spent some time with them developing audio and visual acuity.

Miss Stell then checked Group 5. This group consisted of two children who were slow learners and were not yet ready to read. Miss Stell had allowed them to go to the play corner where they worked with blocks, tinkertoys, and puzzles to better see how shapes fit together. Then Paula, from the upper group, had been assigned to read them a story which they were now concluding.

2:00	*We Play Out-Doors*	The children went to the playground then and for the first ten minutes were allowed to run and leap at will. Then Miss Stell called them together for an original game.
2:30	*We Listen*	The children came into the classroom and settled down at once to listening period. Today Miss Stell had a delightful story about a farm dog. She also showed a short film on Shep, the Farm Dog. She used this film to lead into the development of some arithmetic concepts. On this day it was an exploration of the *4* family.

3:10   *We*   The children evaluated the day and put on their
          Go   wraps to go home.
          Home

What can we note about Miss Stell's planning for the first grade?
By the time children enter the first grade they have a good sense of
the order of a school day. Children in Miss Stell's room were able to
help organize a full day, but they had to have a ready source of
reference to refresh their memories because they could not remember
a whole day after they had planned it. Miss Stell, therefore, was using
her planning period to help her in the teaching of reading.

Notice that Miss Stell also had a master plan. Because she
taught with the purpose of meeting individual needs and developing
individual potential, her plans were very detailed. Miss Stell not only
had planned the day's work; she had also provided many instances
where she and the children would plan one period in greater detail.

The schedule she made out with the children helped them to
know how the day would go from period to period. The plans Miss
Stell made for herself told in detail what would take place during
each period.

A survey of Miss Stell's plans shows she had taken the following
into account:

1. She planned for the whole day in the form of a schedule. "Sixes" are
   able to plan for longer periods of time than "fives."
2. She planned around fixed periods in the day, such as the sharing time,
   lunch time, and recess time. "Sixes" still receive a great deal of security
   and comfort in routine.
3. She planned for short, changing activities. "Sixes" are still very active
   and have short attention spans.
4. She planned a great deal of flexibility between the routine activities in
   her schedule. "Sixes" are very creative and energetic, and she wanted
   to make use of their ideas and their plans.
5. She made allowance for many short periods where the children
   planned in detail. Children need to develop a skill for organizing their
   day and to develop the quality of self-direction, but at the age of six
   they need a great deal of help in doing this.
6. Her planning was sequential. Miss Stell felt children should learn that
   planning is continuous, and the completion of one job frees the way
   to attack another. She helped children to evaluate and to set new goals
   when she did this.
7. Within her larger plans, she allowed for individual planning. During
   the work period and several times during the day, children planned
   for their own work for a short period of time. Group planning is
   necessary for democratic living, as is individual planning.

8. For one period during the day she often made many plans. During the work period children were all working at different jobs. During the reading period, five groups were all busy. Good teaching does not mean all children do the same thing at the same time. Careful planning is needed to allow for individual abilities.
9. She knew her children well. To meet the individual needs and interests of children, the teacher *must* know them well so that she can plan those things they need most urgently.

Planning on a Sixth-Grade Level

Mr. Martin is a sixth-grade teacher in Freeport. His children are studying a unit on Man's Search for Freedom. This unit began when the children exhibited great concern over a local strike in the rug factory. During a discussion it became known that the fathers of these children were working together for greater freedom by striking. This discussion resulted in a sharp interest in the origin of all freedoms. Soon the children had set up questions and objectives for a unit of work. These children were very independent. They had had many years of planning practice and were able to make many plans on their own.

First, the long-term plans for the unit were made. These were broken down into plans for beginning the unit. Then followed plans for developing the unit, for committee work, for reporting, and for culminating activities. These plans were made for the month, the week, the day, and the period.

Mr. Martin's children learned to plan their daily program with their teacher a week in advance. Every Friday afternoon Mr. Martin gave his pupils a dittoed sheet with a rough schedule for each day of the coming week. On this sheet, large blocks of time were left each day for children to fill in their own activities as much as possible. Mr. Martin made a duplicate of this schedule on the chalkboard. On it he wrote in all the periods he would use during each day to (1) have the children together for instruction and (2) have specific groups meeting with him. The children filled in their own plan sheet with the times they would be meeting with Mr. Martin, and then filled in the remaining time with their own jobs. Each morning Mr. Martin had a short planning period at which time he checked each child's program for the day.

Following is a sample of one of the children's planning sheets for two days. All those periods in capital letters designate the time

Mr. Martin put on the board for them to meet specific purposes. The items in lower case letters represent those plans written in by Kevin Edwards, a pupil in Mr. Martin's room.

MY PLANS

NAME: Kevin Edwards   GRADE: 6
FROM: Monday, May 3   TO   Friday, May 7

MONDAY—May 3

A.M.

9:00   PLANNING PERIOD—CONTRIBUTIONS

9:15   UNIT WORK AND OTHER WORK
        ALL—LIST QUESTIONS FOR UNIT ON AFRICA
        CLASSIFY QUESTIONS
        CHOOSE COMMITTEES
        MAP WORK—MR. MARTIN

10:15   CLEAN UP: PREPARE FOR REPORTS

10:30   REPORT PERIOD
        Report on nations of Africa admitted to United Nations—
        my homework. Show collection of pictures from news-
        paper on Africa to class.

10:50   BREAK: SNACK

11:00   LANGUAGE ARTS
        PRETEST: SPELLING—MR. MARTIN
        Make my spelling list.
        Copy questions about Africa on chart.
        Write letter to travel agency for African posters.

11:30   GRAMMAR: MR. MARTIN
        Correct papers—from Friday

P.M.

1:00   READING GROUPS
        1:00: My group—Mr. Martin will give us some work-
           book lessons
        1:40: With Mr. Martin—help in reading (to outline)

2:00   RECESS—OUTDOOR—play ball

2:30   ARITHMETIC
        DECIMAL FRACTIONS—Mr. Martin
        3:00: My group—work at seats on material from Mr.
        Martin.

TUESDAY—May 4

A.M.

9:00   PLANNING PERIOD

9:15   UNIT WORK AND OTHER WORK
SHORT COMMITTEE MEETINGS—ORGANIZE
MAKE UP A PLAN FOR STUDY
MAKE LISTS FOR REFERENCE-RESOURCES
     My committee will meet to organize.
     We will each take a job.

10:15   CLEAN UP: PREPARE FOR REPORTS

10:30   REPORT PERIOD
     Mary's group will report on their assignment—problems
     in Africa—"Africa's Fight for Freedom."

10:50   SNACK

11:00   LANGUAGE ARTS
SPELLING WORDS—Study with Mr. Martin
     Write our reports for the school newspaper.
     Fix bulletin board of clippings in NEWS center.

1:00   READING GROUPS
     With Mr. Martin—new story—read for main ideas—
     "The African King," p. 187.
     1:20: Group planning—roll movie—list scenes—decide
     who will draw each.

2:00   GYM WITH MR. BUNDEE
     Plan May Day Festival.

2:30   ARITHMETIC
     With Mr. Martin—adding and subtracting decimal frac-
     tions—games.
     3:00: Practice sheets from Workbook, p. 86–87.

The teachers cited in the examples above are masters at planning and at helping children develop organizational skills. All teachers can develop this skill. They will begin by planning for single activities and single periods, and gradually expanding these plans until children take over the major responsibilities of planning. Following are some ideas selected from current textbooks, which illustrate how textbooks can be of help in developing pupil planning and creativity at the same time.

Some Activities That Promote Planning in Sixth Grade

1. Have the children make a list of all the things they have for breakfast or dinner. Then have them try to find out what part of the world all these things came from. On a map of the world, have them color in the places where their meals come from.

2. In the encyclopedia, have the children look up Albania, Rumania, Greece, Yugoslavia, and Bulgaria. Do this in groups, and then let each group make a shoe-box scene about each country. Place these scenes around a salt-and-flour map and pin a ribbon from the scene to the place where it would be seen on the map. This will make a nice exhibit.

3. As you finish studying each area of Europe, you may divide your class in groups and have each group construct a diorama that most typically represents the region just studied.

4. Make peep-show scenes of France. To make peep-shows, get a shoe box and cut a hole in one of the small ends large enough to peek into. Then cut slits in the top of the box to allow the light to come in. Different lighting effects may be obtained by pasting colored tissue or cellophane paper over the open slits. Inside the box make a scene, putting one thing in front of the other to provide a three-dimensional effect.

5. You have done many things as you studied each country. Plan an exhibit of all these things, and invite other grades and your parents to see it.

All through this book you have had many opportunities to work together. Learning to work together is important. Here is a chance for your whole class to work together.

6. After you read the stories of Ixchel and Cha, make a list of all the things that happened in the stories, scene by scene. Allow each member of the class to choose a scene and draw it. Two or three class members can cut a stage from a cardboard box to make a roll movie. After the pictures are drawn, label them, then have a committee paste them all on shelf paper. After the shelf paper has been put on rollers, someone can read the stories again while the roll movie is shown to the class.

7. Divide your class into committees. Assign each committee to make a chart on a large sheet of paper of each of the following topics:

a. The food of the Ancient Egyptians.
b. The clothing of the Egyptians.
c. Homes of the Egyptians.
d. Transportation of the Egyptians.
e. The buildings of the Egyptians.
f. The life of the Egyptians.
g. Ceremonies of the Acient Egyptians.

Make your charts as attractive as possible. Use lettering, pictures, and drawings. When they are finished, hold an exhibit and invite another grade.

Summary

As we have seen, pupil-teacher planning is important for many reasons:

1. Children learn to plan and organize by having experiences with these things.
2. Planning together provides both teachers and children with direction and purpose, and a more creative way to work towards the accomplishment of common goals.
3. Children learn more effectively when they are involved in their learnings and understand the purposes behind their work. Planning involves the children in solving daily and long-term problems.
4. Problem behavior is reduced when children know how each part of the day is to be filled and do not waste time waiting to be told what next to do. Boredom is minimized.

TO THE COLLEGE STUDENT

1. In many schools you will visit, movable furniture is often kept in straight rows and children are not allowed to move about the classroom. What does this tell you about the teacher? Does she really understand the concept of the social studies? Is she helping children learn the skills of living together? What do you think her philosophy of social studies is?

2. Many college students of adequate or superior ability flunk out of college or do not work up to their potential. One reason for this is that they do not adequately budget their time and leave too little time for required study. Many colleges teach courses such as

"The Improvement of Learning" to help students learn to program a day and to develop study skills necessary on a college level. Can you see any relationship between this situation and the need to develop planning and study skills in the elementary grades?

3. Creative children are not annoyed by disorder. They are challenged by it. They enjoy bringing order out of disorder. In what ways could you use this knowledge about creative children to put them to work in helping to plan a school day? Could this possibly suggest a way in which the creative child might be more active and accepted in the total group?

TO THE CLASSROOM TEACHER

1. Does your own classroom reflect your philosophy of teaching and your attitude toward developing the creative powers of each individual? Look at it objectively and make a list of ways you can improve your classroom organization by placing children in more open-ended situations than they are in at present.

2. For one day, keep a list of the things children say to each other when they are directly under your instruction. Analyze the list carefully. Do the quotations there indicate that you are developing creative human relations in your classroom?

3. Some educators criticize new team-teaching techniques as being subject-matter centered, with little attention given to developing the individual. Can team-teaching be creative? Can it be uncreative? If you use team-teaching in your school, analyze what you are doing. Decide whether you are developing creativity in children and if you are meeting individual differences.

4. How can teaching by machines be made creative?

TO THE COLLEGE STUDENT AND THE CLASSROOM TEACHER

1. Is it possible to tell what a teacher's philosophy of teaching and her views toward creativity are simply by looking at her classroom organization, even when the children are not in the room? Visit a school after the children have been dismissed for the day, or visit

some classrooms other than your own. Note the differences in seat arrangement, bulletin board displays, work being exhibited, and the materials and their accessibility. Can you tell what goes on during the day? If possible, after you have made such a visit and tried to determine the type of teaching, return to the same classroom when the children are there to check your deductions.

2. Mrs. Wylie is a fifth-grade teacher. She believes children must know the facts presented in the social studies text. Her social studies periods consist of having the children open their books to the topic under study and then reading to find answers to the questions she poses. Each day she gives a review test (written or oral) on the facts of the previous day's lesson. Mrs. Wylie's children know the names of all the states and their capitals, the population of each state, the major rivers and watersheds in the United States, the countries of South America and a whole bookful of dates. What is good about Mrs. Wylie's system of teaching? What is poor about it?

3. Our government, our institutions and our organizations conduct their business through the use of committees. Make a list of the skills you need to work within a committee, such as the ability to say what you feel without feeling threatened, etc. Take a poll of the class members to see where these skills were learned. Were you ever taught them or did you just pick them up through experience? How necessary is group work to you at this point in your life? Do you often wish you could function more effectively in a group than you do? How early in life do you remember working in some sort of group: a high-school dance committee? a yearbook committee? at summer camp? a school paper? doing homework? having birthday parties? church groups? When do you feel group dynamics should be taught in the elementary school?

4. "Preplanning for a school day can be overdone." In the light of what you have learned about creativity, discuss the pros and cons of this statement. Do you think Miss Stell (see page 66) overplanned her day? Why is preplanning necessary?

SELECTED BIBLIOGRAPHY

ASSOCIATION FOR CHILDHOOD EDUCATION. *Space Arrangement, Beauty in School.* Washington, D.C.: The Association, 1958.
ASSOCIATION FOR CHILDHOOD EDUCATION INTERNATIONAL. *Children Can Work Independently.* Washington, D.C.: The Association, 1952.

ASSOCIATION FOR SUPERVISION AND CURRICULUM DEVELOPMENT. *Perceiving, Behaving, Becoming*. Washington, D.C.: The National Education Association, 1959, Chap. 1.

BEAUCHAMP, G. *Basic Dimensions of Elementary Method*. Boston: Allyn and Bacon, Inc., 1959, 146–168.

BERGER, R. M., J. P. GUILFORD, and P. R. CHRISTENSEN. "A Factor-Analytic Study of Planning Abilities," *Psychological Monographs*, LXXI, No. 6, 1957.

CUTTS, NORMA E. and NICHOLAS MOSELEY. *Providing for Individual Differences in the Elementary School*. Englewood Cliffs, N.J.: Prentice-Hall, Inc., 1960.

DEPARTMENT OF SUPERVISION AND CURRICULUM DEVELOPMENT. *Group Planning in Education*. Washington, D.C.: The National Education Association, 1945.

GOODLAD, JOHN and ROBERT ANDERSON. *The Non-Graded Elementary School*. New York: Harcourt, Brace and Company, 1959.

GRAMBS, JEAN. *Group Processes in Intergroup Education*. New York: The National Conference of Christians and Jews.

HACK, LOUISE E. "Using Committees in the Classroom," *Rinehart Educational Pamphlets*. New York: Rinehart and Company, Inc., 1958.

HARAP, HENRY. *Social Living in the Curriculum*. Nashville, Tennessee: George Peabody College for Teachers, 1952.

HARRISON, RAYMOND H. and LAWRENCE E. GOWIN. *The Elementary Teacher in Action*. San Francisco: Wadsworth Publishing Company, Inc., 1958.

LANE, HOWARD and MARY BEAUCHAMP. *Human Relations in Teaching*. Englewood Cliffs, N.J.: Prentice-Hall, Inc., 1955.

LASSWELL, H. D. "The Social Setting of Creativity," in *Creativity and Its Cultivation*, H. Anderson, ed. New York: Harper and Brothers, 1959.

LEEPER, ROBERT M. and ROBERT W. SCOFIELD. "Creative Climate," *Educational Leadership*, XVIII, No. 49 (October, 1960), 5–6.

MIEL, ALICE (ed.). *The Teacher's Role in Pupil-Teacher Planning*. New York: Teachers College, Columbia University Bureau of Publications, 1957.

MILES, MATTHEW. *Learning to Work in Groups*. New York: Teachers College, Columbia University Bureau of Publications, 1959.

OTTO, HENRY J. *Social Education in Elementary Schools*. New York: Rinehart and Company, Inc., 1956.

ROSENBERG, B. G. and C. N. ZIMET. "Authoritarianism and Aesthetic Choice," *Journal Social Psychology*, XLVI, (1958), 293–297.

WILES, KIMBALL. *Teaching for Better Schools*. Englewood Cliffs, N.J.: Prentice-Hall, Inc., 1959, Chaps. vi–ix.

WRIGHTSTONE, J. WAYNE. *Class Organization for Instruction*. Washington, D.C.: Department of Classroom Teachers, American Educational Research Association of the National Educational Association, 1957.

ZIRBES, LAURA. *Guidelines to Developmental Teaching*. Columbus, Ohio: The Bureau of Educational Research and Service, Ohio State University, 1961.

VI Unit Teaching

In order to fulfill their wants, human beings have to CARE ABOUT THE MEANINGS THEY CREATE. When the invitation comes, as it always does, to settle for meanings that are old and familiar and second-hand, the individual has to WANT to respond to the ever-present invitation to explore for his own new meanings. He will not forsake what is known but will integrate it with what he has freshly discovered. That is the function of creativity in living. It is part of the human birthright—something to know and want and value, something to add enjoyment and vitality to everyday encounters in the adventure that is living.[1]

PEGGY BROGAN

TO THE READER

You will get a good idea of a unit and how it works if you will view the film Fundamentals of a Unit of Work *(San Jose, California), and then read this chapter to help you interpret in more detail what you saw.*

Introduction

A review of the history of proposed plans for teaching the social studies reveals that one plan used a few years ago stands up well today in terms of meeting objectives for creative teaching and individual creative development. This is the *unit method* of teaching.

Unit Teaching: Outcomes

The *method* of unit teaching is a creative method and affords many opportunities for developing creative human relationships. Through unit teaching the teacher can develop group skills without sacrificing the development of each individual child. The unit is based on experience and provides the opportunity to meet the teacher's and children's objectives.

[1] Peggy Brogan, "The Case for Creativity," in *Creativity in Teaching: Invitations and Instances,* Alice Miel, ed. (Belmont, California: Wadsworth Publishing Company, Inc., 1961), pp. 20–21.

Through unit teaching a teacher may:

1. Make constructive changes in individual behavior.
2. Meet individual differences of children more realistically.
3. Foster good human relationships among students and adults.
4. Provide a laboratory in which the skills for social living may be developed.
5. Foster self-discipline among students.
6. Develop concepts, understandings, and values among children.
7. Help each individual to live effectively in his world.
8. Develop an understanding and appreciation of other cultures in relation to the knowledge of his own culture.
9. Help children become aware of the problems of their society and their part in solving them.
10. Develop an appreciation of the work of others.
11. Give the child an historical perspective, a time-line concept.
12. Accentuate and use an appreciation of natural resources.
13. Foster democratic ideals and develop the democratic way of life.
14. Develop critical thinking on each level of the child's development.
15. Guide the child toward creative thinking and self-realization.
16. Give to each child the "tools" of his culture in meaningful situations so that he learns to use them in practical applications.
17. Foster mental and physical health.
18. Develop those characteristics of responsibility, independence, sharing, tolerance, cooperativeness, and all other qualities necessary for living effectively in a democratic society.
19. Provide for open-ended experiences which afford children many opportunities to create.

The unit method of teaching is not the only one through which these objectives may be met, but it does seem to make allowance for more of the stated objectives than any other single method. Specifically, it sets conditions for creative development more than any plan yet devised. It provides for self-development; it is a problem-solving method and, if properly used, will provide children with many open-ended situations. Through it children learn many knowledges, skills, and values which they may immediately apply to solving current social problems. Through unit teaching creative and critical thinking can well be developed; convergent and divergent thinking processes can be stressed. Unit teaching provides ample use of all the skills necessary for full creative development—decision-making, passing judgment, critical thinking, evaluation, visual acuity, and comprehension abilities.

The problem-solving approach of unit teaching provides high motivational tension and an opportunity to use all past experiences in new patterns. Children are encouraged to use their own ideas, individuality can be stressed, it can be completely success-oriented. Ideas and objects are manipulated and explored, and the qualities and characteristics indicative of creative people are accepted as important.

Such outcomes imply the utilization of a variety of techniques and practices. The teacher is not only concerned with what the child learns, but with the *techniques* he learns for meeting the problems he faces in his own life *and* the changes the learning process makes on his own abilities and personality. Learning of all kinds generally takes place best as a result of first-hand experience. A good unit provides experiences for children to work together, to solve problems, to be creative, to think constructively, to develop skills, to make mistakes, and to resolve failures.

A unit generally starts with a problem arising in class. Often this is a school or community problem, such as, "What can we do to make our noon hours at school more pleasant?" Or the problem may be concerned with world-community life as well. At the intermediate-grade level, children are often interested in contrasting cultures and may ask simply, "Why are the roofs flat in northern Mexico?" In attempting to answer such problems, the class becomes interested to the extent that a unit may develop. Motivation becomes more than the act of arousing interest in a project—it also involves the act of establishing a purpose that will require cooperative effort on the part of teacher and pupils. It serves as the technique for involving all children in a vital problem: the first step in the creative process.

Teaching a Unit

When Shelley aroused an interest in Mexico in the fifth-grade class, Mrs. Whalen, the teacher, saw her opportunity to teach a unit that would develop the objectives she had set up for her children for the year. The first step in starting the unit is generally to define the major problem clearly. In this instance, after a discussion, Mrs. Whalen wrote the major problem on the board:

How and why is life in Mexico so different from ours?

The children eagerly agreed that they would think of many other questions that would aid in solving the major problem and would think of many ideas that they could use to find out the answers to their questions.

The next day the class met for a planning period. On the board the teacher listed all the questions asked by the children. Each question was recorded regardless of its outward importance, though some were reworded for clarity. After a total of seventy questions was listed, Mrs. Whalen said, "These are good questions and if we answer them, we should find out why life in Mexico is different from ours. Also we will know the ways it is like ours. Our questions are not very easy to work with as they now stand, however. What can we do with them to make it easier for us to use them?"

A discussion revealed that there were many questions in specific categories—some on food, clothing, education, and other definite topics. These questions could be grouped. Using colored chalk, different children took turns going to the board and circling the questions under the various headings. Meanwhile, "secretaries" were appointed within the group who copied the questions from the board onto sheets of paper, one for "food," one for "clothing," and so on. After all the questions had been classified in this manner, the group decided they would put these questions on charts to be used for references. Committees were appointed to make the charts.

The next day, the completed charts were placed across the front of the room. Thus the children saw the questions grouped topically. New questions were added.

"Now that we know what we are going to study," said Mrs. Whalen, "let's talk awhile on *how* we are going to study."

As a result of a discussion, the following chart emerged.

STEPS FOR STUDYING OUR UNIT

1. We list our questions.
2. We classify them.
3. We choose committees.
4. We decide on sources of reference.
5. The committees:
    a. Do research on their topic.
    b. Plan an interesting report.
    c. Present the report to the class.
6. We evaluate reports.
7. We file reports.
8. We do activities together:
    a. We have a Mexican Fiesta.
    b. We have a Piñata Party.
    c. We have a Mexican meal.
    d. We make a Mexican scrapbook.

Mrs. Whalen then led the class into considering the various ideas that could be used to answer each set of questions. A discussion of the questions about shelter went something like this:

MRS. WHALEN:	What could a committee working on these questions do to find the answers and to make their report interesting to us as well?
BILL:	Well, they could find out the kinds of materials used in making the homes in Mexico.
JIM:	Maybe they could make a chart showing these different kinds of materials so we could compare them to ours.
HELEN:	If they find some special kind of material maybe they could tell us about that.
DOROTHY:	They could draw pictures of the different kinds of homes in Mexico.
BART:	Maybe they could show us pictures or films on some of the nice buildings and the different kinds of buildings in Mexico.
JANE:	It would be fun to make some model houses like those found in Mexico.

The value of this type of planning may be noted when committees make their reports. This particular committee prepared an exhibit at the front of the room. They made charts of famous Mexican buildings, of different materials used in Mexican buildings, and the different *types* of buildings. Each child made a report on a building found in the varying climates. One boy gave a demonstration of how adobe was made, and a sand-table Mexican village had been reproduced. Many pictures were mounted and displayed. The committee took a group on a trip through the local community to see the influence of Spanish architecture on the buildings. The questions on the chart were reviewed and answered by a dramatization in the form of a radio quiz program.

When many ideas had been shared by the class, the teacher asked if each child had made up his mind as to the committee on which he would prefer to work. The names were added to the charts. The charts where no committees were formed were put aside for later choice when some committee finished its particular job early.

"Our committees have been formed, and we know some ways they can plan to do their work," said Mrs. Whalen, "but before we have our committee meetings, let's make a list together of all the places where we can go to get information to help us find the answers to our questions."

As a result of this experience, the following chart was made:

OUR SOURCES OF INFORMATION

1. text books
2. reading books
3. story books
4. music books
5. encyclopedias (World Book, Compton's)
6. "Information, Please"
7. dictionary
8. childcraft
9. radio programs
10. television programs
11. films
12. our school library
13. our town library
14. film strips
15. slides
16. pictures
17. people
18. museums

"Now our committees can meet," said the teacher. "Let's review what they are going to do at their first meeting."

On the board she listed the specific duties to be accomplished in this first committee meeting.

Each committee will:

1. Choose a chairman.
2. Choose a secretary.
3. Decide what they will do to answer the questions.
4. Suggest ideas for a final report to the class.
5. Tell the class their plans.

The committees then were assigned meeting-places in the room and met in "buzz" groups to fulfill their duties. The teacher went from group to group suggesting ideas; giving information about films, books, and people each committee might use; and making notes about groups or individuals within the groups. Each group gave a brief report of their plans at the end of the period.

The groups were then ready to go ahead. The next day, the librarian was asked to come to the room and the children and Mrs. Whalen planned with her how they could find materials in the library. Some time was taken to teach new library techniques by going to the library with the librarian and learning how to use the card catalog and the call cards. Then the children gathered material from far and wide. Letters were written to the Pan-American Union, to travel companies and steamship lines. The committees met daily and research began—information was "dug out" of the most remote corners. Each day a short report period was held so the committees were kept informed on each other's progress.

Many times committees desired to take trips which the whole class felt would be valuable: trips to see homes and buildings of various architecture, to commercial film-houses to see moving-pictures of historical value, to museums, and other such experiences.

Finally the committees began to feel they were ready to report their findings, so reports were presented. In this particular unit, each group wanted to contribute something for a culminating activity. After all the reports were made, the whole group participated in a variety of worthwhile experiences which helped draw the entire unit together.

They made a scrapbook of their written reports, poems, original stories, and assimilated news items. In this book, too, were lists of their questions and copies of their planning charts. They filled a cart with real Mexican articles for an exhibit, and displayed it behind a papier-mâché burro.

FIGURE 6–1. *Another booth has a display of real objects from Mexico.*

FIGURE 6–2. *At one end of the plaza a group of players dramatizes* The
Painted Pig.

They held a fiesta in the school gymnasium. The gym was
modeled to represent a market-place and was festooned with the
colored tissue paper hung on strings that is typical of Mexican fiestas.
Around the gymnasium were booths planned by each committee to
show the results of its work. The "life" committee had an art exhibit
and an exhibit of art materials of Mexico. The "products" committee
had a booth where Mexican handicrafts made by the children were
exhibited and sold.

Other booths displayed salt-and-flour maps, charts of varying
information, models made by the children, and displays of the
materials used to study Mexico. At one end of the Plaza, a stage had
been erected with scenery for the dramatization of "The Painted Pig,"
rewritten in script form by the group.

A program had been planned of the Mexican songs, the songs in
Spanish, and the dances and plays learned by the group. All the
grades were invited to the fiesta and the program was presented.

On the day following the fiesta, the group planned and cooked a
Mexican meal This was followed by a Piñata Party, where they

broke the piñata, played Mexican games, and enjoyed their Mexican dances.

The entire group wrote and presented as an assembly program a typical Mexican Christmas celebration. To pull the whole unit together, a few review films were shown, the questions on the charts were checked, and the children and teacher together planned and made a test to summarize what the class had learned.

Throughout all this activity, research, and reporting, Mrs. Whalen acted as a guide for planning each step, for suggesting new ideas and materials, and for *helping the children draw together the concepts and understandings they were developing.* These were checked against an original list the teacher had made and were largely concepts and understandings that can result only as the outcome of experience, such as:

1. All men are interdependent.
2. All countries are now dependent.
3. Mexico is a country with a flavor all its own.
4. Mexico has a history, a culture, a language, and an art that have made unique contributions to the world.
5. Climate has an effect on the way people live.
6. Rainfall has an effect on the way people live.
7. Each country of the world has common problems and unique problems. (*And many others.*)

Such an experience over a six-week period was utilized by the teacher in many different ways. Not only were the children learning to work together but they were learning to think critically, to accept responsibility, to become more independent, to become appreciative and understanding, to learn their specific contribution to group living. They were constantly developing new understandings and arriving at new concepts. Also, such a plan afforded the teacher the opportunity to help individuals. Bill, who was shy and retiring at the beginning of the unit, volunteered for the part of Pedro in the play; the teacher had utilized every possible experience within the unit itself to help Bill gain poise and status with the group. The rewards of her work were forthcoming in the changes in Bill's behavior.

Careful records kept on each child helped the teacher in knowing that Belinda's excessive reading activity was her way of escaping life's realities in an attempt to avoid failure experiences. Belinda's self-concept was low, her home life was such that the child was constantly belittled and everlastingly told she didn't know how to do anything right. The teacher made sure Belinda had many opportunities to do things "right" and rediscover her capabilities. Belinda's failure experiences were carefully resolved and the teacher's anecdotal record cards toward the end of the unit read:

Belinda volunteered to figure up the milk bill today. She said, "I don't know if I can do it, but you will help me if I can't, won't you?" I assured her I would and she set to work. When she brought the bill to the class to report, several of the children checked it and found she was right. Mary said, "Boy, Lindy's a good figurer—I wish I could add like that." Belinda beamed and said, "I'll help you anytime, Mary." It was a wonderful success experience for Belinda, and she did not run to her corner to read once all day.

As in all good teaching, the success of a unit depends largely on the careful planning of the teacher for group and individual experiences. Some samples from the notebook of this teacher give ideas as to how a unit may be carefully planned so that every experience may be utilized to help in developing the teacher's objectives, and yet free her to take advantage of each child's creative contribution and develop each child's creative abilities.

Some Sample Pages from Mrs. Whalen's Plan Book

I. UNDERSTANDINGS AND CONCEPTS TO BE DEVELOPED
   A. To develop in the boys and girls an appreciation and understanding of the early historical and geographical backgrounds of their own culture.
   B. To stimulate an interest in Mexico as a contrasting culture to our own and to discover what we have in common.
   C. To foster an understanding of people from different cultural backgrounds than our own.
   D. To help children form concepts and understandings of the influences of climate and geography on the mode of life, the type of people, the food, shelter, and clothing of a culture.
   E. To help them appreciate the contributions of the early races to our mode of living today.
   F. To help them understand that man is interdependent.
   G. To show how transportation and communication developments have caused the world to shrink.
   H. To show how the geography of a nation has helped determine its history.
   I. To develop an appreciation for the literature, music, art, and type of living in another culture.
   J. To integrate the group and solve certain group problems.
      1. Integrate new children in schoolroom to others so they work and play well together.
      2. Give the girls status in important jobs due to definite minority.
      3. Develop an appreciation of each other's work, etc.

II. TO DEVELOP IN EACH CHILD (LONG-RANGE PLANS):

   A. An appreciation and understanding of worthwhile social relationships.

   B. The ability to think critically and solve problems on his own level.

   C. The ability to carry out worthwhile activities and make good use of leisure time.

   D. His potential in each area and his skills in interest areas.

   E. Skillful use of tools and techniques for good study habits.

   F. Good mental and physical health.

   G. A solution to certain individual problems. Here the teacher listed specific problems on a separate page for each child, such as:

     Bob

     Bob reads poorly—needs to read much familiar material. Be sure he gets much easy reading material. Good at manual things. Artistic—poor in skill subjects, especially arithmetic. Give him jobs measuring scenery—let him increase recipes for Mexican meal. He will be good at painting scenery and making slides.

     Jim

     Jim silly at times. Develop leadership; he has it. Good imagination—help him to apply it practically. If he can be chairman of a committee—good! Good ideas about scenery—get his interest by letting him start here. He will gain status in serious roles.

   H. To develop each child's creative potential through the use of many media: art, creative writing, dance, critical and creative thinking, experimentation and discovery, problem-solving and evaluation.

III. FIRST STEPS IN DEVELOPING UNIT (HER PLANS FOR PLANNING):

   A. The children will list questions on things they want to know.

   B. They will determine how they are going to study their unit and make a chart.

   C. The teacher and children work their plans, making new charts and gathering new material, as the unit develops.

   D. The cumulative activities are decided and used to draw the unit together.

     Note: The teacher makes these long-term plans and from them makes daily plans.

Radio and TV Programs Usable with this Unit:

Tuesday	Nov. 9	*Down Mexico Way*	Music
"	Dec. 14	*Christmas Music*	"
"	Apr. 11	*Saludos Americanos*	"
Wednesday	Dec. 1	*Age of Rubber*	Science
"	Apr. 5	*Caribbean Lands*	Social Studies
"	Apr. 12	*Neighbors to the South*	" "

IV. SPECIFIC UNDERSTANDINGS TO BE DEVELOPED
    [see partial list page 89]
    Main Problem: "Why Is Life in Mexico so Different from Ours?"
                    (anticipated questions to be answered,
                        asked by children, and classified)

Food:

1. What do people of Mexico eat?
2. Do they cook their foods and how?
3. What utensils do they use to eat with?
4. What foods do we eat which come from Mexico?
5. What are the chief products of Mexico?
6. What does Mexico import?
7. What does Mexico export?

Clothing:

1. What costumes do the people of Mexico wear?
2. Do they dress like us?
3. Do they dress differently in the different climates?
4. Do they wear special holiday clothes?
5. What does their military uniform look like?

Similar questions are listed for: transportation and communication; life (amusements, holidays, and religion); government; education; shelter, history, and geography.

V. SOME ACTIVITIES TO CONTINUE THROUGHOUT THE ENTIRE UNIT

1. Keep a list of new words at front of room—a vocabulary chart. These will be used in part for the spelling words.
2. Keep a "unit" bulletin board where new materials may be posted daily.
3. Clip news bulletins, radio and television programs, and theater ads from the paper each week so these may be utilized in the unit.
4. Listen to these radio and television programs; have committees attend the movies (if whole class can not go) and report.
5. Keep a file of all materials after use on the bulletin board—teach child to file early in the game.
6. Keep a list of all stories, books, and materials available on the unit in the school.
7. Map work—repeatedly.

This particular teacher arranged her notebook so that an outline of the subject-matter she felt her children should know appeared on the left-hand side of the page; the suggested activities and references for teacher and pupil appeared on the right-hand side of the page. This arrangement provided a simple method of quickly gaining access to materials, ideas, and resources so that her teaching could be more flexible.

In modified form such teaching is applicable to older children. In simplified form it can be utilized for younger children. Many teachers of primary-grade children utilize unit techniques in the kindergarten, first, second, and third grades, but the subject-matter is differently planned. Recognizing the inability of children to read extensively for information, other resources are used to answer questions. The teacher may record questions in the kindergarten, for instance, and then, in planning for a trip to the fire station, may give each child the responsibility of finding out the answer to one question.

In a first grade where a group was reading at various levels, the teacher printed on the board each question that was asked, and the child copied his question on a 3 x 5 card. Then the child was responsible for reading his card to find the answer to the question when the group went on their trip.

Primary-grade teachers who have their objectives clearly in mind fulfill these objectives by a series of experiences rather than through a detailed subject-matter unit such as that written above. These teachers often plan their work by listing these objectives vertically on a large sheet of paper and then horizontally blocking off experiences which they will plan with their children to fulfill these objectives throughout the semester. In this fashion, the short interest span of the young child is considered, and each experience provides a contribution toward developing activities to meet the objectives. The objectives provide purpose for the various experiences of the year.

An idea of the planning an early primary teacher can do is obtained from this sample sheet of a kindergarten teacher's plan.

Sample Pages—Kindergarten Teacher's Plan Book

I. OVERALL GENERAL KINDERGARTEN GOALS AND OBJECTIVES FOR THE YEAR

    A. Help children to solve their problems.

    B. Increase their knowledge.

    C. Improve skills.

Through a wide variety of experiences

    D. Develop desirable habits and attitudes.

       1. Responsibility.

       2. Independence.

       3. Social awareness, cooperation.

       4. Creativity.

       5. Self-discipline.

 E. Help develop in each child a sense of happiness and security in his introduction to elementary school.

 F. Help develop readiness for skills and knowledge to come later.

II. SPECIFIC OBJECTIVES TO BE ACCOMPLISHED

Through a series of units closely related to the child's everyday life, plan to develop the following specific outcomes:

Objectives:

1. To build in the child the realization that people are interdependent and that we need each other to live effectively.

 a. To help him understand that each person has freedoms and responsibilities to perform in order to make life good for all.

 b. To help him understand that it is important to be helpful and considerate of people less fortunate than himself.

 c. To help him realize that living together is pleasanter when certain accepted social courtesies are observed.

2. To teach children how to work effectively in a group.

3. To develop basic concepts of quality and quantity: to give each child a meaningful base in numbers.

 a. To teach him to understand number value.

 b. To teach him to count.

4. To help each child develop oral language skills.

 a. To help him to be comfortable in speaking before a group.

 b. To provide opportunity for him to express his own ideas.

 c. To guide him in clear, colorful, and correct expression.

5. To develop an appreciation and love for music.

 a. By teaching him many songs suitable for his age level.

 b. By giving him experiences with musical instruments.

 c. By helping him to develop his body through the use of rhythms.

These units are so arranged that the current and natural interests of children may be used to accomplish the objectives regardless of the content. A flexible shifting from one unit to another is possible if some topic of immediate interest is introduced on any particular day. Materials have been arranged so the teacher has at her fingertips those books, songs, games, and suggested activities which can develop any topic of interest to the children, and a shifting from one topic back to another to fill in the undeveloped objectives is possible with the waxing and waning interests of children, their flexible and uncertain attention-spans.

EXPERIENCES FOR MEETING OBJECTIVES

Objective	Unit I	Unit II	Unit III
	Living Together in School	Living Together in the Home	Fall
1	Talk about school. Tour school—meet principal, nurse, janitor, etc. Note rooms. Talk about room. Set up centers. Assign lockers—have each draw a picture. Select workers—introduce chart. Collect pictures of jobs at home.	Film: *Patty Garman, Little Helper* Responsibilities of different members of family. How kindergarten child can help at home. Read to children, books: *Daddies, What They Do All Day,* *Not a Little Monkey*	Help rake leaves at home. Plant bulbs. Feed squirrels and chipmunks at home or school. Build a simple bird-feeding station.
2	Have daily committees. Plan work period— Sharing materials. Asking for help. Plan small and large group work. Plan together how to run day—set lunch table, clean up, etc. Plan trip through school. Plan use of playground area.	Plan together a puppet show, "A Family Outing"	Plan and take an excursion around neighborhood of school to look for seeds, colored leaves, caterpillars, etc.

3	Through use of blocks, colored paper, doll-house furniture, etc., develop concepts of 3, 2, 5, 10, 8. Flannel board for number stories and symbolic experiences. Count napkins, cups, cookies, etc., at snack time.	Count members in your family. Count different kinds of jobs fathers have.	After teacher mounts one of each kind of leaf on bulletin board with caption, children count the kinds. They then compare future leaves brought in with the ones mounted.
4	Have each child tell about his summer. Introduce "show and tell"—each child bring something from home. Draw pictures of school and tell about them. Tell stories and poems learned at home.	Have children tell what they did to help at home. Compose invitation to another class to come and see the puppet show.	Talk about objects found on excursion or brought in at other times by children.
5	Sing songs learned at home. Learn some new school songs. Plan rhythm band—explore each instrument, etc.	Rhythms: climbing stairs, reaching, home games, building a house.	Play in leaves in the street. Learn songs about leaves (see list).

Objective	Unit IV Hallowe'en	Unit V Neighborhood Helpers	Unit VI Pets
1	Plan a Hallowe'en Party (carry out responsibilities they agree upon).	Films: *Helpers Who Come to Our House.* *The Mailman.* *Our Post Office.* *Chimp the Fireman.* Discussion: Careful about fires in home or elsewhere. Follow policeman's traffic directions.	Take care of classroom pet or pets. Take care of aquarium. Show film: *Farm Animals* Show filmstrip: *Stories About Pets; Too Many Pets.* (Bring in colony of ants for children to watch.)
2	Work together on party decorations, etc. Filmstrip: *Celebrating Hallowe'en*, followed by a discussion to see whether we can use any ideas suggested in filmstrip for our party.	Make a roll movie as a class project (see Objective 8)	Plan for the care of pets, what to feed them, who should do it, when, etc.
3	Count what we will need for party.	Count helpers who come to home, to school.	Count different kinds of pets children in room have. Find pictures of each kind and make display of "Our Pets."

4	Plan-the-party would fit in here also.	Tell about helpers who come to their homes. Dictate captions or script to go with role movie pictures, so teacher can write same.	Tell about our pets at home.
5	Care in carving Jack-O-Lantern lanterns—danger of fire from candle in same.	See Objective 1. Also might show film: *Fire Safety Is Your Problem* —if not shown before in Unit II.	Keep animals well. Do not pet strange dogs. Handle animals so they won't bite or scratch us.

Subsequent pages of this teacher's plan book show that she has a wealth of material handy to use at any time. Following are some excerpts taken at random from her plan book:

SONGS

Unit I—Living Together in the School

1. "Time for School," p. 126, *Our Singing World—The Kindergarten Book:* Pitts, Glenn & Watters: Boston, Ginn & Co., 1957
2. "Watch the Lights," p. 136
3. "Stop, Look & Listen," p. 136
4. "Skipping Song," p. 129

Unit II—Living Together in the Home

(All from *Our Singing World—The Kindergarten Book*)
1. "Drink Your Milk," p. 33
2. "Get Up," p. 44
3. "Good Morning," p. 44
4. "Hiding," p. 45
5. "I'm a Spinning Top," p. 127

POEMS

Unit II–Living Together in the Home

Vol. I—*Childcraft*
1. "A Mother's Song," p. 67
2. "After a Bath," p. 72
3. "Animal Crackers," p. 71
4. "Breakfast Time," p. 69

Vol. II—*Childcraft*
1. "It Was," p. 12
2. "Moving," p. 17

Poems to Grow On
1. "Kitchen Tunes," p. 41
2. "Moving In," p. 39
3. "Moving Out," p. 38
4. "Our House," p. 44
5. "Surprises," p. 41

BOOKS

Unit VI—Pets and Other Living Creatures

1. Dennis, Wesley. *A Crow I Know.* N.Y.: Viking Press, 1957
2. Francoise. *Chouchou* (Story of a Donkey) N.Y.: Charles Scribner's Sons, 1958
3. Lenski, Lois. *Davy and His Dog.* N.Y.: Oxford Univ. Press, 1957
4. Podendorf, Illa. *The True Book of Pets.* Chicago: Children's Press, 1954

GAMES

Games for all uses

1. Pussy Wants a Corner (5 players at a time—exchange corners)
2. Musical Slipper (stand in circle, pass slipper)
3. Mulberry Bush
4. London Bridge
5. Drop the Handkerchief
6. Looby-Loo

FILMS

Unit I—Living Together in the School

1. *Beginning Responsibility: Taking Care of Things*—#1756—11 min., Coronet—Gr. K-5; $2.00 (At home and school: cleaning up, accident prevention, etc.)
2. *Kindness to Others*—#2936 —11 min., color, Gr. K-3, $3.75
3. *Our Teacher*—#145—11 min., K-4, $2.00

4. *Safety on Our School Bus—*
   #2916—11 min., K-6, $2.25

FILMSTRIPS

Unit VII—Christmas, Hannukah
   1. *Celebrating Christmas* (see Celebrating Holidays Series under Fall)
   2. *Feast of Lights with Jesus* (color) SVE, 1953 (How Jesus as child might have celebrated festival of Hannukah)

Unit XI—Valentine's Day
   1. *Celebrating St. Valentine's Day* (see Celebrating Holidays Series under Fall)

The Scientific Method as Creative Social Learning

In unit teaching the approach has been based on a scientific method. This is the unique contribution of science to the social studies and to creative thinking. No longer are children expected to accept dogmatic statements made by a teacher or a textbook. Critical and creative thinking do not result if such techniques are overused.

A scientist has a creative, exploratory mind. He learns to observe carefully and to examine critically; he tests his beliefs. These qualities are also possessed by the creative person.

Although the area of science has its own body of knowledge, the main purpose for teaching science in the elementary school is to develop creative minds by using the scientific approach to problems.

This scientific method is not confined to the subject-matter of the physical sciences alone. In the above discussion on unit teaching, the scientific approach was used in a cultural-social problem: Why is life in Mexico different from ours? The basic steps in the use of the scientific method might be listed as follows:

1. A problem is presented.
2. An hypothesis is formed concerning the problem.
3. Data are collected to prove or disprove the hypothesis.
4. Material is classified.
5. The hypothesis is tested in light of the data collected.
6. Conclusions are drawn; understandings are developed.

Children who are taught to study by use of this procedure are working creatively and constructively toward solutions to their problems. Some of the specific objectives which may be met through utilizing the scientific method might appear to be something like this:

Through use of the scientific method—

1. Children learn to think creatively and critically.
2. Children learn to become more observing—observation becomes a habit.
3. Curiosity about the environment is aroused.
4. A healthy thirst for knowledge results.
5. Children are equipped with techniques for finding out answers to their own problems independently.
6. Experimentation is encouraged as a means of learning "why" and "how."
7. New interests are constantly being developed.
8. Children learn to differentiate between fact and fancy; superstition is dispelled.
9. The joy of exploration and the thrill of discovery are encouraged.
10. Children learn to appreciate and enjoy the works of others.
11. Children develop the ability to see relationships.
12. Children acquire the habit of basing judgment on fact.
13. Children develop open-mindedness.
14. Children develop good social attitudes.
15. Children obtain practice in logical, convergent-thinking problem-solving, and in divergent, creative problem-solving.

Selecting Unit Content

The foregoing discussion indicates how large bodies of knowledge may be organized for creative teaching. Selecting the bodies of knowledge to be used with children has invited controversy in the past.

The imaginative, creative teacher can use *any* body of content to develop all the objectives of education through unit teaching. How much of this accumulated knowledge of the world should children know? It is from this question that the debate stems. Many schools have loaded their curricula with so many facts and so much knowledge that nothing of the value or application of the knowledge is used. Other schools have gone the other way and have omitted important knowledge from the child's background, depriving him of things he must know in order to live effectively in a democratic society.

It is the job of the educator to select from the knowledge available what is important to the period of history and the culture of which the children are a part. Part of the confusion regarding the content of the social studies curriculum comes from the lack of clear-cut objectives or guidance in selection of topics from many state courses of study. A recent review of many courses of study from various states showed some shocking weaknesses in their structure and content. Only a few contained units of relevance on any level regarding the contribution of other cultures to the American way of life. Because the fight for civil rights is one of the major problems of this generation and will be for a few generations to come, education for the proper attitudes, the necessary understandings of civil rights and their meaning in a democratic society, and an understanding of subcultures is essential. The school neglects its duty by not including all those content areas which will help to develop these understandings in our young children.

Scientists tell us that one of our greatest problems is water. The pollution of our lakes, rivers, and springs has become a serious problem. The total problem of conservation is one of major importance, especially in light of the uncontrolled use of insecticides and man-made chemicals and the effect they are having on our wildlife. Yet few of the social studies outlines for elementary school today contain units on water pollution—some do not even have units on conservation in general.

Scientists also tell us that within twenty years the chief source of our natural resources will be the sea. From it we will obtain food, medicine, water, minerals, and recreation. Yet the author of this book found very few units of work on the sea in the state courses of study that he examined.

At different periods in history focus must be put on different places in the world. Current social studies textbooks devote a large portion of their space to Europe and the Old World and a few pages to Africa. Most of the illustrations in the section on Africa are of animals or jungles. Both pictures and text give the impression that Africa is a backward, dark continent, when in reality it is a nation fighting for its independence as we were in 1775. It is an emerging nation, rich in resources, and its future is closely interwoven with our own. Our children should be learning all there is to know about Africa and Southeast Asia. The future lies in these countries as much as in Europe.

A reassessment of unit topics is also needed in order to fully develop the social studies content. In the lower primary grades community helpers are often studied. This is a sound approach to meeting social studies teaching objectives if it is properly carried out. However, when the policeman or fireman is presented as a kindly man who will give his life to help everyone because he is "our helper" and a sentimental, unreal atmosphere is created about community helpers, much of the value of the unit is voided. Children can understand from the beginning that all people are human and therefore not always kindly. They can begin to understand economics when they are taught that the fireman or policeman does what he does because he is paid to do it—and that their mothers and fathers pay him through their taxes. He is not a god. He is a public servant. So are teachers. It has been pointed out that the social studies are those areas of the social sciences which are selected for instructional purposes. The social sciences include economics, civics, political science, history, geography, sociology, etc.—and *all* areas of the social sciences can be taught at every grade level in accordance with the ability of the child to form concepts and develop understandings.

The following criteria are suggested for the selection of content for the social studies program:

1. It is meaningful to children and is related to previous learnings and understandings.
2. It is pertinent to their life in the Space Age.
3. It helps them better understand the problems of their own life.
4. It is important because it develops knowledge in all areas of the physical sciences.
5. It provides opportunity to develop skills, values, knowledges, and understandings essential to living in a democratic society.
6. It provides the background of knowledge necessary to deal with controversial issues.
7. It offers ample opportunity for creative problem-solving.

Summary

The effect of a sound social studies program in the elementary school is expressed in the social living of the children from day to day in the regular classroom. The social studies program provides children with truths and contributes to behavior changes which result in more creative and constructive human relationships.

The unit method of teaching contributes directly to the development of creativity in the following ways:

1. It allows children to be inventive, original, and imaginative.
2. It gives the opportunity to develop fluency of thought.

3. It provides for evaluation, necessary for the total creative act.
4. It provides for concentration.
5. It makes provision for putting knowledges and facts into divergent thinking situations—to apply them to new situations.
6. It is based on integration—the ability to see unity and to perceive structure and new design, the ability to relate and connect experiences.
7. The unit is flexible and allows for spontaneity and individuality.
8. Opportunities are afforded for children to analyze, abstract, and synthesize.
9. All types of experiences (verbal, symbolic, evaluative, figural, etc.) are provided to place children in situations where creative thinking and doing is at a premium.
10. Creative acts are guided by a goal or purpose.

TO THE COLLEGE STUDENT

1. Poll your class to see if any of the students in it remember being taught by the unit method. If so, have them tell what they remember about any given topic. Compare this to the memories the rest of the class have about learning the same topic. Did the experience approach help check forgetting?

2. If you viewed the film, *Fundamental Skills of a Unit of Work,* consider the following problems:
   a. How many ways did the teacher use different media to develop creativity?
   b. How did the teacher meet individual differences?
   c. Think of all the ways the children showed evidence of developing creative human relationships.
   d. Did you feel the teacher was creative? Did she set conditions so children could be creative? Discuss the total role of the teacher as shown in this film.

3. Planning a unit of work is essential before teaching it. Some reasons are listed below:
   a. Education is a selective process. The teacher must know what (from all the information available on each topic) is suitable for use with her group.
   b. The teacher must have an awareness of the subject-matter of the unit so she can guide children in finding it and can check the authenticity with which they report it.
   c. The teacher must have goals and objectives in mind for herself and for individuals. This does not mean that the children

will not also have objectives of their own. It does mean the teacher may have some objectives the children do not have.

d. The teacher must know the resources available in the school and in the community in order to fulfill her objectives.

e. The teacher must be able to organize a large body of material into workable form.

List some other reasons why planning ahead of time is necessary. Try planning a unit to teach to a classroom of children you have recently observed, or, better yet, if you plan to do your student teaching soon, plan a unit to teach to your own group.

TO THE CLASSROOM TEACHER

1. Review your school objectives and note which ones can be met by content and which by method. Check your own program to determine how many of these objectives you are working on. How can you expand your program to meet more of them?

2. In terms of the objectives of a good social studies program as outlined in the last two chapters, can you justify the following practices, which were observed by the author in a recent school survey on which he worked?

a. Class schedules were posted outside each door and each teacher stopped teaching one subject at the end of each scheduled time and began another, *even though she rarely reached a logical stopping-place in her teaching.*

b. A school that was totally subject-centered.

c. All the children were reading from the same social studies textbook.

d. Only the bright children were allowed to work on activities.

e. The only form of measurement used were teacher-made tests administered in every subject every Friday.

3. In what ways does a unit provide for open-ended experiences in which a subject-centered curriculum does not?

4. Check yourself for a few days on each of the following questions to see if your teaching leans toward the creative or the conservative type.

a. Do I give more answers to questions than the children do?

b. Does my room reflect the children's work or my own (bulletin boards, exhibits, etc.)?

c. Does the furniture in my room get rearranged into new patterns during the day?

d. Do my children have the opportunity to talk or do they spend most of their time listening to me?

e. Do the children's creative products appear daily on my desk or on the bulletin boards (poems, stories, paintings, etc.)?

f. Am I tolerant of mistakes and do I help children turn their mistakes into successes?

g. Did I help *each* child in some way each day?

h. Did I learn something from the children each day?

TO THE COLLEGE STUDENT AND THE CLASSROOM TEACHER

1. Review the purposes of unit-teaching as listed on page 81 and decide how the teacher who taught the unit on Mexico fulfilled these purposes.

2. Parents often do not understand the purposes and objectives behind modern education. Review the pictures in this chapter. If you were a parent and you dropped into the school to visit and saw only what you see in the pictures, might you think how different this school was from the elementary school you attended? You might well ask, "What are they learning?"—meaning, of course, what subject-matter are they mastering? Limiting yourself to the pictures, answer this question: tell what subject-matter they learned and list the skills the children are also learning.

3. In a rural community, an intelligent but uneducated farmer came to school at the invitation of his fifth-grade son to attend the culminating activity of a unit that was a dramatization and exhibit of Alaska. In the exhibit was a great deal of art work painted by the children. He made this comment, "I don't see why Harry has to spend so much time in school foolin' around with paint—he ain't ever goin' to be no artist—he's goin' to work on my farm. Seems to me you folks waste a lot of time and tax money lettin' kids fool around with all this art stuff."

How would you defend your program to this taxpayer? Does his comment indicate the need for an adult education program?

4. Of the following plans of organization, which are more likely by their very nature to foster creative teaching situations?

    a. The ungraded school.

    b. The self-contained classroom.

    c. The multigraded school.

    d. Team teaching.

    e. Machine teaching.

    f. Homogeneous grouping (for reading and other areas of the curriculum).

    g. Segregated classes for the bright or slow students.

    h. Television teaching.

SELECTED BIBLIOGRAPHY

ASSOCIATION FOR CHILDHOOD EDUCATION INTERNATIONAL. *Children Can Work Independently*. Washington, D.C.: The Association, 1952.

CUTTS, NORMA and NICHOLAS MOSELEY. *Providing for Individual Differences in the Elementary School*. Englewood Cliffs, N.J.: Prentice-Hall, Inc., 1960.

GROSS, RICHARD E., RAYMOND E. MUESSIG, and GEORGE L. FERSH. *The Problems Approach and the Social Studies,* Curriculum Guide Number 9, rev. ed. Washington, D.C.: National Council for the Social Studies, 1960.

HANNA, LAVONE, GLADYS L. POTTER and NEVA HAGAMAN. *Unit Teaching in the Elementary School*. New York: Rinehart and Company, Inc., 1955.

JAROLIMEK, JOHN. *Social Studies in Elementary Education*. New York: The Macmillan Co., 1959, Chap. IV.

KLEE, LORETTA (ed.). *Social Studies for Older Children: Program for Grades Four, Five and Six*. Washington, D.C.: National Council for the Social Studies, 1953.

MICHAELIS, JOHN. *Social Studies for Children in a Democracy*. Englewood Cliffs, N.J.: Prentice-Hall, Inc., 1956, Chap. V.

MILES, MATTHEW. *Learning to Work in Groups*. New York: Bureau of Publications, Teachers College, Columbia University, 1959.

PRESTON, RALPH. *Teaching Social Studies in the Elementary School*, rev. ed. New York: Rinehart and Company, Inc., 1958, Chaps. 5–7.

SMITH, JAMES. *"Teaching Through Process Units,"* in *Social Studies for the Middle Grades,* C. W. Hunnicutt, ed. Washington, D.C.: National Council for the Social Studies, 1960, Chapter 6.

STRANG, RUTH. *Group Work in Education*. New York: Harper and Brothers, 1958.

THORNDIKE, ROBERT. *"How Children Learn Problem Solving," Learning and Instruction,* National Society for the Study of Education, Forty-ninth Yearbook, Part I. Chicago: The University of Chicago Press, 1950, 192–217.

WESLEY, EDGAR B. and MARY A. ADAMS. *Teaching Social Studies in the Elementary School*. Boston: D. C. Heath and Company, 1952, Chap. XIV.

Creativity Is Individualism

Only men can create, for only men have the capacity to turn signals into symbols.[1]

HAROLD RUGG

TO THE READER

List all the organizational plans you have heard of in recent years and think about each. Which allows for creative development? After you read this chapter try to plan a day with one or more of these plans to provide for creative development.

Introduction

Every major organizational change in the American public school in the past two decades has stemmed from one goal: *to give each child an education that is commensurate with his ability.* As a democratic nation and a free society we are committed to this cause. We are the first group of scholars in all of history to be concerned with the development and education of *every* individual. Our political ideology is designed around this concept: in a free society individuals count.

To develop the concept of meeting individual differences among our children, creative people have frequently designed new plans of instructional organization or new methods of teaching. We have adjusted materials to the child; impoverished or enriched the curriculum; altered promotion policies and changed grade standards; homogenized children by ability levels and other criteria; introduced the Joplin Plan, the Denver Plan, the Amidon Plan and a score of others; ungraded and multigraded our schools; employed television-teaching and programmed learning; utilized core curriculum and unit teaching; departmentalized our elementary schools; teamed our teachers for team-teaching; mechanized our syllabus; programmed courses of study and used self-instruction, individualized reading, and pre-designed "contracts."

[1] Harold Rugg, *Imagination: An Inquiry Into the Sources and Conditions that Stimulate Creativity* (New York: Harper & Row, Publishers, 1963), p. xii.

Each of these plans has been successful when it was used in a situation where it was carefully applied and evaluated. Many have been disastrous in the communities where they were applied simply because change was held to be important for change's sake and was necessary so that a particular school could claim it was in the swim.

With all our attempts to meet individual differences and develop individual potential, we are still not doing an outstanding job. The reason may very well be that the basic way to help each person to become an individual is through the development of his *creative* powers. In developing the child's creative powers, we may find that he is able to meet many of his own needs without all the organizational plans, and the gadgets and gimmicks of modern education. For if children have their creative powers developed within them from preschool times, even little children will be inventive enough to help themselves more than they presently do. Rigid conformity to an organizational plan may be as detrimental to the development of creativity as conformity to traditional teaching methods. The socialization process of every child is accomplished largely within the existing structure of his school. That structure will have a decided effect on his creativity as well as his other social abilities. That we have not been as successful as we had hoped to be is evidenced by the continued rise in the number of drop-outs from our schools; the rise in delinquency and vandalism; the number of school failures, including nonreaders; and the failure of many pupils to be motivated to learning.

The social studies is the curriculum area in which democratic concepts are developed and which prepares boys and girls for their *child and adult* roles in a democratic society. While much attention has been given to individual differences (largely in ability) in reading, spelling, and arithmetic in the elementary classroom, little attention has been directed toward *developing the uniqueness* of individuals in the social studies program.

Before the problem can be attacked meaningfully, an examination of some of the common fallacies of most grouping plans is in order:

1. Individual differences are still regarded in many schools, and by many teachers, as a nuisance rather than an asset to the schoolroom society. Planning for individual differences requires a great deal of time, which many teachers are reluctant to give. Until individuality is seen as an *asset* to a free society, and until the attitude of the teacher is changed so that she regards it as a precious commodity and

a base for the operations of free men in a free society, *no organiza-tional plan for meeting individual differences has a chance of being effective.*

2. All the organizational plans mentioned above have one basic fault. They assume there are enough likenesses among the differences in a group of children so that children can still be put in some kind of group where these differences can be met *better* than they can through individual help. Often there is little allowance made for individual differences within the smaller groups.

3. Grouping for individual differences has taken place without clear-cut objectives. When a teacher asks, "Shall I have three of four reading groups?" she is showing her lack of understanding of the purposes behind grouping. The only purpose in grouping is *to help each child learn in harmony with his ability to learn.* Often grouping is used simply because it is easier for the teacher and not because it is more beneficial to the child! Segregation, at times, may create more problems over a long period of time than it solves. Some educators find it difficult to see much difference between segregation by intellect and segregation by color of skin, and they wonder if democratic concepts are being developed in *any* kind of segregation.

4. Every plan developed to date interprets meeting individual needs to mean, "How can we arrange, organize, and teach our children so they can absorb the material *we* feel they must know, or amass the skills *we* feel they must master?" *Not one of these plans attempts to get to the inner personality or unique learning patterns of each child and develop him as he is.* Instead, we try to make him over so that he will conform to our stereotype of the acceptable student. Consequently, many children often feel rejected because of their individuality. Every human being on the face of this earth must bring of himself to his learning, and it is his *whole* self, not just his mind, which changes as a result of his learning. *We need to talk less about meeting individual needs and more about developing individual differences.*

5. The concept of meeting individual differences *or* developing individual differences has been regarded almost totally as a small group process where similar problems are attacked by the teacher. One important element of individuality has gone unheeded: *individu-ality only shows when it displays itself in a group.* Individuality needs a background of conformity so that it will stand out. In a good social studies program there will be many opportunities to develop indi-viduality and to meet individual differences *in a large group situation.*

Reference to many of the illustrations presented in Books II and III of this series[2] will show with dramatic impact the necessity of a large group situation for this type of creativity (or individuality) to be developed. By their very nature, many of the new organizational plans prohibit this type of grouping and therefore deny the child the challenge of creative thinking "on his feet" before an audience.

When we consider the facts mentioned in Chapter I of this book—that all children are creative, that there are degrees of creativity, that creativity is related to intelligence, that creativity is individualism, that creativity is a process and a product, that creativity is a series of characteristics and traits—we have as sound a set of criteria for grouping within a classroom as the criteria currently used for many of our grouping plans.

Effective grouping to develop precious individualism calls for a change in the attitude of teachers. Teachers, too, must be individual —their roles must change from mimetic ones to creative ones. Objectives for teaching the various curriculum areas must also change in keeping with the philosophy of the times; the past objective for developing *correct* communication in the language arts, for instance, must change to that of developing *effective* communication.

Effective grouping also means that developing individual differences must be considered from the standpoint of each individual rather than as a form of curriculum modification, or as an organizational plan, or as giving teachers more free time. It means that sometimes a child will be taught alone, sometimes in a small group, and sometimes in a large group. Sometimes he will be in a group of his own interest or ability, or with the children who live on his street. But *the plan must suit the child*—it is not the child who must be manipulated to make possible the successful working of the plan.

This calls for new concepts and creative ways of grouping. Why not, for instance, group together for certain lessons children who respond to certain ways of teaching better than to others? Recent studies indicate that some children respond and learn best in situations where there is considerable structure and many rules and directions, while others learn best in a less structured, more permissive situation. Some children learn better in a creative situation while others are threatened by it. And some children can be more creative in a structured situation than in another type.

[2] James A. Smith, *Creative Teaching of the Language Arts in the Elementary School* and *Creative Teaching of Reading and Literature in the Elementary School* (Boston: Allyn and Bacon, Inc., 1967).

No matter what the situation, teaching, organization for teaching, and learning can be individual if the teacher is creative. Therefore, effective grouping to develop individual differences demands creative teachers. And creative teachers will recognize that individual differences are precious and that they must set conditions so these differences can emerge and be legitimately accepted in the classroom. There have always been creative teachers, but one of the greatest tragedies of our times is that too many of them are forced to teach under some organizational plan that restricts their own individual talents.

Grouping for Individual and Creative Development

The success of any organizational plan always depends on the teacher. Because the self-contained classroom still stands up under criticism as being a structure in which sound education can be developed if creative teachers who remain flexible and who know their children well are in charge, I have chosen as illustration one self-contained fifth-grade classroom as a good example of creative living where the children's individual differences were developed by the conditions set by Miss Smith, a creative teacher.[3]

A School Day

A.M.

9:00   The children have come. They have brought many things. As they enter, the teacher greets each one and examines him critically, but in a friendly manner, for any signs of illness or uncleanliness. She notes that Mary's eyes are heavy, and asks Mary if she feels well. Mary tells of a restless night.

The teacher suggests she go down to see the nurse in the office and perhaps rest on a cot in the nurse's room. To John, she says, "I bet you played ball on the way to school, Johnnie. How do I know? You guess!" And Johnnie, grinning, runs off to wash his hands.

The teacher goes to the front of the room and sits waiting; as the children see her there, one by one they stop their work and join the circle. They look over the list of things on the board that were left from yesterday which they plan to do to-

[3] James A. Smith, D. T. Donley, and R. L. Lorette, *Independent Learning Activities* (Albany: Capital Area School Development Association, 1958), pp. 16–20.

day. Together they plan the day and check their plans to be sure they alternate between sitting and activity.

Then the teacher says, "Do we have any contributions today?" Each child who has something shows it to the group and tells what he knows about it. No contribution is ignored. Helen brings in a painted pig, which a friend has brought her from Mexico. The class is studying Mexico and is interested. Bobby stands up and shows a rock he has picked up on the way to school. The teacher is inwardly overjoyed—for Bobby has never contributed before. This is a great moment for which she has been striving, but she meets it calmly and gives vent to her emotions on the 3 x 5 card she carries which she will later drop in his folder. "Bobby brought a rock to school today and presented it to the group! His first time before the group!" To insure further participation by Bobby, she asks questions about the rock, and the children also ask questions. Bobby cannot answer them so teacher says, "Let's put these questions on the board! Then some of us may find the answers in other places, like our science books. Perhaps Bobby would like to look up some of the answers in work period?"

Bobby says, "I can't read the science books." So teacher reassures him at once with, "It is hard, but perhaps you and I can read it together."

9:20   The class goes to the planned work period which they set up the last part of the previous afternoon. A group that is slow mentally is making a mural of Mexican industries. A group with a high I.Q. is doing research on government agencies and education in Mexico. They plan to make graphs and present a report. Three children are writing letters to the Pan-American Union to ask for resource materials. One girl who is not yet socially adjusted to all the children works on a scrapbook cover for the reports on Mexico. One group of boys makes papier-mâché Aztec masks for a play they will present. One very bright girl writes the script for the play. Others prepare reports to be made in the conference period. Teacher gets a book on science and reads to Bobby.

Bobby tells teacher the answers to the questions on the board from what she has read, and she prints the story simply on a sheet of paper in his words. This he is able to learn to read quickly, and he then joins the group making the mural to do his part on it. Teacher circulates, taking notes, helping where she can, and jotting down ideas for future work, for individual help, and for group help.

10:30   The group comes together for a conference. One group is reporting on "Shelter in Mexico." They use activities to make their report. Bobby, who cannot read well, gives a demonstration on how to make adobe. Harry, another poor reader, has collected pictures or drawn pictures of different homes in Mexico. Sarah and Michael, who read very well, read the written report that answers the questions asked by the class on the board as a result of their research. The report is evaluated by the class—checking with a chart they have made, "What Makes a Good Report?" The work period is also evaluated in this manner.

Bobby gives his report. Each child briefly tells what he has done during the work period and what he must do tomorrow. This is listed on the board. A list is also made of "materials we will need tomorrow."

11:00   Time out for lunch, and the teacher teaches a new Mexican hat game she has found in her reading.

11:15   Words to learn are taken from the Vocabulary Chart. This is Monday, so a pretest of the words is given to determine which ones each child will have to study. Each child makes out his own list of words to study for the week. For the slow learners, the teacher underlines the most important ones so they can begin there.

11:30   The remainder of the morning is used in studying scripts and learning how to write them so that those writing scenes for the plays will know the right techniques. The teacher noted the previous day that no one was doing this correctly, so some scripts are read and examined and a chart is made bringing out the main points in writing a script. Then the teacher and the pupils write a short act together on the board, putting to use what they have learned.

P.M.

1:00   Children come to front of room, check off jobs done in A.M., and review plans for P.M.

1:10   Reading groups—
Group 1: (Good achievement) continue research in difficult questions asked of research for unit.

Group 2: With the teacher, reading on a second-grade level, make charts to read together and read some stories from an easy reader.

Group 3: Weak in selecting main points in a story, are doing mimeographed exercise prepared by the teacher.

Group 4: Three or four individuals, capable but not up to grade level, getting help from Mary, who is a good reader. Mary has been coached by the teacher and is telling words to the children who do not know them. They are reading a story silently, will later read the stories aloud to each other striving for speed.

Teacher finishes with her group and checks all the others, giving needy individuals help.

2:00   The group has made arrangements to have the gym teacher help with a Mexican dance they are learning to present to the parents.

3:00   The class is working on a Mexican meal they are to have. Joe has brought in a recipe for chili con carne; they must increase it four times to feed a class of 32. The recipe has been printed by teacher on a large chart. She puts it before the group and utilizes it to teach concepts about fractions. Increasing 1 and ¼ cups kidney beans four times presents a problem which each works out in his own way until answers agree. Teacher shows an economical way to add 1 and ¼ four times and the children have fun trying some of those examples. Those who "catch on" help those who don't. Teacher helps those who need her.

3:30   Quick evaluation of the afternoon: "We did a lot today." "We learned much." "We had fun." "What is there to do tomorrow?"

This simple review of a day in a modern school demonstrates how grouping functions. Children meet in different groups for different things. Each child contributes to the best of his ability, and each works at his own level; the group dynamics of the class are organized so that each child may progress at his own rate, and yet each is challenged. An examination of the chart in Figure 7–1 will show pictorially the operation of the group pattern throughout the school day in the class discussed.

A closer examination of this chart shows some interesting facts. How, for instance, does the slow child fit into such a picture as this? The dotted line in the chart represents the activities pursued by a slow child, Bobby, in this room.

At 8:30 Bobby comes into the classroom. He immediately goes to work on the mural he is helping to paint. At 9:00 he joins the teacher and the group in front of the room and helps plan the day. He shares a picture of a Mexican donkey he has found in a magazine with the class. Teacher suggests he put it in the Mexican Scrapbook as the title page for the section dealing with Mexican animals. Bobby also presents the rock which he has picked up on the way to school. Bobby is asked to help find some of the answers the children asked about the rock. At 9:20 he meets with teacher by her desk. He finds a science book and is able to locate pictures of the rock. Teacher reads him what it says. Together they make a new story about the rock which the teacher prints on a sheet of paper

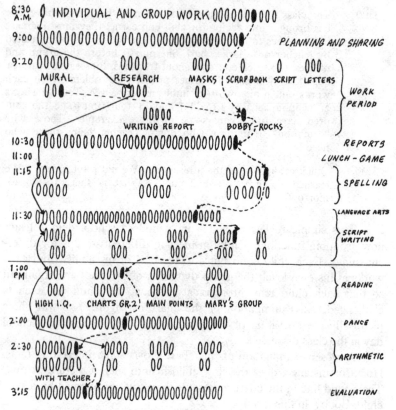

FIGURE 7-1. *Grouping through a school day.*

for him in his own words. She tells him what the words say. He reads them back to her. Then she goes to paste his donkey on a piece of paper for the title page in the scrapbook. He then joins a group in painting the mural on shelter in Mexico.

At 10:30 the group cleans up materials and comes together at the front of the room. Bobby participates in a report on Mexico, showing the class how to make adobe. He helps evaluate his committee's report. Then he reads his report on the rock and shows the page he made for the scrapbook. He listens to the reports of the other children.

The conference period is over and Bob helps serve the milk. Teacher plays a record while they are having crackers and milk. It is some music from a Mexican hat dance. When they finish they make up a few steps to go with the music. They will work more on this later with Miss Jones, the physical education teacher.

Bob helps select words from a vocabulary chart in the front of the room. He takes a pretest of the words. He misses many, so he copies them correctly in his spelling notebook. Teacher comes around and draws a red line under six words she thinks are most important for him. These he will study first.

At 11:30 Bobby meets with the group and listens to some plays read. He helps put ideas about script-writing on a chart. He helps with ideas for the first act of *The Painted Pig,* which teacher read. Then he volunteers for a committee to write a scene. He joins the committee for planning. Sarah is chosen to write the script for his scene, for Sarah is a good writer. Mickey reads well so he is chosen to reread the plot and use the chart at the front of the room to be sure they are doing it correctly. Teacher drops around to be sure all is going well.

It is time for lunch. After lunch, Bob joins the group in the front of the room to evaluate and replan their work. He then joins Group 2, which meets today with the teacher. They make up a story about the donkey picture Bob brought in the morning to go in the scrapbook. They then make up another story about donkeys and read in a Grade 2 reader. She introduces new words and the class reads the story, answering questions as they go along. Through a hole cut in a cardboard box to resemble a TV set, children then play Storytime on TV, and take turns reading to other members of the group in an audience-type situation.

It is time to meet with Miss Jones and Bob joins the other groups in the gym to learn the hat dance.

At 3 o'clock, everyone meets to increase the recipe for the Mexican meal. Bob helps to find how much ¼ is when increased four times by using a measuring cup at the front of the room and filling it ¼ full of water four times and pouring it into another measuring cup. He gets help from Mickey in doing some problems later on.

Then he helps decide what the class has to do the next day before school is dismissed. He wants to stay after school to finish his work on the mural.

Bob has made many valuable contributions to his group; he has gained status in ways other than scholastic. He is a contributing member with status. He does not feel left out or failing. He is free from tension. His needs are being met. He is comfortable in his situation. His mind has been freed to learn to the best of his ability.

In a similar manner, the solid line in the chart shows the activity of Mickey, a very intelligent child, throughout the day.

Mickey enters the room at 8:30 and goes to work on a chart he is making with a committee showing the government agencies of Mexico. At 9 o'clock he joins the group for planning. Here he decides what he will do for the day. He contributes a book he had found in the library which will help his committee (and other committees) find pertinent information. He listens to the contributions of the others and lists questions on the board about an interesting rock Bobby has brought to school.

During work period, Mickey's committee reads together from the book he has brought. They find the answers to some questions and they proceed to work on the chart. One chart shows the number of years of schooling the average Mexican had before and after the drive to erase illiteracy. Another graph depicts the number of grammar schools, high schools, and colleges in Mexico. The children decide to dramatize a day in a Mexican school after their charts are finished.

During report period Mickey hears a report on shelter and then reports for his group on the work they are preparing. He then makes suggestions for evaluating the work period.

Lunch period follows and Mickey is part of a clean-up committee which takes the empty milk bottles downstairs. When he returns he joins in plans for a hat dance the class is preparing.

At 11:15 the children take their seats and the teacher helps them choose words for their spelling. Mickey then takes a spelling test. He misses three words, so he copies them correctly from the vocabulary chart in his spelling notebook. After that, he reads part of a play to the class and helps the teacher make a chart on script-writing. He is chairman of a committee to write a scene for the play, so he takes a copy of the book and meets briefly with his committee, reading parts of the book when they need his help.

In the afternoon Mickey and some of the other boys and girls continue their research in the library while teacher meets with some of the other groups to read.

All of the class goes to the gym at 2 o'clock to work with Miss Jones on the hat dance. When they return to the room, the teacher has charts of their recipes for the Mexican meal across the front of the room. The class works on the recipes together. Mickey discovers that when ¼ is increased four times it is the same as adding top numbers (numerators) and bringing down bottom numbers (denominators). He tries out some of these in a workbook exercise suggested by the teacher and is overjoyed to discover he can do them easily. He then goes to help Bobby and three others in a group who are having a little trouble.

After going over the day's work and deciding what is to be done tomorrow, Mickey runs happily out-of-doors to play ball with a group of boys.

In a program where teachers and pupils plan their work, all the reading groups or arithmetic groups do not necessarily meet at one time. Other activities may be in progress while the teacher meets with a group, just as she helped Bobby in the above illustration while the rest of the class was having its work period. Each child knows from his own plan or the board plan where he is to be and what he is to do at various times throughout the day.

Another look at the chart shows there were many types of grouping going on through the school day. So many teachers fail to realize that constant ability grouping attaches stigmas to the child and breaks down the social structure of the classroom. A further look at the chart shows both Bobby and Mickey engaged in a large number of groups, organized for various purposes throughout the day.

8:30	*Heterogeneous* grouping of choice.
9:00	*Family* group—all class members meet.
9:20	*Interest* group— choice of activity.
10:30	*Family* group again for reports and evaluation.
11:00	*Heterogeneous* grouping—eat with whom they like.
	Family group to learn a dance.
11:15	*Individual* work for spelling test.
11:30	*Family* group to read play—make charts.
	New Interest groups for scene in the play.
1:00	*Family* group for planning.
1:10	*Ability* group for reading.
2:00	*Family* group in gymnasium.
3:00	*Family* group for arithmetic.
	New Ability group for work on arithmetic.
3:30	*Family* group for evaluation.

The likelihood of identification of any one child with any specific group is diminished when the emotional-social rapport of the room is wholesome and when each child appears in such a variety of groups throughout the day. A child in this school day participated in the following grouping:

7 times for *Family* grouping, each for a different purpose.
2 times for *Ability* grouping.
2 times for *Individual* work (minimum).
2 times for *Interest* grouping.
2 times for *Heterogeneous* grouping—*free choice* of group.

Grouping is not confined to classroom activities alone in a modern school. Groups are formed among the grades for various purposes, such as publication of a school newspaper, a dance group, garden club, paper drive, etc. Grouping, committee work, and use of group dynamics have become a technique of the democratic society and can begin in the early elementary school. Children who have experiences such as these ought to be better able to employ group dynamics in adult life to help them solve community problems.

Grouping contributes to maximum involvement for each child,

and consequently to maximum progress. Each child comes to feel he belongs, because each contributes to the functioning of the classroom. Belongingness is a security necessary to encourage creativity. In using flexible grouping the teacher sets conditions for individuality and creativeness to emerge.

Summary

Basic to all creative aesthetic living is the design of the schoolroom and the organization of the school day. The appropriate physical environment, the social-emotional climate of the class, the ability of the teacher to plan and organize the classroom to meet group and individual needs, and the degree to which children become involved in their own learning create the type of situation where the objectives listed by the teachers in Chapter II of this book can be developed.

In classrooms such as those described in this chapter, teachers are teaching facts as well as developing attitudes, building skills, establishing values, instilling appreciations, promoting abilities and forming character. Within the creative organization of a classroom, creative methodology also helps the teacher to meet the goals for social living.

Creative development is fostered when children have the opportunity to explore and manipulate ideas and materials. In Chapter III it was pointed out that some degree of stress and tension is essential for creative thinking. Too much homogeneity lessens this stress and tension. The reproduction of the total society of mixed abilities, races, ideas, religions, and creeds may do more to create the necessary tensions for creative thinking and creative living than the placement of children in groups that are too much alike.

TO THE COLLEGE STUDENT

1. We often hear of brilliant or gifted people who never finished their schooling because they were expelled as problem children. Does the information on page 109 explain this phenomenon to some degree?

2. Try this in class: Spill a little paint or ink on the center of a few sheets of paper. Fold the paper to make ink or paint blots. Make five such blots. Put them before the class one at a time and have each

class member tell what the blots remind them of. Categorize the answers (a committee may do this). Then analyze them—which ones seem to be unique or different from the others? Do you think the people who wrote these answers are more creative than others? Why?

3. List the merits of self-instruction as it pertains to the development of a child's creative ability. What specific group of children are most benefited by self-instruction devices?

4. The statement is made in Book I of this series[4] that the teacher needs materials in her classroom which are appropriate for *all* ability levels. Each individual brings something different to these materials and uses them according to the dictate of his own creative ability. Paint, clay, and colored paper are examples of such materials in art. Make a list of the materials that might fulfill this criterion in social studies.

TO THE CLASSROOM TEACHER

1. Various psychologists have observed these traits in creative children: a willingness to take a calculated risk, an ability to sense and question the implicit, a capacity to be puzzled, an openness to the seemingly irrational in himself, considerable sensitivity and exuberance, and a greater acceptance of himself than is the norm. How do you regard the children in your class who possess these traits? Do you value them or consider them problems?

2. Sound human relationships are among the most creative of all acts. In our many ways of grouping, we have not put children together geographically—that is, grouped them by neighborhood when they come on the bus. This might be a good way to group children because the relationships made in school would be reinforced outside of school in the neighborhoods. Discuss this as a creative idea. Is it a practical one?

3. School personnel generally set up a list of objectives they hope to meet, then they determine a method of teaching to meet their objectives. To this they add the necessary tools, supplies, and resources to enhance the methodology. Then they set up an organizational plan whereby the determined methodology may function. Does

[4] James A. Smith, *Setting Conditions for Creative Teaching in the Elementary School* (Boston: Allyn and Bacon, Inc., 1966).

your school plan its organization as carefully as this, or has it adopted some of the new plans without first defining goals and methods? Has the effect of your total school organization ever been evaluated in terms of the goals and objectives of the school? Should it be? How would you go about it?

4. If you could wave a magic wand and have what you want, what sort of organizational plan would you want in your school? Your classroom?

5. What things about your school would you like to change? What do you regard as valuable and would like to keep? How can change be instigated? Think of plans that might rouse the faculty to make some needed changes.

TO THE COLLEGE STUDENT
AND THE CLASSROOM TEACHER

1. Make a list of instances you can think of where creativity develops best in solitude. Make a list of those where it develops best in a group situation.

2. "Some things are better taught individually, such as reading, handwriting, and grammar usage. Other things cannot be taught individually or they are ineffective because they are basically concerned with the relationships among people; for example, oral expression, listening, and social studies." Consider this statement and decide what implications it has for teaching the social studies. Does it mean we do not take care of individual differences in the social studies?

3. Rigid schedules in a school can be a detriment to creativity. How? Devise an organizational plan that would best help you meet the objectives you set up for a classroom of your own.

SELECTED BIBLIOGRAPHY

ANDREWS, M. F. (ed.). *Creativity and Psychological Health.* Syracuse: Syracuse University Press, 1961.

ASSOCIATION FOR CHILDHOOD EDUCATION. *Space Arrangement, Beauty in School.* Washington, D.C.: The Association, 1958.

ASSOCIATION FOR CHILDHOOD EDUCATION INTERNATIONAL. *Children Can Work Independently.* Washington, D.C.: The Association, 1952.

ASSOCIATION FOR SUPERVISION AND CURRICULUM DEVELOPMENT. *Perceiving, Behaving, Becoming.* Washington, D.C.: The National Education Association, 1962, Chap. X.

BAKER, S. S. *Your Key to Creative Thinking.* New York: Harper & Row, 1962.

BERGER, R. M., J. P. GUILFORD, and P. R. CHRISTENSEN. "A Factor-Analytic Study of Planning Abilities," *Psychological Monographs,* LXXI, No. 6, 1957.

BURKHARDT, R. C. *Spontaneous and Deliberate Ways of Learning.* Scranton, Pennsylvania: International Textbook, 1962.

CARLSON, RUTH K. "Stimulating Creativity in Children and Youth," *Elementary English,* XXXIX (1961), 165–169.

CRUTCHFIELD, R. S. "Conformity and Character," *American Psychologist,* X (1955), 191–198.

CUTTS, NORMA E. and NICHOLAS MOSELEY. *Providing for Individual Differences in the Elementary School.* Englewood Cliffs, New Jersey: Prentice-Hall, Inc., 1960.

DEPARTMENT OF SUPERVISION AND CURRICULUM DEVELOPMENT. *Group Planning in Education.* Washington, D.C.: The National Education Association, 1945.

FOUNDATION FOR RESEARCH ON HUMAN BEHAVIOR. *Creativity and Conformity* (report on research on creativity and conformity in organizations). Ann Arbor, 1958.

GARDNER, J. W. *Self-Renewal.* New York: Harper & Row, 1964.

GARRETT, A. B. *The Flash of Genius.* Princeton: Van Nostrand, 1963.

GLASS, S. J. "Creative Thinking Can Be Released and Applied," *Personnel Journal,* XXXIX (1960), 176–177.

GOLDNER, B. B. *The Strategy of Creative Thinking.* Englewood Cliffs, N.J.: Prentice-Hall, 1962.

GOODLAD, JOHN and ROBERT ANDERSON. *The Non-Graded Elementary School.* New York: Harcourt, Brace and Company, 1959.

GRAMBS, JEAN. *Group Processes in Intergroup Education.* New York: The National Conference of Christians and Jews.

GRUBER, E., G. TERRELL and M. WERTHEIMER (eds.). *Contemporary Approaches to Creative Thinking.* New York: Atherton Press, 1962.

HACK, LOUISE E. "Using Committees in the Classroom," *Rinehart Education Pamphlets.* New York: Rinehart and Company, Inc., 1958.

HAEFELE, W. *Creativity and Innovation.* New York: Reinhold, 1962.

HARAP, HENRY. *Social Living in the Curriculum.* Nashville, Tennessee: George Peabody College for Teachers, 1952.

HARRISON, RAYMOND H. and LAWRENCE E. GOWIN. *The Elementary Teacher in Action.* San Francisco: Wadsworth Publishing Company, Inc., 1958.

LANE, HOWARD and MARY BEAUCHAMP. *Human Relations in Teaching.* Englewood Cliffs, N.J.: Prentice-Hall, 1955.

LASSWELL, H. D. "The Social Setting of Creativity," H. Anderson, ed., *Creativity and Its Cultivation.* New York: Harper and Brothers, 1959.

LEAPER, ROBERT M. and ROBERT W. SCOFIELD. "Creative Climate," *Educational Leadership,* XVIII, No. 49 (October 1960), 5–6.

MacKinnon, D. W. "Characteristics of the Creative Person: Implications for the Teaching-Learning Process," *Current Issues of Higher Education*. Washington, D.C.: National Education Association (1961), 89–92.

————. "The Highly Effective Individual," *Teachers College Record*, LXI (1960), 367–378.

Mead, Margaret. *A Creative Life for Your Children*. Washington, D.C.: U.S. Department of Health, Education and Welfare, 1962.

Miel, Alice (ed.). *The Teacher's Role in Pupil-Teacher Planning*. New York: Columbia University Bureau of Publications, Teachers College, 1947.

Miles, Matthew. *Learning to Work in Groups*. New York: Columbia University Bureau of Publications, Teachers College, 1959.

Myers, R. E. and E. Paul Torrance. "Can Teachers Encourage Creative Thinking?" *Educational Leadership*, XIX (1961), 156–159.

Otto, Henry J. *Social Education in Elementary Schools*. New York: Rinehart and Company, Inc., 1956.

Rosenberg, B. G. and C. N. Zimet. "Authoritarianism and Aesthetic Choice," *Journal of Social Psychology*, XLVI (1956), 263–267.

Stein, I. and Shirley J. Heinze. *Creativity and the Individual*. Glencoe, Illinois: Free Press of Glencoe, 1960.

Torrance, E. Paul. *Education and the Creative Potential*. Englewood Cliffs, N.J.: Prentice-Hall, Inc., 1963.

Torrance, E. Paul. *Guiding Creative Talent*. Englewood Cliffs, N.J.: Prentice-Hall, Inc., 1962.

Wrightstone, J. Wayne. *Class Organization for Instruction*. Washington, D.C.: Department of Classroom Teachers, American Educational Research Association of the National Education Association, 1957.

Zirbes, Laura. *Guidelines to Developmental Teaching*. Columbus, Ohio: The Bureau of Educational Research and Service, Ohio State University, 1961.

Using the Textbook to Develop Creativity

. . . Although the American school takes the long view and the long chance, in the creative aspects of its program it is demonstrably defective. The lock-step of curriculum, textbook, and a teaching habit of all eyes front is hard to break. What many critics derisively speak of as progressive education is simply an attempt—often a good attempt—to break through this crust of conformity and passivity. Memorized forms, as useful as bricks are to a building, create nothing. Steel, concrete, and glass may be made into the meanest of structures, failing in all respects, and the reference is not to changing styles. So for the pupils, row on row.[1]

GEORGE STODDARD

TO THE READER

Current textbooks, as a rule, do little to develop creativity. Their main function, in most instances, is to provide information for students. Make a list of all the purposes for which a regular classroom textbook can be used. Then look through the introductions preceding each chapter of this book and make a list of all the ways you have been encouraged to use this textbook. From these two lists check those ways which develop creativity. How else could a textbook be used to promote creativity?

Introduction

In Book I of this series, Chapter VII,[2] the overuse of the textbook was listed as a barrier to creative development. Incorrect use of a textbook also is a barrier to creative development.

The era of textbook teaching is on the way out. Textbook teaching has never fulfilled the objectives of the American educational system, particularly in the social studies program. In many subject-matter areas, especially in the social studies, new knowledge is being

---

[1] George Stoddard, "Creativity in Education," in *Creativity and Its Cultivation,* ed. Harold H. Anderson (New York: Harper and Brothers, Publishers, 1959), pp. 187–188.

[2] James A. Smith, *Setting Conditions for Creative Teaching in the Elementary School* (Boston: Allyn and Bacon, Inc., 1966).

amassed so quickly that parts of textbooks become obsolete between the time they are written and the time they leave the printing press. A recent popular sixth-grade social studies series printed in September and released in February contained no mention of nine African nations that had been formed within that period of time, nor were any of the maps of Africa up to date. This puts great responsibility on the shoulders of the teacher, where it has rightfully belonged all along. Too many courses of study in schools have been determined from textbooks and not from the needs of the children or of any particular community.

Oscar Handlin[3] points out that the basic assumption of the textbook is that learning consists of remembering and that the text supplies the material to be remembered. Mr. Handlin cites some exceptions in a list that acknowledges the excellent service provided by textbooks in developing map skills in children; the contributions some make to children's critical thinking; the suggested activities in some texts which *could* develop *social* skills in children, if they were used; the organization of material in textbooks which saves the teacher endless hours of research; the vast amount of material they place at the disposal of children and teacher; the continuity they provide; the excellent visual aids available in some texts; and the material provided in some textbooks which helps to develop basic values in children.

Teachers can use textbooks creatively and many do. But it is not an easy task when most textbooks in themselves are so unrelated to diverse types of learning and uncreative in their presentations.

Can textbooks be creative? This author believes they can. George Stoddard says this about textbook teaching:

. . . Now we know that memory has a part to play in learning: speaking any language, including our own, involves a vast number of correlated impressions on call. The trouble is that in textbooks far removed from original sources, we are fed fragments that conform neither to the logical demands of an intellectual discipline nor to the psychological needs of the learner. Devoid of form, many a textbook renders its authors wholly unexciting. Our search for creativity therefore demands a new role for the textbook—a lesser one in the totality of the school day, but a deeper one. Its main purpose should be introductory. It should stir the student to ask, and find answers for, key questions. It should send him to original readings, experiments and experiences not otherwise occurring to him; it should transport him across the barrier of words to sights,

[3] Oscar Handlin, "Textbooks That Don't Teach," *Atlantic Monthly*, CC, No. 6 (1957), pp. 110–113.

sounds, feeling, and emotions. Such a work viewed as a map, ticket, or guidebook is defensible; not itself creative, a good textbook can show the way to creativeness.[4]

This author believes that the textbook of the future *must* be guided by the concept stated above by Stoddard. It is his firm belief that textbooks (and so-called workbooks) *can* be designed to take an active part in the creative development of teachers *and* children. Creative uses for the textbook as they now exist and suggestions for changes in their design follow in the hope that teachers will supplement the textbooks used in their classrooms with their own intelligent, creative ideas.

Social studies textbooks are primarily a summary of facts intended to impart knowledge and build concepts. We have learned that communication on the conceptual level is difficult without the common experiences which underlie these concepts. For this reason, children encounter concept words (approximately 200 per page) in the social studies books which they do not readily understand, and communication often breaks down.

The imparting of information is *one* aspect of the social studies program, but it is only one aspect. Children who have difficulty in reading can obtain information in many ways: through films, filmstrips, still pictures, interviews with people, observation, field trip experiences, and sharing with other children.

The textbook can generally be used with children of average or above-average abilities to gather information for reports, for checking factual knowledge, to read for specific items, and for developing research skills.

Used as an aid to the social studies program rather than the core of it, the textbook takes on new dimensions. It can help in developing many skills in children. It becomes a springboard for creative learning.

The Textbook as a Resource Material

Textbooks have their primary value in serving as resource material for children. As resources of information they can be used in the following ways:

[4] George Stoddard, "Creativity in Education," in *Creativity and Its Cultivation,* ed. Harold H. Anderson (New York: Harper and Brothers, Publishers, 1959), p. 182.

1. To gather material for a debate, a discussion, or a report.
2. To provide information for children doing research in order to report to the rest of the class.
3. To summarize and culminate a unit of work. Often textbooks help organize the material the children have presented and pull it together. The textbook also fills in gaps in the children's information.
4. As a check for material gleaned from less reliable sources.
5. As instruments for testing children's knowledge.
6. To provide material for details—such as making scenery for dramatizations set in a foreign locale, for determining correct props, etc.
7. As a resource to gain ideas for worthwhile activities and thought-provoking questions and study skills.
8. As an overview for an organized body of knowledge.

But the textbook can be put to more creative uses. A few current textbooks are not concerned solely with imparting factual knowledge; they attempt to develop creativity by posing open-ended problems and learning situations that set conditions for creative thinking and creative doing by putting the knowledge to work.

On the following pages are types of materials that could be developed in textbooks or are being used in current textbooks to develop the following skills:

1. Putting acquired knowledge to work.
2. Stimulating various creative kinds of research.
3. Providing supplementary material rather than serving as the core of the unit.
4. Building concepts through creative thinking and experiences.
5. Helping children in making choices and in passing judgments.
6. Helping children with problem-solving.
7. Helping to promote creative thinking.
8. Helping to develop critical thinking.

Putting Acquired Knowledge to Work

It is an essential element of creative development that: (1) children acquire a great deal of knowledge and (2) that knowledge be put to new uses in problem-solving. Figure 8–1 shows excerpts from pages in primary companion books which illustrate how knowledge can be put to work.[5]

[5] James A. Smith, *I Have Friends, Companion Book* (Syracuse, New York: The L. W. Singer Company, Inc., 1957), pp. 53–57.
———. *I Know People, Companion Book* (Syracuse, New York: The L. W. Singer Company, Inc., 1957), pp. 28, 44, 114.
———. *I Live With Others, Companion Book* (Syracuse, New York: The L. W. Singer Company, Inc., 1957), pp. 5, 6, 23.
* The author is indebted to the L. W. Singer Company, Syracuse, New York for permission to use sample materials in this chapter from The Singer Social Studies Series, Grades 1–6.

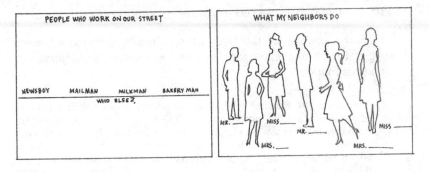

PEOPLE WHO WORK ON OUR STREET

NEWSBOY   MAILMAN   MILKMAN   BAKERY MAN
WHO ELSE?

WHAT MY NEIGHBORS DO

MR.___   MISS___   MR.___   MISS___
MRS.___   MRS._____

PROPER BICYCLE SIGNALS

THINGS WE GET FROM CATTLE

A VISIT FROM A DADDY

AT THE FARM
THINGS WE SEE ON A FARM

DO YOU KNOW THE ANIMALS?
HORSE
PIG
CHICKEN
TURKEY
DUCK
BEAR
SHEEP
DOG
CAT
SQUIRREL
COW
BIRD
RABBIT

WHICH ONE ARE FARM ANIMALS?

WAYS WE HELP DADDY

FIGURE 8–1. *Sample pages from a primary social studies book. Knowledge put to work.*

Some samples of the types of activities that textbooks might suggest for putting knowledge to work in creative problem-solving situations follow:

1. You have just finished reading many stories about the Indians. All of these stories did not happen at the same time. The Incas, for instance, lived many hundreds of years after the Mayas. With your teacher's help arrange the stories in order so that you will know which happened first, which happened second, and so on. You will then be able to tell what was happening in South America when the Indians roamed North America. Putting things in order is called a sequence. You are making a *sequence chart*. Develop this chart as you read this book so you can keep in mind the events that were developing in different places at the same time. (Grade 4)

2. After reading about the mill wheel as a source of power, have a group of boys construct one and demonstrate it to the rest of the class. (Grade 5)

3. What kind of dances did the pioneers dance at the mill-raising, do you suppose? Do some research on this and ask your physical education teacher to teach you some of these dances. (Grade 4)

4. Do you ever wonder what happened to the Indians who once owned this country? Watch your papers carefully and collect newspaper items about the Indians. Also look in your encyclopedia under the topics "Indians" and "Reservations" and find out where the Indians are today. Keep clippings that show the kinds of problems the Indians have with the United States Government. Discuss these problems and give your opinion on them. (Grade 4)

5. From your readings up to this point, start to develop a list of things that are always true of hot countries, cold countries, temperate countries, high countries, low countries. Examine your lists and decide how geography affects the life of the people in terms of clothing, transportation, occupations, amusements, religion, education, and shelter. (Grade 6)

6. The Apache and the Hopi Indians were both desert tribes but they were very different. Make a chart like the following and list ways they were different.

Hopis	Apaches
Farmers	Wanderers
Peaceful	Warlike

Then make a chart of the ways they were alike. (Grade 4)

7. Some things people must do in order to live together comfortably are: (1) make up rules to protect each other's freedom, (2) work out ways to give people equal rights, (3) work out ways so each family can have enough food, (4) plan a way so all families have a place to live, (5) agree on some way to communicate, (6) appoint someone who can be a good leader. What are some other things people must do in order to live together? Find parts from the story of Red Hawk to show how his people had taken care of these things. Then discuss how these things are taken care of in your community today. (Grades 5–6)

8. Now that you have read about the Industrial Revolution, hold a class discussion on this topic: "There is an Industrial Revolution going on today." Is this true? (Grade 6)

9. You can see that there were times when people did not keep records, so we have no way of knowing for sure exactly what happened to them. We have to play detective and find clues that help us know about them. From these clues we can make guesses about their history. Think of all the reasons you can why there might be no records of a special race of people or a time in history. (Grade 5)

10. In this book you will read how man began to change his world. Before you do this, make a list of five great inventions that you think changed the world a great deal. (Grade 5)

11. Watch your newspapers for headlines and for advertisements that are propaganda. Collect propaganda material and make three charts: "Propaganda for Good," "Propaganda for Bad," and "Propaganda that Has Little Effect." Paste the headlines and advertisements on the proper charts. (Grade 6)

Stimulating Creative Research Activities

A characteristic of creative children is that their learning is often self-initiated. One way to develop creativity in all children is to encourage them to learn for themselves by providing stimulating problems and by teaching them the skills for seeking out the answers in many ways. The following types of exercises suggest a need for many kinds of research skills and a motivation for research to many children. Often research leads to discovery, and discovery is a great impetus to creativity.

Many sources for research are suggested in the following examples and in other chapters of this book. Many types of research are implied, all of which can be used comfortably by children. Among them are: refined observation techniques (empirical—3–4–5 below);

historical research (6–7); research through experimentation (see page 213); action research (2–3); analytical research (see Chapter IX of this book); and applied research (see pages 86–87).

1. Before you take your trip to the airport, have your teacher list on the chalkboard all the things you want to know about the airport. Then have each person copy one question on a 3 x 5 card. Each person must find the answer to his question and report to the class. (Grade 6)

2. Ask your grandmother and grandfather these questions and then discuss how their lives were different from yours:
   (1) What kind of school did you go to when you were my age?
   (2) How did you get to school?
   (3) What amusements did you have then?
   (4) How did your mother cook dinner?
   (5) Where did your parents shop?
   (6) How did you learn the news each day?
   (7) How did you heat your houses?
   (8) Where did you get most of your food in the winter?
   (9) In what kind of house did you live? (Grades 2–3)

3. Invite an older person in your town to come to school and show you how the following things were done when they were a boy or girl: (Grades 2, 3, 4)
   (1) Making butter.
   (2) Making candles.
   (3) Making a patchwork quilt.
   (4) Tapping shoes.
   (5) Canning vegetables.

4. If you live in a part of the country where maple trees grow, try to locate a farm where the trees are tapped and maple syrup is made. Plan a visit to this place. You can then tap trees and boil some maple syrup. (Grade 4)

5. If there is a great canal near your school, visit it to see how boats are lowered or raised over hills by locks. The invention of locks was a great idea. Does the Suez Canal have any locks in it? (Grade 5)

6. You may want to study further some of the ideas mentioned in this chapter. Your class may want to take some of the following topics and work as committees. Or people who finish their work before others may want to look up these topics and report to the class: irrigation, Rosetta Stone, hieroglyphics, ancient Thebes, deltas, Cairo, the Ezbekia Gardens, the Sphinx, the Great Pyramids, the flag of each country, Babylon, the beginnings of our alphabet, life on an oasis, the Suez Canal, and others. (Grade 6)

7. In a little book, *The Chinese Knew*, there are pictures of all the things the Chinese had discovered how to do long before the rest of the

world knew. Have one of your classmates get the book from the library and make a report about it to the rest of the class. (Grade 6)

8. How much water do you think each person in the United States uses in one day? See if you can find the answer to this in your school library. (Grade 6)

Providing Supplementary Material

Textbooks may be used effectively as supplementary material. After a teacher has launched a unit and the children are gathering information, the teacher may want the children to first gain a unique "feel" for a country or place. Literature contributes greatly to the feeling about a country. Children's literature today contains stories about every country in the world which paint delightful word pictures and use illustrations that give vigor and reality to the countries being studied. A teacher may prefer to use literature (or a film or filmstrip) as the principal way to introduce the factual material or a feeling for a country. The textbook is used to fill out the details of the overall impressions the children get after their original exposure to the topic. Teachers who use this approach to unit teaching prefer to have many kinds of textbooks available in the classroom rather than thirty copies of one set.

When social studies texts are used with good pieces of children's literature a new world opens to children! Below is a passage from a social studies book which tells about Switzerland. Compare it to the passage from *Heidi* which follows it. Can there be any doubt as to which passage will reach the heart and free the imagination of any child?

In beautiful mountains

The pictures on pages 85–89 were all taken in Switzerland. The kind of scenery they show has attracted many thousands of tourists. Summers are delightfully cool in the mountain valleys. In winter, there is wonderful skiing on mountain slopes. The picture on page 86 shows a hotel in which people stay, both in summer and winter.

Years ago, the Swiss considered it a great disadvantage that more than a fourth of their country was barren mountain land, covered with ice and snow much, or all, of the time. The mountains now are the chief natural resource on which the tourist industry depends. The Swiss have advertised their mountains all over the world, inviting people to spend their vacations in Switzerland. This is one way in which the Swiss have tried to turn a disadvantage into an advantage.

Farmers in the mountains

Many stories have been written about how Swiss farmers make a living. For example, some men and boys herd cattle and sheep in the high mountains during the summer. One of these places is shown in the picture on this page. This pasture is above the tree-line. Highest of all, of course, are the snow fields on the high peaks. Even in midsummer, the snow does not melt.

The picture at the bottom of page 87 was taken a little lower than the one on this page. There, farmers grow crops of hay and a few grains. As the picture shows, cutting hay is still done largely by hand. The fields are too small and the slopes too steep for use of big machines. Most of the hay, of course, is fed to dairy cows in winter.

Other Swiss farmers live in valleys which are still farther down the slopes. These valleys may be broad and rich. The farmers in these valleys grow more field crops. Many have orchards or vineyards. Yet most of them, like the farmers in the high mountain valleys, make a living largely by selling dairy products.

Swiss farmers face many difficulties in their mountainous country. Most of the soils are not rich. Much land is too stony or too steep to be farmed easily. Winters are long and cold. Summers are short and cool. But there is plenty of rainfall, and the grass is good. So, the farmers have turned to dairying. At home and abroad, they find a good market for high-quality dairy products. . . .[6]

Now, let us look at an excerpt from *Heidi:*

Heidi meanwhile had unfastened her apron and rolling it carefully around the flowers laid it beside Peter's wallet inside the hollow; she then sat down beside his outstretched figure and looked about her. The valley lay far below bathed in the morning sun. In front of her rose a broad snow-field, high against the dark-blue sky, while to the left was a huge pile of rocks on either side of which a bare lofty peak, that seemed to pierce the blue, looked frowningly down upon her. The child sat without moving, her eyes taking in the whole scene, and all around was a great stillness, only broken by soft, light puffs of wind that swayed the light bells of the blue flowers, and the shining gold heads of the cistus, and set them nodding merrily on their slender stems. Peter had fallen asleep after his fatigue and the goats were climbing about among the bushes overhead. Heidi had never felt so happy in her life before. She drank in the golden sunlight, the fresh air, the sweet smell of the flowers, and wished for nothing better than to remain there forever. So the time went on, while to Heidi, who had so often looked up from the valley at the mountains above, these seemed now to have faces, and to be looking down at her like old friends. Suddenly she heard a loud harsh cry overhead and lifting her eyes she saw a bird, larger than any she had ever seen

[6] Harlan H. Barrows, Edith Putnam Parker, and Clarence W. Sorenson, *Old World Lands* (Morristown, N.J.: Silver Burdett Co., © 1964), pp. 84–85. Used by permission.

before, with great, spreading wings, wheeling round and round in wide circles, and uttering a piercing, croaking kind of sound above her.[7]

Textbooks can never hope to accomplish what *Heidi* does. Used with *Heidi,* however, texts take on a new creative meaning.

The teacher who read *Heidi* to the children had the children list all the things they had learned about Switzerland from reading parts of the book together. They checked this list with the original questions for their unit. The textbooks were then used for resources to find other material.

Building Concepts by Stimulating Creative Thinking

Concepts are generalizations built after many specific experiences; they stay with children after specifics are forgotten. Some words in themselves are concepts (such as "hot," "region," "area," "desert," "range," etc.). Because concepts are built as a result of many experiences, communication on the concept level is always the most difficult type of communication. Often the same word may have a different meaning to two people because their field of experience is not the same.

Textbooks give children many specific facts and experiences. Often the teacher is left to develop concepts from these experiences. A creative teacher will set conditions for new ideas to recur in her classroom in new situations until concepts are formed.

Recently some textbooks have successfully attempted to help in the development of these concepts. Such textbooks can make a major contribution to creative learning in a classroom.

Following are some activities teachers can use to set conditions for concept development in the classroom:

Activities for Concept Development: Intermediate Grades

1. Collect pictures of all kinds of weather and landscapes. Your book says, "Almost all kinds of climate can be found on the great continent of South America." Place a map of South America on your bulletin board and pin your pictures around it. Now with colored string or ribbon make a path to the place where that scene or weather picture might be found. You will have to use what you learned about geography and climate to figure out some places. Your teacher can help you with others.

2. Here are a list of words, phrases, and names which most people associate with France. Do you know what they mean?

[7] Johanna Spyri, *Heidi* (New York: World Publishing Company, 1946).

WHERE DOES CLOTHING COME FROM?
Sub-Committees

cotton

Wool

leather

silk

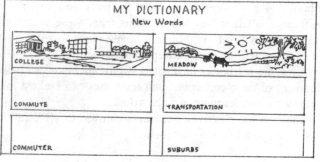

COMMITTEE CHARTS
Ways We Use Cotton

SOAP

OIL

FERTILIZER

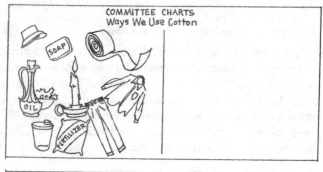

MY DICTIONARY
New Words

COLLEGE

MEADOW

COMMUTE

TRANSPORTATION

COMMUTER

SUBURBS

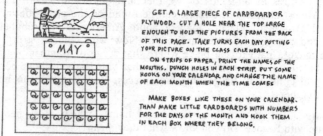

Make a Calendar

MAY

GET A LARGE PIECE OF CARDBOARD OR PLYWOOD. CUT A HOLE NEAR THE TOP LARGE ENOUGH TO HOLD THE PICTURES FROM THE BACK OF THIS PAGE. TAKE TURNS EACH DAY PUTTING YOUR PICTURE ON THE CLASS CALENDAR.

ON STRIPS OF PAPER, PRINT THE NAMES OF THE MONTHS. PUNCH HOLES IN EACH STRIP. PUT SOME HOOKS ON YOUR CALENDAR AND CHANGE THE NAME OF EACH MONTH WHEN THE TIME COMES

MAKE BOXES LIKE THESE ON YOUR CALENDAR. THAN MAKE LITTLE CARDBOARDS WITH NUMBERS FOR THE DAYS OF THE MONTH AND HOOK THEM IN EACH BOX WHERE THEY BELONG.

FIGURE 8–2. *Concept development: sample pages from a primary social studies book.*[8]

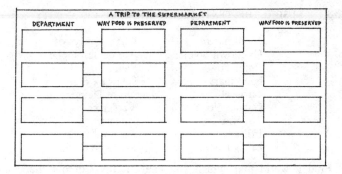

[8] James A. Smith. *Companion Books* (Syracuse, N.Y.: The LW Singer Publishing Co., Inc., 1957), sample pages.

Montmartre	Champs Elysees
Unknown Soldier	Arc de Triomphe
Eiffel Tower	Seine
book mart	sidewalk cafe
carousel	Notre Dame
Chanel No. 5	Versailles
Tuileries	Riviera
Brittany	Maginot Line
Louis Pasteur	Madame Curie

3. Find a world map which you can cut up. Cut out the country of Russia and then lay it on other countries in the world. How does it compare in size?

4. How did the people of Egypt learn to live with their geography? List several ways. (Grade 6)

5. Draw pictures that show what these new words mean: (Grade 4)

snow snake	cradle board
porcupine quill	traps and snares
embroidery	clan
tumpline	pitch
birch-bark mocucks	mide

6. Look up the words "chow mein" and "chop suey." Are they really Chinese dishes or American ideas as to what Chinese food is like? (Grade 4)

7. Collect pictures of all the recent inventions you can find. At the top of a large sheet of paper draw or place a picture of each of the inventions mentioned in this chapter. Then paste your pictures under the one big invention that started all the others. For example: on one sheet of paper you might paste an electric light. Under that would come neon lights, the radio tube, television tubes, etc. (Grade 4)

8. Pretend you are the governing body of one of the backward countries. How would you plan to make it more modern and more productive? (Grade 6)

Pages in textbooks could be designed so that each page develops a concept and stimulates creative thinking. Figure 8–3 is an example of such a page.

Making Decisions and Passing Judgments

The ability to make decisions and pass judgment are two skills that are a necessary part of the creative process. The artist must make decisions continually in choosing the right color for the right space.

WAYS WE ARE ALIKE

1. WE ALL LIKE ADORNMENTS
2. WE LIKE BEAUTIFUL THINGS
3. WE ALL NEED FOOD
4. WE ALL LIKE TO DANCE
5. WE LIKE A GOOD STORY
6. WE ALL LIKE MUSIC
   WHAT OTHER WAYS?

FIGURE 8–3. *Concept development: every person in the world likes the same things.*

FIGURE 8–4. *Developing the skill of making decisions and passing judgments.*

The poet must concern himself with the right word in the right place, the architect, with the right material or design in the right place. All creativity relies on these two skills. The social studies program offers unlimited opportunities to develop these skills which are also essential to democratic living. People must choose jobs, decide on school-bond issues, vote for political candidates, and judge persons on trial.

There are many small ways children naturally make decisions in a modern classroom all through the day:

Decision-making Situations

Painting	Planning the daily program
Creative writing	Solving arithmetic problems
Choosing games	Evaluation of each class period
Map study	Construction activities
Modeling	Choosing committees on which to work

Planning trips, parties, programs, etc.

But as soon as children are able to handle these routine tasks, conditions should be created for them to continue to experience judgment and decision-making.

Following are some examples of contrived experiences which put children in decision-making situations. They could be incorporated into textbooks to develop critical thinking.

THIS IS SENEB

YOU MET HIM ON YOUR VISIT TO ANCIENT EGYPT. COULD HE HAVE LIVED THERE? DO YOU THINK HE REALLY DID OR DID THE AUTHOR OF THE BOOK CREATE HIM TO MAKE THE BOOK MORE INTERESTING?
HOW CAREFULLY DO YOU READ? CAN YOU TELL "REAL" FROM "MAKE-BELIEVE"? IN THIS CHAPTER WHAT IS REAL FACT? WHAT DID THE AUTHOR MAKE UP TO MAKE THE BOOK MORE INTERESTING?

FIGURE 8–5. *Developing the skill of critical thinking.*

FIGURE 8–6. *Developing a concept and putting it to work in critical thinking.*

Decision-making Situations—Intermediate Grades

Children: Here is a problem for you to think about!

CHILDREN SHOULD HELP TO MAKE UP SCHOOL RULES!

This is a problem on which all people will not agree. We call it a "controversial" problem. That *big word* means you could have a dispute or a controversy over it.

Let's see how you can share ideas. Can you listen to other people's ideas and opinions? Can you wait for your turn to talk?

To see that everyone gets a chance, divide your class into small groups of about six people in each group. If your chairs are in rows, face each other. If you sit around tables, group them. Choose a chairman to call on people. Choose a secretary to write down your ideas. Have the chairman keep a list of ideas *for* the argument and a list *against* the argument. Discuss this for ten minutes. Then let the secretary from each group report to the whole class.

This is how your dad works with other men. This is how your teacher works in her teachers' meetings. This is how your mother gets things done in the P.T.A. Can you do it? It is an important way to work together.

Some Things to Think About (Grade 4)

1. In Part IV of this book we are going to read how man began to change the world. You have been reading history in this part of your book. Did the people in this history change their world at all? The Eskimos, the Hopis, the Apaches, the Chippewas, the Mayas, the Incas? How?

2. One of the things we all have to learn in order to become adults is how to make judgments. Making judgments means making a decision. But it means more than that because it means trying to make the wisest decision. Below are four sets of statements. Using the last four chapters in this book, decide which one you think shows the best judgment for the people about whom you read.

Statement 1. Chapter 11

Brave Hawk was foolish to believe that the rain dance would bring rain.

or

Brave Hawk helped his people believe in their gods by believing in the rain dance.

Statement 2. Chapter 12

Fleetfoot was unwise to live in a wigwam in the winter.

or

Fleetfoot's parents made the best use of materials they had to make a warm winter shelter.

Statement 3. Chapter 13

Aztec's father was foolish to work for the Lord Serpent for one whole day every once in a while when he needed the time for his own cornfields.

or

Aztec's father was wise to work for the Lord Serpent.

Some Problems to Solve

1. This chapter gives you a chance to make a special kind of chart. Write a series of facts along one side of a sheet of paper leaving room along

the other side to write how we know these facts are true. Then write "Things We Think We Know" along the left side of another sheet of paper. Across from each thing we think we know write why we think we know it.

Example:

We think the Mayas were serpent-worshippers.

All their carvings are full of serpents.

2. Collect some stamps from different countries and study the pictures. Do any of them tell anything about the geography or climate of the country? (Grade 5)

3. Take a problem from your classmates about something that happened at school or at home. Have a group act it out for the class. Then have other groups of children act out ways to solve the problem.

4. Fewer trains are running in America today than ten years ago although more people are traveling. How do you account for this? Let your class have a discussion about this. (Grade 6)

5. Here is a list of statements that are generally true but are not true in the case of Egypt. Explain why. (Grade 6)
   (1) When rivers overflow they cause great damage.
   (2) Almost nothing grows in the desert.
   (3) Lack of rainfall means that growing things cannot live.
   (4) Very few people live in desert regions.
   (5) The heaviest rainfall in Egypt is 8½ inches per year. Almost nothing will grow with so little rainfall.
   (6) Travel is difficult in a hot, arid land.

A Problem For You to Think About: A Controversial Issue

In a democracy the majority of the people rule. That means that if *all* the people do not want a law it is put to a vote. If *most* of the people vote for it then it is passed. "Most" of the people is a majority. Another way to say it is that a majority is one more than half the votes.

Some people feel this is unfair. They say that when a vote is very close a majority is not enough. A law needs support of the people, and if nearly half the people in a country do not want it, then it will not work. There will be too many people who do not support it. They feel it is more democratic to get what is called a "consensus." A consensus means that people work on a law together and change it until nearly all are satisfied with the change. What do you think about this?

PROBLEM: If the rights of nearly half the individuals in a country are suppressed by a small majority vote, is this really democratic?

Divide your class into groups and talk about this. Then come together and share your opinions.

The group that is not the majority is called the minority. In a real democracy the rights of the minority are also considered. Can you think of some ways minority groups might secure *their* rights also? Discuss this problem, and share your ideas about it.

The Textbook Can Help Children with Problem-solving

Unit teaching is designed to provide children with situations in problem-solving. Discovering facts in science is problem-solving. Creating is problem-solving. Working arithmetic meaningfully is problem-solving. The curriculum of the modern school is designed to be a problem-solving one.

Problem-solving is important because research shows that positive tensions created in the learner stimulate him to learn. His learning releases the tensions and satisfaction results. Learning by problem-solving is sound methodology because it involves the learner. Only by involvement with a problem does a learner learn.

In social situations these tensions may be very strong. Often they are negative, or even destroying, tensions. This does not mean they are less valuable as learning situations. The creative teacher sees the social problems of her classroom as natural conditions for developing sound learning experiences rather than as discipline problems. In the next chapter sociodynamics will be discussed. Sociodynamics are those ways teachers have learned to deal with intense social-emotional problems.

Textbooks can help in the solution of social problems. Recent textbooks recognize that social studies programs must involve those learnings which help children to understand and deal with social problems. Here are some of the ways they help teachers set conditions for creative problem-solving:

Problem-Solving Situation Ideas for Textbooks—Intermediate Level

1. Show how some simple tools help to save energy. For instance, try to drag one of your classmates across the floor in a flat-bottomed wooden box. How many children does it take—how hard do they have to work? Now put some dowels under the box. Keep putting dowels in front of the box as you move it across the floor. How many children are needed now to push the box? How difficult is it? You can see that a simple roller can move heavy objects more easily than a strong push. The Egyptians knew this. Where did they use this knowledge? (Grade 4)

2. Try this. Fasten a strong rubber band on the front of a heavy toy truck. Lift the truck and measure the length of the rubber band as it

FIGURE 8–7. *Problem-solving situations from primary social studies text-books.*[9]

[9] *Ibid.*

stretches. Now lean a board against a chair and pull the toy truck up the board by the rubber band. Again measure the stretch of the rubber band. What do you notice? The tilted board makes it easier to lift the truck, doesn't it? It makes the weight of the truck less so the stretch of the rubber band is less than when you lifted the truck directly. The Egyptians knew this, too. Where did they use this idea? (Grade 4)

3. One simple way you can show how water pressure is greater on the bottom of the sea than on the top is this: take a tall tin fruit-juice can. Puncture holes from the top to the bottom along one side in a straight row. Now fill the can quickly with water and hold it above the sink. Notice that the water squirting from the hole in the bottom shoots the farthest. Why? (Grade 5)

4. Try some more experiments to show how tools preserve energy with a pulley, a wedge, a pencil sharpener, a window shade, a blackboard eraser, a safety pin. (Grade 4)

5. You can demonstrate action and reaction simply by blowing up a balloon. When you let go of the balloon the escaping air is *action* and the moving of the balloon in the opposite direction is *reaction*. How else can you show action and reaction? (Grade 5)

6. The Mayas discovered some of the facts and skills which we still use today, such as building time around changes in the moon, measuring direction by the north star, and building a system of numbers. List all the things you can find that the Mayas used which we still use. (Grade 5)

Promoting Creative Thinking

Creative thinking was defined on page 9 as that thinking which involves the production of new ideas. Creative production depends upon a background of related experiences. It comes from the growth of an urge to express one's self, the accessibility of a variety of materials, time, and a permissive atmosphere for creative work.

Setting conditions for creative thinking in social studies means providing all the kinds of experiences mentioned in this book. Textbooks could make giant steps in stimulating creative thinking through a variety of suggested activities. Some suggestions follow:

Promoting Creative Thinking: Intermediate Grades

1. What did the people in early times do for fun? Do you think they mixed work with pleasure sometimes and had fun? Would the mill-raising described in this chapter be fun? What do you think the women did at a mill-raising? The children? People had house-raisings, quilting-bees, church-raisings and corn-huskings. They were all fun. You will enjoy reading about them.

ON THE WAY TO SCHOOL
THINGS I SAW THIS MORNING

MY STORY
WHEN I GROW UP

A PICTURE FOR MY FRIEND

TOMMY'S STORY

Things to do on a Rainy Day
OTHER IDEAS   A PUPPET SHOW

MONEY, MONEY!
What did Ann and Sally do? How did the story end?

FIGURE 8–8. Developing creative thinking: a primary textbook.

2. Can you think of any reasons why the first roads to Fairland were not good enough after Fairland became a big town? Can you find out what the first roads were made of? How were they built? Compare them to the way we build roads today. What has made the difference possible?

3. How long ago was "Long, Long Ago"? The pictures in this chapter may help you understand. (Grade 4)

4. What do you think happened in your town a long time ago? Wherever you live, you can be sure that there is plenty of history. (Grade 4)

5. How did your town get its name? Can you find out about the first settlers to come into your town? Perhaps you can start making a picture history of your town like this one of Fairland. (Grade 4)

6. Many people say, "The Indians are the only true Americans!" What do they mean? What do you think?

7. If you live near a library visit it and ask to see some real old newspapers. Then look at the advertisements. Notice the differences in tools, clothes, materials, and services for sale. Notice, too, the difference in prices. What brought about all these changes? (Grade 4)

8. Make a list of all kinds of materials that the people in your class are wearing. Which ones are new or different since your teacher went to school? (Grade 4)

9. A magic carpet can go anywhere. Write some stories telling about some places in the ancient lands you visited on the magic carpet which we did not visit. You will have to read about them first.

10. Can you make up a "saga" about the Vikings' trip to America and have one of your class "skalds" recite it? (Grade 4)

11. Pretend that you were a boy or girl living in Pompeii on August 24, 79 A.D. Write a story or play telling what happened. (Grade 4)

Developing Critical Thinking

Critical thinking is generally defined as being more objective than creative thinking. It is problem-solving, as is creative thinking, but it is more directed toward some goal. It is taking a group of facts, making decisions, and passing judgment consistent with those facts.

Critical thinking can be stimulated by situations in which children find themselves forced to pass judgments or make decisions. Sometimes the motivation for critical thinking comes from the questions teachers ask or those listed in a textbook.

Many questions asked by teachers and textbooks serve the sole purpose of checking comprehension. The answers can be found simply by rereading parts of the text. This is not to be confused with critical thinking. When social studies are taught by the reading of a textbook through a question and a read-to-find-the-answer period, little can be claimed for it in terms of meeting social objectives. The program is little more than a series of lessons in reading comprehension using a social studies text.

Following are some questions taken from various social studies texts which were listed under the pretense of developing critical thinking but which actually are only comprehension questions:

1. Why did the pioneers often take their stoves west in their wagons when space was so precious?
2. Why did people migrate west?
3. What are the various means of transportation and what goods are shipped by each means?
4. At sixty miles per hour, how long will it take to travel across Texas?
5. Why is Alaska growing in importance?

The following questions were taken from the plans of two teachers who were concerned that their children learn to think critically. The difference between this type of question and the type listed above is obvious.

Questions That Provoke Critical Thinking

1. What effect has the St. Lawrence Seaway had upon our country?
2. What were the desirabilities and undesirabilities of plantation life?
3. Why were a desert state (Nevada) and a swamp state (Florida) the two fastest growing states in 1960?
4. What were some of the differences and similarities of settlers in Virginia in 1607 and in California in 1849?
5. Where would you want to live if you moved to Alaska? Why?
6. Do you suppose Russia is sorry that she sold Alaska to us?
7. What has happened that has made it possible for people to live on the desert now?
8. The coldest and hottest places in the world are in the temperate zone. Why isn't the coldest place in the Frigid Zone and the hottest place in the Torrid Zone?
9. Why do homes in northern Switzerland have such steep-sloping roofs?
10. What has made it possible for homes in the temperate climates of North America where there are severe winters to have flat roofs?

Here are some ways textbooks might set conditions for critical thinking.

Some Problems to Solve

In Chapter I you learned much about geography. Geography helps us to understand why the world and the universe are as they are. It helps us to understand why people in some parts of the world are alike and why they are different. You have already seen many still pictures, moving pictures, and television shows of people from other places doing things differently than you do.

Here is a big problem for you:

1. Collect all the pictures you can of people who are doing things differently than you do in your town. Also collect pictures of people who dress differently than you do. Make a big bulletin-board display of these pictures. Then see if you can answer these questions about the people in your pictures.

   a. If they are working, why are they doing the work they are doing? Is it because the land where they live is different from the land where you live? Is it because the weather or climate is different?

   b. Can you tell by your pictures what part of the world these people come from?

   c. Can you guess what zone they might live in?

   d. Can you tell which places are hot all the time, which are cold all the time, and which are in-between?

   e. If people in your pictures are playing, can you tell if the climate and geography determine how they shall play?

   f. See if you can make lists of facts that are *sometimes* true of cold countries but not always (such as: There is generally ice there), of hot countries (such as: They generally do not have snow), of temperate countries (such as: They generally have cool or cold winters and warm or hot summers), of high countries (such as: They are generally cooler than low countries), of low countries (such as: They are generally near the seacoast).

2. Here is another problem that will make you think. Arrange a bulletin board or a chalkboard with signs as follows:

Found *only* in hot countries	Found *only* in cold countries	Found *only* in temperate countries
Found *sometimes* in hot countries	Found *sometimes* in cold countries	Found *sometimes* in temperate countries
Never found in hot countries	*Never* found in cold countries	*Never* found in temperate countries

Now take the following list of words and fit them in the proper spaces. After you have done this, make up lists of words of your own and put them in the proper spaces:

mining	palm trees	equatorial forests
roses	westerly winds	hurricanes
whales	the equator	bananas
ice caps	fishing	apple trees
oranges	sponge fishing	evergreen trees
jungles	deserts	lakes
glaciers	snow-capped mountains	lemons
hailstones	icebergs	pelicans
cactus	dates and figs	pearl divers
bathing beaches	snowstorms	sandy beaches
alligators	oysters	polar bears
seaweed	wheat	corn
dairy farming	igloos	sugar cane
bamboo	sunburns	pinapples
sailboats		rice

3. Ask your mothers and fathers to tell you the answers to these questions and you will see how quickly things change:
   a. What was your favorite television program when you were ten years old?
   b. What kind of automobile did your father have when you were my age?
   c. How long did it take a large passenger airplane to travel from New York to San Francisco when you were ten years old?
   d. What materials were used to make your clothes when you were my age?
   e. When you were in the fourth grade, what kind of school did you go to and what subjects did you study?
   f. What happened to people who had polio when you were young?
   Now see if you can figure out why there are so many changes from the time your mother and father were your age up to now.

4. Here are some statements. Using this chapter, see if you can find material that shows these statements are true:
   a. People work all the time to bring order in their world.
   b. Most people have religious beliefs.
   c. People depend on each other for their living.

5. Find passages in this chapter which make these ideas true:
   a. People try to bring order to their world by making laws about living together.
   b. People are always trying to make their lives interesting and happy.
   c. Inventions and discoveries change people's ways of living.
   d. People live as they do because of the world around them.

6. How good are you at remembering facts? You will have to be a *real* good reader in order to do this problem. In each of the following

statements only one word makes the statement false. Can you find that word?

   a. The Chippewas first lived in New York State but were driven east by another tribe.
     The wrong word is _____.
   b. Redbird's family lived in a wigwam all the year round.
     The wrong word is ———.
   c. Redbird always stayed indoors when the snow came down and worked on her embroidery.
     The wrong word is _____.

Activities That Evoke Critical Thinking

1. Make a picture chart of all the food Man can get from the sea. Don't forget salt. (Grade 4)

2. In 1959, Premier Khrushchev of Russia visited the Western world to study the American way of life. Compare his visit with that of Peter the Great. What were the similarities? The differences? (Grade 6)

3. One of the freedoms we now have is freedom of the press. People can print what they want to. But do they always print the truth? Look at the clippings and advertisements in Figure 8–9, taken from a famous newspaper. Is what they say really true?

FIGURE 8–9. *Is freedom of the press sometimes abused?*

FIGURE 8–10. *Does freedom of the press sometimes lead to a violation of people's rights?*

4. Figure 8–10 shows two reports taken from different newspapers. Which one gives the truest account of exactly what happened? Which one gives the reporter's opinions as fact? Which newspaper violates the freedom of the press? Why? What laws protect people from misuse of freedom of the press?

5. Headlines and guidelines in your newspapers give you a clue about the article that follows. If your teacher gave you this assignment, "What was the great crisis in the Suez Canal situation?" which of the articles headlined in Figure 8–11 would you read to find the best answer?

FIGURE 8–11. *Which article would you read?*

6. POPULATION OF ASIA
Figure 8–12 shows three graphs taken from three books. They tell the population of some of the countries of Asia. None of them agree.

    a. Which one is correct?

    b. How would you go about finding which one is correct?

    c. Ideas:
       Check the authors. Check with other books of authority. Write the publishers. Check with a recent atlas. Check the dates of the books. We must check many things in order to read critically.

POPULATION FIGURES INDIA•CHINA•JAPAN (FROM 3 DIFFERENT BOOKS-1963)
REPORTED BY MILLIONS

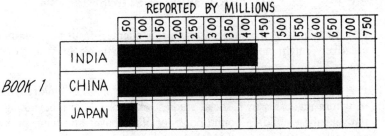

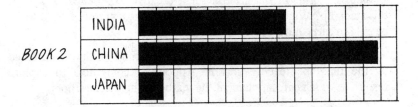

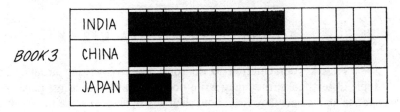

FIGURE 8–12. *Which graph is correct?*

Summary

Within the framework of unit teaching it is possible for teachers to be creative and to develop creativity with the academic materials they use. Chief among these materials is the textbook. The role of the textbook in the modern school is changing. This changing role calls for a more creative use of the textbook and a more creative outlook on the part of the teacher.

TO THE COLLEGE STUDENT

1. Which of the suggestions in this chapter on using a textbook creatively might apply to the use of the textbook in your college classes?

2. Your author once taught a fifth-grade class of children, each of whom made his own social studies textbook. At the beginning of the year these children bound books of blank pages and then, through research, discovery, and experimentation, filled the books in with pictures, graphs, maps, and written material about the units they studied. In terms of the criteria for a creative experience, how does this stack up? What sorts of resources did the teacher need in order to be able to carry out a project of this kind?

3. Many modern textbooks contain information that is outdated by the time the teacher gets it. Appoint a committee to explore resources which can supplement the textbooks in the classroom.

4. Which of your college textbooks do you enjoy? Analyze the reasons.

TO THE CLASSROOM TEACHER

1. Ask your children to do some creative writing around the topic of textbooks; they may write poems, essays, criticisms, plays, or stories about how they feel about their textbooks. Analyze the writing to see if you can detect their attitude about these texts. Then ask yourself whether or not they learn much from them if they do not like

them. What could you do to supplement the textbooks you use to make them more attractive, or how could you supplement them to make them more useful to children who like them?

2. What origins, other than textbooks, do you use as a source of information for the children?

3. American textbooks are the most attractive and best-planned books on the market. Children should like them. Do they? If not, it is the use of them that has built a negative attitude. Check your use of textbooks and decide whether or not you are using them to the best advantage.

4. Hold a discussion with the children on textbooks. Ask them to suggest ways they feel the textbook might be used in interesting ways.

TO THE COLLEGE STUDENT
AND THE CLASSROOM TEACHER

1. List all the ways you can use television and radio creatively to help keep your textbook information current.

2. Make a survey of all the children's literature that can be used to supplement each unit of the social studies program.

3. Take the questions with answers from any chapter of any teacher's manual that accompanies a social studies textbook and think of creative ways for children to apply this knowledge.

4. Study the activities suggested in the teacher's manual of a social studies book and analyze them. Which ones provide creative development and critical and creative thinking? Which ones help children to grow in their ability to make decisions or pass judgments? Which ones are just busy work?

5. Make a list of skills, attitudes, values, and appreciations which *may* develop when a teacher uses more than one resource book in teaching a unit rather than a single textbook.

6. Do the suggestions at the beginning and close of each chapter in this textbook help you to use this book more creatively? Could similar ideas be used in children's textbooks? Design such a textbook.

SELECTED BIBLIOGRAPHY

ANDERSON, HOWARD R. (ed.). "Teaching Critical Thinking in the Social Studies," *Thirteenth Yearbook of the National Council for the Social Studies.* Washington, D.C.: The Council, 1942.

BARNES, FRED R. "The Textbook Dilemma," *Teachers College Record,* LV, No. 7 (April, 1956) 369–383.

CRAWFORD, R. P. *The Techniques of Creative Thinking.* New York: Hawthorn Books, 1954.

CRONBACH, LEE J., *et al. Text Materials in Modern Education.* Urbana, III.: University of Illinois Press, 1955.

DALE, EDGAR. *Audio Visual Methods in Teaching,* rev. ed. New York: The Dryden Press, 1954.

DALE, EDGAR. "Teaching Critical Thinking," *Education Digest,* XXIV (May, 1959), 29–31.

JAROLIMEK, JOHN. *Social Studies in Elementary Education.* New York: The Macmillan Co., 1959, Chap. VI.

KLEIN, A. F. *Role Playing.* New York: Association Press, 1956.

LOGAN, LILLIAN N. and VIRGIL G. LOGAN. *Teaching the Elementary School Child.* Boston: Houghton Mifflin Company, 1961, 180–186.

LORGE, I. "The Teacher's Task in the Development of Thinking," *Reading Teacher,* 13, 1960, 170–175.

MICHAELIS, JOHN. *Social Studies for Children in a Democracy,* 2nd ed. Englewood Cliffs, N.J.: Prentice-Hall, Inc., 1950, Chap. XIII.

THOMAS, R. MURRAY and SHERWIN G. SWARTOUT. *Integrated Teaching Materials.* New York: Longmans, Green and Company, Inc., 1960.

THOMAS, R. MURRAY. *Ways of Teaching.* New York: Longmans, Green and Company, Inc., 1955, 150–153.

Values and Character Development

Creative workers have devised many techniques through the years to aid themselves in overcoming their habits and stiff attitudes. In this work we will define, as a *creative technique, anything that will give or lead us to a fresh point of view.* A creative technique is not to be considered as giving a *finished* result, unquestioned in quality. It is, rather, a technique to start us on a new path of thinking that may well lead to a successful conclusion.[1]

EUGENE VON FANGE

TO THE READER

How do you think your own attitudes, values, and appreciations developed? Do you ever remember anyone "teaching" them to you or were you expected to acquire them through the act of growing up? Make a list of all the ways you can think of that you might "teach" these things. Then read this chapter and add to your list.

Introduction

Levinger has pointed out that unit teaching provides for the integrating experience that is a prerequisite to developing the intensity of experience necessary to create and to come up with answers.[2]

It has been said that within the general framework of unit teaching the goals of creative teaching may be realized. Unit teaching not only makes it possible for children to explore and learn large bodies of knowledge, it also provides a flexible structure wherein freedom to capitalize on children's interests and ideas is available. This method makes possible the development of many skills and abilities in children. It also opens the way for teachers to develop certain attitudes, values, and appreciations in the children. The teachers of Freeport, mentioned on page 27, believed that part of

[1] Eugene Von Fange, *Professional Creativity* (Englewood Cliffs, N.J.: © Prentice-Hall, Inc., 1959), p. 34.

[2] Leah Levinger, "The Teacher's Role in Creativity," *American Journal of Orthopsychiatry,* XXIX (1959), pp. 291–297.

the cultural heritage which should be passed along to each child should include all these things.

Perhaps the most obvious way to develop character that incorporates these values, traits, attitudes, and appreciations is to live in an atmosphere where they are held sacred by the teacher. But children come from many types of homes: some come from homes where they are rejected; others from homes where they are physically deprived. Many children come from homes dominated by one parent; others come from homes where they are overly accepted. Some come from parent-child-centered homes.

Each of these homes is likely to possess a different set of values and appreciations. And each child brings to school those attitudes, traits, values, and appreciations held in his own home. Confronted by group pressure in school, he learns to change some of them. But this is a haphazard way of developing values and a wanton waste of human resources, should sound values and attitudes not develop. Certain values and appreciations must be taught—their development cannot be left to chance. Appreciation of freedom and an understanding of the rights of children and men are examples. Teachers can employ many sociodynamic devices to help children build the character traits that are necessary to the perpetuation of human rights.

Dramatization

Dramatization can be used in many ways to help teachers build values and attitudes in children. Any social eruption taking place within the classroom (which is a group problem) can be dramatized in order to give the class a first-hand experience with the situation. Once the group *sees* the problem presented by the dramatization, a discussion on the facts of the situation (which are clearly known) can take place.

Mr. Anderson, a fourth-grade teacher, found two boys from his classroom running in the hall, chasing another boy for a hat. Running in the hall was against school rules. Mr. Anderson brought the boys into the classroom to talk over the problem. Each seemed to feel the other was to blame for the situation. Mr. Anderson asked them if they felt they could remember enough of what had happened to dramatize it before the class. The boys were willing to do this.

After they had dramatized the situation that brought on the hat-snatching, Mr. Anderson stopped the dramatization at the point where he had stopped the running in the hall and asked, "Now how do you boys feel? Now that you have acted out the situation, do you see it any differently?" Each boy felt the other was still to blame, so Mr. Anderson turned to the class to ask for opinions.

Mr. Anderson did not express his opinions to the class. He did not moralize. He did not make the children feel guilty. He simply approached the situation as a social problem for which his fourth-grade class had a responsibility. And the children took the responsibility. At the end of the discussion, they had thought of five ways the boys might have handled the situation without breaking a school rule.

Dramatization can also be used very effectively with children to show comparisons. In a sixth grade the children were trying to decide which was the best of two different plans. One group felt they would like to go to the school library to look up material for their unit each day during their room work period. The other group felt the library rules would cramp their style and would kill the opportunity to discuss their findings among themselves, to move freely about, to get materials, etc. They felt that books kept in the classroom would afford a much better opportunity to accomplish their goals.

The teacher suggested that a committee from each group drama-tize the scene which they did *not* want to happen. This was done, and in the discussion that followed the children immediately agreed that the library situation offered too many restrictions on accomplishing their goals, so a library was set up in the room.

Dramatizations help children prepare for trips taken in the social studies program. Miss Marsden, a first-grade teacher, was taking her children to a small circus. Since many children had never been to a circus, the children arranged their chairs as they would find them arranged at the circus and then dramatized buying their tickets and taking their seats. Later, at the circus, they performed with all the poise and security of veteran circus-goers.

Miss Rockwell, a second-grade teacher, used dramatization to help evaluate a trip to a pony farm. In spite of careful planning and excellent preparations, the trip had not gone well. Some of the boys had not carried out their responsibilities at the farm, and the bus ride home had been noisy and unruly.

Miss Rockwell talked to the children about the trip on the following day. First they discussed all the good parts of the trip. Then Miss Rockwell asked them if there were any parts of the trip which they felt had not gone so well. Immediately, many of the children said they felt some of the boys had not done what they were supposed to do, nor had they behaved well on the bus. Miss Rockwell said she had felt this too.

"I wonder what happened," she asked. "We planned well, we talked about problems that might come up, we talked about how we should behave, and still we had trouble. I wonder what went wrong?"

One of the boys who had been responsible for the trouble on the bus was the first to volunteer. He felt some other boy had "picked on" him. Soon a discussion was going on as to what happened to bring about the disorder on the bus. Miss Rockwell suggested the boys dramatize the bus scene to see whether or not the class could find out why their plans had failed, and what they might do to make them better next time.

Chairs were lined up to resemble a school bus and the scene unfolded. Children were quite free about reconstructing their roles. Soon the trouble center was spotted; four boys had set it off.

Miss Rockwell stopped the dramatization and held a discussion. The four boys who began the trouble were allowed to talk first. Almost at once it came to light that they had been terribly bored and were just trying to relieve their boredom. Gerry gave the clue to the problem when he said, "I've been to that old pony farm so many times I'm sick of it anyway."

"Why," said Miss Rockwell, "I thought no one in the class had ever been to the pony farm. Have others of you been there, too?"

The four boys who had created the problem had all been there many times before. Further discussion brought the class (and the teacher) to the realization that this had been an oversight in their planning. The class decided that the next time they planned to go on a trip they would find out at the very beginning who had been there before.

"Once we know this, what will we do about it?" asked Miss Rockwell.

"Well," said Charlie, one of the trouble-makers, "you could have given us sumpthin' to do besides look at all that old stuff again."

"A very good idea," agreed Miss Rockwell. "Charlie, Gerry, Jody, and Hank could all have been guides for our small groups. Even when I've seen something many times I get a thrill out of showing it to people who have never seen it before. How do you boys feel about that idea?"

They felt fine about it. It was agreed by the class that one weakness in planning their trip was in making proper assignments to individuals and that the next time they would be more careful about it.

Dramatization can also develop empathy and help children understand other people's feelings and problems. Acting out famous stories or poems gives children a feeling for them that reading does not do.

Following are some ideas used with children to develop certain concepts and values through dramatization. Properly used, they help to set conditions for the creative development of attitudes.

1. One child was accused of something he did not do. A dramatization helped develop the concept of fair play and the idea of withholding judgment.
2. One class committee wasted a work period, and the work they were to finish was not completed so the class could use it at the proper time. A dramatization brought out the importance of accepting responsibilities and the need for fulfilling them.
3. Through a dramatization of the home life of a child in a wartorn country, the children came to realize the values of the richness in their own lives and decided to send boxes to these needy children.
4. One child who had been in the hospital for a long time persuaded some of the children to act out one of his lonely days there. As a result, the children decided to send cards and games to children's hospitals.
5. After a dramatization resulting from a discussion of the problems of old people in the homes of the children, one group was organized and went to sing Christmas carols in the old-people's home.
6. One child was severely hurt on the playground. In dramatizing the scene the other children clearly saw how the accident could have been avoided. A newly organized safety patrol, safety rules, and precautions resulted.

Role-playing and Role-reversal

Other forms of dramatization also provide opportunity to develop understandings. Most popular among these is role-playing.

A careful observer of children at play will notice that after playing through a situation once, they replay it with a shifting of roles. Thus, a child who was mother in a dramatic play often becomes the father, or the baby, or the postman. Through their play children learn what it is like to be a postman, a milkman, a dog—or to be dead. They are not only content to see and hear the various roles of life being enacted around them, they must *feel* what it is like to be a mother, a father, a postman, a dog—or dead! Through mimicking words and actions as they see them, they come to feel like the dog who cannot talk. They feel how it is black and quiet when one is dead. They feel how tired the milkman may become jogging from place to place in a monotonous routine. They also *feel* how mother becomes angry at children who do not do as they are asked. They *feel* how it is to be nasty, to be sympathetic, to be loving, to be hated. And through these imitations and these feelings they learn a great deal about human nature and the reasons behind action.

It is this ability which children have to *feel* that makes it possible for them to understand. Through empathy they come to realize the other fellow's viewpoint. This is a creative approach to the understanding of problems which breaks down emotional barriers and develops emotional understanding.

Role-playing is a conscientious attempt on the part of the teacher to use these natural tendencies of empathy for constructing natural group relations. In the first grade, two children have a quarrel over the possession of a ball. Instead of verbalizing the conflict, the teacher may ask each child to become the other one and then to give reasons why he should claim ownership. Thus each child is pressed into feeling and acting like his opponent and is therefore more understanding. In a succeeding verbalization of the feelings, the children, more understanding at this point, are often able to arrive at their own solutions and work out a way to handle the situation. The teacher has encouraged understanding and left the solution up to the creativeness or inventiveness of the individuals concerned. She is leading them to an independent solution of their problems and to emotional maturity.

In the fourth grade a child feels he has been treated unfairly at home and comes to school with a chip on his shoulder. He is ugly and cross. Finally, when confronted with the need to account for his actions, he spews forth his ill-feelings concerning his father who was overdemanding of him before school time. By being encouraged to play the role of the father while another child plays his role, he may be able to understand more readily his father's actions—to identify the true reasons behind them. Thus he learns through empathy plus analytical discussion that what appears to be malice toward him is really his father's own bitter feeling coming out, which may have been caused by his father's boss's overdemands of him. Thus a feeling of understanding replaces one of hostility.

Role-playing differs from straight dramatization of a problem in one major respect. In role-playing children are placed in a situation where they must see (and defend) a viewpoint different from their own. Through this technique they learn to project themselves through empathy. Often they are able to understand why there is disagreement between themselves and other people.

In a fourth grade two boys were arguing. Ivan thought that Carl had taken his pen. Carl flatly denied this and said he had just received the pen as a gift from his father. It was just like Ivan's because he liked Ivan's pen and had asked his father to get one just like it.

Miss Kelly, the teacher, said she *could* settle the problem, but first would the boys mind changing roles? Carl was to accuse Ivan of stealing a pen. Miss Kelly did not know or care at this point whether or not Carl had stolen the pen. She wanted to build better relationships among her students by having them realize that it was damaging to friendships to accuse someone of taking something without being sure first.

In changing roles, Carl let loose on Ivan. Ivan had to defend himself. Considerable emotional tension was drained out of the situation in the process. Without prompting from the teacher, Ivan drew in his fangs and apologized to Carl.

Shortly after, Ivan's pen was found on the floor under the piano. Ivan was especially sorry after his pen was found, but Miss Kelly pointed out that this was not really important. The important thing about a situation of this nature was never to infringe on anyone's rights or character before making certain about any given situation.

Role-playing can be combined with problem stories, problem pictures and dramatization to make effective social situations in which children develop values and understandings.

Some suggestions for the creative use of role-playing are:

Lower Grades

1. A playground fight over the swings—sharing.
2. A safety hazard, such as fighting over a turn on the slide.
3. One child blaming another for an accident, such as spilling the milk at snack-time.
4. Helping one child feel better by developing understanding among the others in a situation as when a child is tardy for school.
5. Children do not understand why certain school rules must exist, so the teacher and the children exchange roles to better realize each other's situation.

Intermediate Grades

1. Children are careless about cutting across the corner of a neighbor's lawn on the way to school.

2. Children are resentful about some regulations passed by the school principal.
3. Children choose the same team all the time making the teams uneven.
4. Some children use certain materials all the time depriving other children of their use.
5. Children cause the janitor unwarranted work by being careless about cleaning up their room.
6. Children do not cooperate with the safety patrol.

The Sociodrama

The sociodrama is a type of role-playing which deals with a social problem. The *general* plot of a sociodrama may be planned, but that is all. The actors experience the situation they are role-playing in the very creative sense that they make up the plot as they go along. In this situation, children bring past experiences to a new problem and use both reproductive and productive thinking to solve the problem at hand.

The children in Miss Hire's sixth grade were very concerned over the fact that some parents would not allow them to attend a seventh-grade dance to which they had been invited because the dance was to be held on the evening of a school night. Miss Hire felt the children were not understanding of the parents' viewpoint, so she set a series of scenes as follows:

Scene I: Sally Peters' (a fictitious girl) home—the kitchen. Sally comes home to tell mother about the invitation.
Scene II: Living room of the Peters home. Sally, her mother and father talk over the dance.

The scenes were played impromptu. In this case Miss Hire allowed two casts to play it two different ways. A better understanding of the parents' attitude resulted from the discussion that followed.

Children then directed their energies toward a possible solution to the problem. Some brain-storming resulted. A committee was finally organized and sent to the seventh-grade room to discuss the problem. The seventh-graders could not change the night because the gym was to be used for other functions, but they did set the dance for an hour earlier so that the sixth-graders could attend the first hour and still be home early. The teachers cooperated by assigning no homework on that night.

The Structured Dramatization

The structured dramatization differs from role-playing in that it has been written beforehand. Children memorize the lines or simply read the lines and "walk out" the play. The illustration given in Chapter I of this book involving Helen Arens is a classic example of the use of the structured dramatization.

These dramatizations are situations dealing with social problems. They are useful in building values, appreciations, and understandings. Children's plays that pose a social problem can often be used. Many upper-grade children can be encouraged to write their own.

Generally, a teacher uses a structured drama in the classroom when she is having problems in social behavior which are founded on a lack of a sense of values or appreciations. She finds (or writes) a play built around a theme that shows a lack of a sense of the same values or appreciations. In a reading class or social studies class, children read the parts, and a discussion follows. Again, it is not the purpose of the teacher to moralize, but to provide an open-ended experience. The children discuss among themselves ways in which such a situation might be handled, and thereby determine their values or help develop values.

Children in the upper grades especially enjoy these dramas and often write their own. Some commercial ones are available, most of which deal with teen-age problems. Let's see how one creative teacher used a structured drama to build understandings in his sixth-grade children.

Mr. Martin was concerned about the attitude of his students toward a new boy who had come to school. Mike had not been accepted by the boys in the sixth grade. The sixth-grade boys had definitely divided themselves into two gangs. But Mike was from a city school. They were suspicious of him and did not like his aggressive ways. At first Mike did not seem to mind this—then the effect of social rejection began to show. He began "buying" his friends with candy or by giving a few boys his prized possessions. He resorted to dare-deviltry to gain status and attention; hoping to gain approval from the boys, he "sassed" Mr. Martin, who had caught him behind the evergreen trees in the yard showing the boys how to smoke. In spite of all of this, Mike was never chosen voluntarily by any group, he was never asked to any of the other boys' homes, and he was never asked to be on any committee in school. Often he worked alone.

Mr. Martin had made many attempts to draw Mike into the children's activities in the natural ways that had worked most of the time in similar cases. But in this case it did not work.

Mr. Martin recognized the problem as one in human relationships—*acceptance and friendliness to a stranger.* After Mike had been in the school a month and the condition had not improved, Mr. Martin decided to take the bull by the horns. He felt he knew his class well enough to talk frankly about this social problem, part of which was theirs, part of which, Mike's.

He decided to introduce the problem through the use of a dramatization. Finding no commercial one that dealt with the problem of acceptance, he wrote one. Then one day he told the children he had a play that he would like them to read during their work period. A cast was chosen and the children "walked out" the play. From the discussion that followed, the social responsibility of accepting new members in a group was clearly brought out by the children, although Mike's name was not mentioned once.

Several months later, Mr. Martin looked back on this instance as the turning-point in Mike's behavior. He was convinced that the play had helped to build values and appreciations in the children when a girl of their age from another country moved into the town and the children suggested that they should plan ways to help the girl feel at home.

Mr. Martin's Dramatization

Cast of Characters:

TOM WILLIAMS: a sixth-grade boy
JODY: his best friend
MRS. WILLIAMS: Tom's mother
MR. HERRING: Chief Counselor at Camp Mohawk
TED HAINES: Counselor of Sioux Wigwam
PAUL, BILL, SANDY, TONY, SAMMY, and BUTCH: the boys in Sioux Wigwam

Scene 1

(Tom's bedroom, one afternoon after school. When the curtain rises, Tom is busy packing clothes into a suitcase. His best friend, Jody, enters on the run.)

TOM: Oh, hi, Jody.
JODY: Hi, Tom. Thought I'd come over and see if I could help you with your packing.

TOM: Gee, that's nice of you, Jody. If you mean it, you can stamp my name on that pile of sheets Mum got ready for me.

JODY: Okay. Where's the stamp? How do I do it?

TOM: With the stamp pad and that rubber stamp Mum bought me. It's a stamp with my name. It's neat.

JODY: (*tries it out*) Sure is—real neat. Gee, Tom, I wish I was going to camp. You're pretty lucky to be going to camp. Do you know it?

TOM: Yeah, I know it. Dad is real great to let me go. It's going to cost a lot of money.

JODY: I know it. That's why I can't go. My Dad told me if I got my bike I couldn't go to camp. I had to make a choice and I chose the bike. But I still wish I was going to camp!

TOM: Well, I'm pretty lucky, I guess.

JODY: Say, how long is it before you go, Tom?

TOM: In a week; just one more week. School is out Friday, then I'll have three days to get ready and then—off I go! I can hardly wait!

JODY: Boy, it sure sounds great. What's it going to be like at the camp, Tom? What you going to do?

(*He stops working and sits on the edge of the bed, dreamy-eyed, listening to Tom.*)

TOM: Well, from what we read in the folders Dad sent for, it's a real swell place. There's a big lake, and the camp is built right on the nicest part. There's a big assembly hall and dining-room in the center of the camp. Then all around in the woods there are small cabins. Eight boys live in each cabin. We have an older guy who's a counselor. And there's everything to do—swimming, boating, campfires, crafts, art work, hikes, parties—oh! just everything. (*Tom has also stopped and is sitting in a chair, dreaming.*)

JODY: Sure sounds great.

TOM: I plan to do so much! I'm hoping I can learn to swim better and to dive. And Dad says they have a man who will teach me how to man a sailboat. And, oh, I forgot—we have a field for games too. And I'm going to learn to play tennis and badminton!

JODY: Man, oh, man!

TOM: It sounds good, doesn't it?

JODY: Sure does! Say, when does the camp open?

TOM: Oh, it opens this week. I'll go almost two weeks late but that doesn't matter. Kids come and go all summer.

JODY: How long will you be gone, Tom?

TOM: Four whole weeks—isn't that great?

JODY: Yeah, great for you, but not for me. I won't have anybody to play with or anything to do! Some summer!

(*Tom's mother calls from off stage.*)

MOTHER:	Tom, Tom!
TOM:	I'm up in my room, Mum. Jody's here with me.
MOTHER:	Good, I'm coming up. I've some things I want to talk to you about.
TOM:	Okay. (*to Jody*) You know, Jode, I'm going to miss you, too. That's the only part about going that's not nice.
JODY:	Well, we can write to each other.
TOM:	Yeah. And when I get home I can teach you how to play tennis and badminton.

(*Mother enters with sewing box.*)

MOTHER:	Well, Tom, it looks as though you've done a lot of packing today. Hi, Jody.
JODY:	Hi, Mrs. Williams.
MOTHER:	How's your mother, Jody?
JODY:	She's fine, thanks, Mrs. Williams.
MOTHER:	Well, I'm glad to hear that. Tom, what I want is all those summer shirts so I can sew the labels on them. I'd better take your shorts, too. Then I guess we'll have about everything ready that we can do until a day or so before you go.
TOM:	Here are the shirts—what about my sleeping bag, Mum?
MOTHER:	Dad's going to pick it up at the Army and Navy Store tomorrow. They promised him it would be in by then.
TOM:	Good!
JODY:	Tom sure is lucky, Mrs. Williams. I wish I was going to camp!
MOTHER:	I wish you were, too, Jody. Tom is going to miss you!
JODY:	It'll be a lousy summer around here.
MOTHER:	(*Puts her arm around Jody*) Now, Jody, don't say that! You'll make many new friends and besides it'll only be for four weeks. Remember you've got that lovely new bicycle to ride all summer. You'll have lots of fun.
JODY:	Tom's sure lucky!
MOTHER:	Yes, he is, Jody. Tom's father is very good to him. But we're proud of Tom. He's very good to us, too. So we try to do everything for each other that we can.

(*She sits beside Jody.*)

	We're proud of you, too, Jody. We're very happy Tom has such a fine boy to play with. And some summer you and Tom will be able to go to camp together!
JODY:	Thanks, Mrs. Williams. I sure hope so!
MOTHER:	And now, how about you bringing that pile of shorts, Jody. Tom, you bring that pile of shirts. We'll go downstairs and get some cookies and milk. They're homemade ones—just baked them this afternoon!
JODY:	Oh, boy!
TOM:	Hot dog! C'mon, let's go!

(*The boys dash out of the room with the clothing. Mrs. Williams smiles after them, looks around the room for a minute and then follows.*)

Scene 2

(*A small log cabin at Camp Mohawk. There are four sets of double bunk beds along the walls. A writing table is under one large window at the rear of the stage. Near the window is a door; both of them open out onto a beautiful woods. A large table in the center of the room is covered with books and magazines neatly stacked. Under each bed is a closed suitcase. By each bunk hangs a towel and wash cloth. All the bunks but one are neatly made with blankets folded very precisely on the end of each bed. The stage is empty when the curtain rises, though laughter and voices can be heard outside in the distance. Then two voices seem to be drawing near. Soon the door opens and the chief counselor, Mr. Herring, enters with Tom. Tom is carrying a suitcase and has a bed roll on his back.*)

MR. HERRING: Well, we're glad to have you with us, Tom. Now this is the cabin you'll share with six other fellows and your counselor, Ted Haines. It's called Sioux Wigwam. That'll be your bunk over there.

TOM: Gee, thanks, Mr. Herring. Where is everybody?

MR. HERRING: Well, this is a bad time to arrive, Tom. All the fellows are with Ted down on the beach practicing for next week's diving contest. They have to get ready for chow soon though, so they ought to be here any minute. Sorry there isn't a reception committee for you.

TOM: Oh, that's all right, Mr. Herring. It will give me a little chance to get unpacked.

MR. HERRING: Not "unpacked," Tom. Up here it's "squared away."

TOM: (*laughing*) "Squared away?" Gee, what does that mean?

MR. HERRING: It means "all's in order," Tom—Marine talk!

TOM: Oh, I see. Okay. I'll get "squared away."

MR. HERRING: Good! You do that! I've got to get along now. The fellows will be in soon.

(*He goes to the door.*)

Well, so long, Tom. If you need anything, let me know.

TOM: Gee, thanks, Mr. Herring. I'll do that.

(*Mr. Herring exits.*)

(*Tom goes to the window and looks out at the woods. He stretches deliciously and says, "Boy, Sioux Wigwam! Boy! At last!" Happily he goes about unpacking his suitcase. He stacks the pile of shirts on the middle table, dumps some of his clothes on his bunk, unrolls his sleeping bag on his bunk, and is busy humming a tune and unpacking when loud voices are heard approaching Sioux Wigwam. Suddenly, with a burst of laughter and noise, the door opens and Ted Haines enters followed by noisy boys. All are dressed in swimming trunks and carrying towels. Tom stands back and smiles as he faces them. All the boys become quiet and stand looking Tom over. Ted Haines is about twenty-six years old. He walks up to Tom and looks at him with a sneer on his face.*)

TED: Well, if it ain't the new kid—finally got here. What's your name, kid?

TOM:	Tom—Tom Williams.
TED:	It's Tom, fellows—Tom Williams. (*He walks around Tom looking at him from head to foot.*) He's not much to look at, is he—a little on the puny side.
	(*The boys laugh.*)
TOM:	Oh, I'm not so puny. I'm real strong.
TED:	He's real strong. Well, that's something. Say, kid, will you tell me one thing? How come you got here a week and a half after all the rest of us?
TOM:	Well, my school didn't let out until last Friday—and then I could only come for four weeks on account of the expense, so I chose these four.
TED:	Oh, you did? Didn't you read the catalog which said that in order to get on the teams you had to be here at the *beginning* of the season? What's the matter with your old man? Couldn't he dig up enough dough to send you one week earlier like the rest of us? We've all been practicing diving, and tennis, and everything for a whole week and a half—now you're way behind. The fellows in Sioux Wigwam decided we were going to win *all* the competitions this summer—didn't we, fellows?
BOYS:	Yeah! 'Ray! You bet!
TED:	So you've got a lot of catching up to do, see? First thing, I guess you better meet the gang. This is Paul—Paul Angle.
PAUL:	Hi! Say, Tom, how well can you dive?
TOM:	(*crestfallen*) Well, not at all really. I hoped to learn this summer.
PAUL:	Holy mackerel! He can't dive at all! There goes the diving competitions, you guys!
	(*They all groan.*)
TED:	It's worse than I thought. Well, that next kid, he's Bill Manner.
TOM:	Hi, Bill.
BILL:	Say, Tom, how good are you at baseball. Can you pitch?
TOM:	(*eagerly*) Oh, I play baseball real good. I play second base on my little league team back home.
BILL:	Yeah, but can you pitch? What we need is a pitcher!
TOM:	Well (*quietly*), I never really tried pitching.
BILL:	Well, he won't be much help to us there.
TED:	I'm afraid not. Well, that next kid—he's Sandy Hopkins.
TOM:	Hi, Sandy.
SANDY:	Hi, Tom. Say, how are you at tennis?
TOM:	I don't play yet, but I want to learn!
SANDY:	My gosh! (*mockingly*) He wants to learn! Well, fellows, there goes the tennis cup!
TED:	Say, kid, can you do *anything?*
TOM:	Well, I swim fairly well.
TED:	You've got to be better than fair here. You've got to be

	good! Well, that black-haired fellow over there is Tony Demperio. He's our star badminton player.
TONY:	Yeah, Tom—how are you at badminton?
TOM:	Well—I (*he is so discouraged he hangs his head and shakes it slowly "no"*).
TONY:	Good night! He can't play that either!
TED:	And nearly two weeks already gone by! Why do I always get stuck with the dopes! Well—that kid over there is Sammy Cohen.
SAMMY:	Hi, Tom.
TOM:	Hi.
SAMMY:	I don't suppose you know anything about sailing a boat? (*Tom shakes his head sadly.*)
SAMMY:	Well, maybe I can teach you.
TOM:	(*smiling eagerly*) I'd like to learn.
SAMMY:	Tom, this is Butch Kelly.
TOM:	Hi, Butch.
BUTCH:	Hi. Say, did you ever pitch horseshoes?
TOM:	A few times.
SAMMY:	A few times? Gees!
TED:	Well, it looks as though we've got a job on our hands, you guys. We'll do our best to win as many of the honors for Sioux Wigwam as we can. (*He looks at Tom and shakes his head sadly.*) Though, I must say, our chances seem to be smaller and smaller! (*He looks around room.*)
SAMMY:	It looks to me like we better give old Tom–boy the word —how about it fellows!
BOYS:	Yes—you bet. Give him the word, Ted!
TED:	Well Tom, old boy, you stand at attention while I give you the word!
TOM:	I don't understand.
TED:	Well, you'd better understand! At attention means feet flat on floor, back straight, stomach in, chest out, chin up, eyes straight ahead, arms straight along sides. Attention! Good old Marine Corps!

(*Tom stands at attention.*)

(*Ted roams around table picking up Tom's clothes and dropping them back on the table.*)

TED:	Bill, old boy, you give Tom the word about the clothes.
BILL:	(*steps forward and stands at attention*) In Sioux Wigwam every man puts all his clothes away and out of sight at all times! Any brave caught with his clothes in sight during the day gets three demerits on his birchbark honor card.
TOM:	Oh, I'm sorry. I . . . .
TED:	(*interrupting*) Brave! Quiet! No man talks when he is standing at attention! He listens—do you hear?
TOM:	Yes, sir.
TED:	Now Tony, you give him the word about suitcases.
TONY:	(*steps forward*) In Sioux Wigwam every man has his

suitcase placed out of sight under his sack every day. A messy suitcase means three demerits on his birchbark honor card.

TED: Look you guys, get a load of that sack! You better give him the word about the sacks, Paulie.

PAUL: (*steps forward*) In Sioux Wigwam every man makes his sack first thing every day. All blankets are pulled tight with one blanket folded neatly at the end of the sack. Any man caught with wrinkles in his sack or improperly folded blankets, or with his sack not squared away, gets ten demerits on his birchbark honor card.

TED: That leaves you to tell him about the towels, Sammy.

SAMMY: (*steps forward*) All towels must be folded and hung in the racks, Tom.

TED: Yeah, or that's two demerits. Now, Tom old brave, answer me—do you get all this?

TOM: Yes, sir!

TED: Well, it's about time for our free swim. (*to Tom*) But seeing as how you are late, Tom, old boy, and seeing as how you already have eighteen demerits on your honor card, and seein' as how you're the newest one, we'll not let you go for a free swim today. You square this place away, hear? And then you can shine every fellow's shoes for church, see—and then you can sweep out the wigwam —and then, if you do that real well, Tom, old boy, we may let you go to chow with us when we come back. And you stand at attention right there until you can't hear us any more. Got it? Now c'mon, fellows, to the lake!

(*He charges out and the boys follow—all but Sammy. He falls behind and stands before Tom.*)

SAMMY: It's all right, Tom. You get used to it. It's only the first few days that are hard. Ted's really a nice guy. You'll like him after a while. And Tom, I'll help you with the diving and all!

(*He dashes out.*)

(*Tom stands at attention until all is quiet. Gradually his body relaxes. He looks helplessly and unhappily around the cabin. Slowly he goes to the table and begins to put his clothes in his suitcase. Then he rerolls his sleeping bag and starts to make his bed. But his lip trembles and finally he can stand it no longer. He falls down on his partly made bed and bursts into tears.*)

TOM: I wish I was home. I wish I was home with Jody!

End.

MR. MARTIN'S SOCIODRAMA

Discussion Questions

1. How did you like this play?
2. Which characters in the play did you like best?

3. Were there some that you did not like too well?
4. Why did you like Jody, the mother, and Sammy?
5. Do you know people like Jody? Like Mother? Like Sammy?
6. Why did you dislike Ted Haines?
7. Do you know anyone like Ted Haines?
8. What was there about Ted Haines that you did not like? Can you describe his character?
9. Why do you think the boys in Sioux Wigwam acted the way they did?
10. Would a different leader have made them act differently, do you think?
11. Do you think Ted Haines was a good leader? In what ways? In what ways was he a poor leader?
12. Do you know boys like those in Sioux Wigwam? What do you think about them?
13. If you were Tom, what would you do?
14. Which person in the play do you feel is most like you?
15. What could the boys in Sioux Wigwam have done to make camping pleasant for Tom?
16. What could Tom have done to make it easier to live in Sioux Wigwam?
17. Does the way people feel decide what they do?

Structured dramas are also very effective when used on an adult level. Many commercial plays are available for use at P.T.A. meetings and Mothers Clubs. They contribute a great deal to building better understandings between home and school when properly used.

Puppets

Puppets can sometimes be used very effectively for building social relationships. A puppet show is a dramatization with puppets instead of people. The advantage in using puppets rather than people is sometimes very definite. If the problem to be acted out is one where children have developed strong guilt feelings, they may be reluctant to act their feelings before the class—or they may not put into the dramatization the emotional ingredients that appeared in the actual incident.

Puppets, therefore, become a projective technique. By getting down behind a table or in back of a puppet stage where faces cannot be seen, children will be better able to reproduce a scene because they, too, are seeing the puppet act out their emotions. This is more objective and often more realistic than the real-life drama.

The Open-ended Story

Another excellent technique for moulding opinion and developing values is the use of the open-ended story, which deals with a social problem in the lives of the children. The story never comes to any solution; it merely poses a problem. It can be used in the same manner as dramatization. After the story has been read, the children discuss possible endings.

In 1959 Dorothy Spoerl edited a book called *Tensions Our Children Live With*.[3] This book is a compilation of stories dealing with the tensions of children in today's world. Discussion aids are suggested to go with each story. Teachers have reported unusual success in using these stories with children.

Following is one sample of an open-ended story. It was written for use in the third or fourth grade. The discussion questions at the end will suggest how children, through empathy, come to understand each other's feelings and build values of human relationships.

AN OPEN-ENDED STORY

The Case of the Broken Tulips

All the children in the fourth grade were excited. Tomorrow they were going to have the Spring Festival, and today was the day they were going to decorate the gym for it!

Marcy could hardly wait! She was chairman of the decoration committee. She knew the gym was going to be beautiful. Mr. Sellers, her teacher, had met with her committee and they had made all the plans together. She thought about them all the way to school, and she could see the gym transformed into a garden just as they had planned it.

Marcy's mother had helped her a great deal. She had promised her that she might borrow the large lawn umbrella to be placed in the center of the gym. Marcy and her committee planned to put crepe paper streamers from the tip of each point on the umbrella to the sides of the room. Each streamer was going to be a beautiful spring color. Mr. Sellers had given them some money from the P.T.A., and they had gone to the store and bought the crepe paper the night before. Marcy smiled as she thought of the beautiful pinks, the bright yellows, the soft blues, and the lovely violets in the crepe paper.

The children were going to hang huge murals of spring flowers on the walls of the gym. They had painted them in art class. Each one would be framed in green crepe paper. Then, most beautiful of all, they were going to bring the first spring flowers from their home gardens to bank

[3] Dorothy T. Spoerl, ed., *Tensions Our Children Live With* (Boston: Beacon Press, 1959).

around the base of the umbrella and around the refreshment stand at one end of the room. Marcy hoped that they could get enough flowers!

Mr. Sellers was giving directions on how they would work in the gym, when Marcy's mind drifted back to the reality of the fourth-grade room.

"After we get all the crepe paper and the paintings in place," he was saying, "you may bring the flowers from home. In this way, they will not get crushed and they will stay fresh until the festival. . . ."

Before Marcy could realize it, they were in the gym and everyone was working just as they had planned to do. At noontime Mr. Sellers called them together. "Boys and girls," he said, "you have done a wonderful job! Doesn't our gym look beautiful? All that remains is to put the flowers in the middle of the room and around the refreshment stand. When you go home for lunch I think it would be safe to bring them back."

Marcy was the first one back in the afternoon. She came with her arms loaded with flowers from her mother's garden. As chairman of the decoration committee, she eagerly accepted the flowers which each child brought and carefully arranged them at the base of the umbrella in the center of the gym. Long before the last child had returned from lunch, however, Marcy knew that there were not going to be enough flowers to do the job. In her imagination she had seen one big mass of color under the umbrella. Instead, there were individual bouquets. More flowers were needed to fill in the empty spaces.

Marcy could not keep the disappointment from her voice when she told Mr. Sellers that there were not enough flowers. "Well, Marcy," said Mr. Sellers, "the gym looks beautiful and even if we don't get more flowers I think it will be all right. However, if you feel that we need more, perhaps some of the children will be able to find some and bring them to school in the morning."

So Marcy went from child to child asking for more flowers. But their mothers had already given them most of the new spring flowers from their gardens and almost no one could promise to bring any more.

Marcy was so disappointed she did not feel like going to school the next morning. When she entered the room her greatest fears were realized. There were almost no new flowers waiting for her. She was about to resign herself to bitter disappointment when Angie Botts saved the day. Angie came into the room with her face beaming and her eyes sparkling. Her arms were loaded with red and yellow tulips. There were enough to do the job.

Marcy squealed with delight as she took the tulips from Angie. "See," Angie said, "now you can have it just like you wanted and I brought them to you, didn't I?"

Marcy hustled Angie off to the gym. In no time at all they had arranged the flowers around the base of the umbrella. Marcy praised Angie and told her how wonderful she was and how she alone had saved the Spring Festival from disaster.

Marcy could not understand why Angie had been so eager to please her. Certainly Angie was not one of her friends. In fact, Marcy and the girls had often made fun of Angie. She was not like the rest of the girls. She did not have nice clothes and she never belonged to the clubs or went

to the parties that the other girls attended. Marcy ignored Angie most of
the time, although Angie was always trying to give her something or to
sit with her to eat her lunch on the days when they ate in the cafeteria.
Marcy felt a little guilty as she watched Angie beaming at her while she
arranged the flowers.

When they returned hand-in-hand to the fourth-grade classroom
Mr. Garson, the principal, was talking to Mr. Sellers at the front of the
room. They seemed to be very serious and the children were very quiet.
Marcy and Angie took their seats.

Mr. Garson turned to look at the boys and girls. "Children," he said,
"Mr. Sellers and I have a serious problem to discuss with you. Our good
neighbor across the street, Mrs. Parsons, has just telephoned me. Someone
has broken off all of her prize yellow and red tulips and all of the blossoms
are missing. Mrs. Parsons noticed many of the children carrying flowers
to school yesterday and today and she called me to ask if we might help
her find out what happened to her favorite blossoms."

Panic seized Marcy's heart. From the corner of her eye she took a
quick look at Angie. Angie was looking right at her, smiling. Her face
glowed with happiness.

End

Questions for Discussion

1. What do you think happened next in the story?
2. Why was Marcy so anxious to have the gym look so well?
3. Why was Angie so anxious to please Marcy?
4. Do you think Angie took Mrs. Parsons' flowers?
5. If you think she did, do you think she knew it was wrong to take
   them?
6. If you think she didn't, why did Marcy feel panicky when Mr. Garson
   told the children about the broken tulips?
7. If Angie took the flowers, and she knew it was wrong, *why* did she
   take them?
8. Why did Angie like Marcy so well?
9. Can you think of a happy ending to the story?
10. On what basis do you choose your friends?
11. Have you ever wanted to be someone's friend and that someone
    would not play with you?
12. Have you ever wanted a friend so badly that *you* would do anything
    to get one—even something you thought was wrong?
13. Is there something we could each do to help keep things like this from
    happening?

The Problem Story

Similar to the open-ended story is the problem story. The problem
story poses a problem with a "What-would-you-do?" type of ending.

Its purpose is to help children build values and make decisions and judgments.

Problem stories have been used successfully as early as the kindergarten. Shaftel and Shaftel[4] tell of the use of problem stories in their pamphlet, *Role Playing the Problem Story*. This little book will provide the teacher with many problem stories to use in her own classroom.

Problem stories may be detailed, or so short they merely present a problem. In one sixth grade where considerable falsehoods were being told, the teacher used the problem story below. Her goal was to help children understand that social pressures sometimes force us into situations where we behave in unaccepted ways. The teacher recognized the telling of falsehoods as a symptomatic behavior for some unmet tension. In order not to put any one person in the spotlight, she used a story that was not involved with falsehoods but with stealing. In the discussion following the story, the children built up some concepts and understandings about correct social behavior. The teacher also helped build rapport with children by providing ways for them to meet their problems within her classroom.

A Problem Story: The Case of the Christmas Stocking

The children in Miss Anderson's sixth grade decided they would collect money to help support a school in a foreign country. This particular school was in a disaster area. The children wrote to the principal of the school, who sent them a list of supplies such as balls, paint, crayons, paper, and paste. The children were going to buy these articles with their money and send them to the school for Christmas.

They hung a Christmas stocking in the front of the room with a sign on it which said, "Fill the Stocking for Christmas," and then they brought their pennies and nickels to put in it.

One night Miss Anderson decided to count the money in the Christmas stocking. She counted eight dollars and ninety-six cents. On the following morning Miss Anderson reported to the boys and girls and complimented them on their good work.

After school that evening Miss Anderson went to the library to secure some books for the children. As she returned to her classroom she met Helen, a sixth-grader from another class, coming out of her room.

"Why, Helen," said Miss Anderson, "what are you doing in my room? Can I help you some way?"

"No," said Helen, "I was just going by and saw your pretty bulletin board, so I came in to see it." And with that Helen darted down the hall.

Miss Anderson was puzzled. She entered the room and looked around.

[4] George Shaftel and Fannie R. Shaftel, *Role Playing the Problem Story* (New York: The National Conference of Christians and Jews, 1952).

Her eyes picked up a piece of paper on the floor. It was the sign on the Christmas stocking, which had been knocked down. Miss Anderson went to the front of the room and, taking the sign from the floor, she started to pin it back on the stocking. Suddenly she was aware that the stocking seemed very flat compared with what it had been like earlier in the day. So Miss Anderson dumped the contents from the stocking onto her desk and counted it. There were exactly three dollars and sixty-five cents.

If you were Miss Anderson, what would you do?

The Problem Picture

Problem pictures are a projective technique that can be used to help children understand the world around them, and to better interpret the feelings and problems of others. Figures 9–1 and 9–2 were taken from the cover of a popular magazine. Each presents a social problem, with a sense of humor for some of the parties involved, but perplexity and confusion for other parties involved.

These pictures give the teacher an opportunity to build a discussion around a situation that involves a great deal of empathy and develops a better understanding of the behavior of all people.

Below is a conversation, written from recall, as it developed in a third-grade classroom. Mrs. Bond, the teacher, had been disturbed over some lunchtime conversations she had heard wherein the children in her class complained about their parents not giving them more privileges. She felt the picture had possibilities for developing appreciations for the role of the parent and the responsibilities that went with it.

Class Discussion

MRS. BOND: Today I want to talk about a picture I found which I like very much. Are you all sitting where you can see the picture? When I show it to you, study it hard for a few minutes to make sure you understand what it is trying to say. This one picture is really made of three small ones and you will begin by looking at the top picture first. (*Shows picture.*) Who can tell me the story of this picture?
(*Many hands are raised.*)
MRS. BOND: Bill, you tell me the story of this picture.
BILL: Well, it's about two boys who are having a pillow fight. They are in their bedroom on the third floor. Their father is way downstairs, but he hears them because they are yelling and screaming and making a lot of noise. So he goes upstairs to

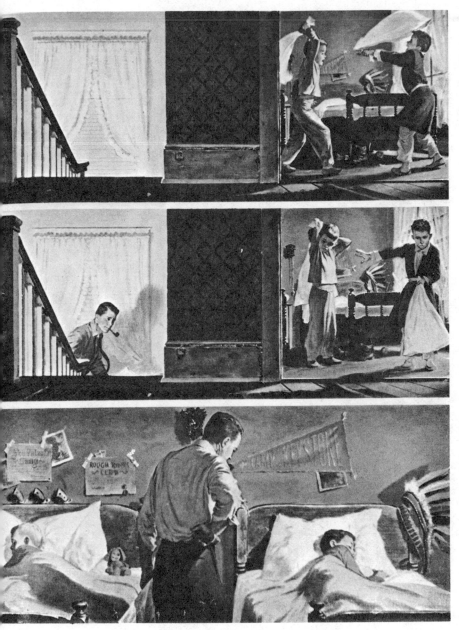

FIGURE 9–1. *The pillowfight.*[5]

[5] Cover by Tom Utz, reprinted with permission from *The Saturday Evening Post,* © 1955 The Curtis Publishing Company.

FIGURE 9–2. *Valentines.*[6]

[6] Cover by Dick Sargent, reprinted with permission from *The Saturday Evening Post,* © 1956 The Curtis Publishing Company.

	stop them, but they hear him coming. So when he gets up there, they pretend they are fast asleep.
MRS. BOND:	Well, that was a good story, Bill. Does anyone have anything to add to the story?
BOB:	Well, they aren't really asleep. They're just pretending.
MRS. BOND:	Why do you suppose they feel they must pretend to be asleep?
JOE:	Because they'll get heck if they get caught.
MRS. BOND:	Why will they get heck?
MARY:	Because they're being naughty!
BETTY:	They're supposed to be asleep and they know it!
SALLY:	I think their father is angry!
MRS. BOND:	Kevin, do you think the father is angry?
KEVIN:	Yes.
MRS. BOND:	Why?
KEVIN:	Because it's past the boys' bed-time and they're supposed to be asleep.
MRS. BOND:	Does this make *your* fathers angry?
CHILDREN:	Yes, oh yes, it sure does.
MRS. BOND:	Do you think your fathers ever had pillow fights when they were little boys?
	(Silence—Rudy volunteers)
RUDY:	Well, I bet they did!
MRS. BOND:	I bet they did, too! Then I wonder why they get angry when their own little boys have pillow fights?
	(another silence)
BILL:	Because that's the way fathers are!
MRS. BOND:	You think all fathers are like that, Bill?
KEVIN:	Mine isn't.
JANET:	Neither is mine.
MRS. BOND:	You two people think only *some* fathers are like that.
HARRIET:	I think fathers don't like to be disobeyed.
SHAWN:	They want everybody to do what they want them to.
ERIC:	My father is always telling me to do something and if I don't he yells at me.
MRS. BOND:	You feel that fathers are all bossy at times. Is there a reason?
JOHN:	Well sometimes kids are bad and then fathers have to get tough.
MRS. BOND:	Let's look at our picture again. You said the father was angry because the boys were supposed to be asleep. You said fathers were bossy and that sometimes kids are bad. Do you think the boys in the picture are being bad?
MARY:	No, they were just having fun.
MRS. BOND:	Then what is the father really mad about? What makes fathers angry besides the times when people don't do as they say?
RUDY:	Maybe he's angry because he wants them to get their sleep and they are still awake.
MRS. BOND:	Rudy thinks the father is as much worried as angry.

HELEN: Yes, I think he is worried.
MRS. BOND: Look closely at his face. Make a face like it. Now make an
             angry face. Are they alike?
BILL: Something alike. I think the father is worried.
HARRIET: He wants the kids to get to sleep.
MRS. BOND: Can you think of any reasons why he wants the boys to go
             to sleep?
JOE: 'Cause—'cause they've got to get up in the morning to go
             to school, and they won't want to if they don't get to sleep.
MRS. BOND: Joe thinks the father is worried that the boys won't get
             enough sleep.
MARY: Yes, that's it—the boys want to play, but the father knows
             they need sleep.
MRS. BOND: You said that the father wasn't angry; that he was worried.
             You said that he really is concerned over the boys' health.
             Is he coming upstairs because he is angry at them or because
             he loves them a lot?
MARY: He loves them a lot. He is looking out for them.
MRS. BOND: We said the father really acted as he did because he loved
             the boys a lot. Is that what we said when I first showed you
             the picture?
BILL: No, sometimes you don't see the whole story at first. You
             have to think about it.
MRS. BOND: Did some of you change your idea of the story?
CHILDREN: Yes.
JOHN: The father is really looking after the boys, because they
             aren't being sensible.
MRS. BOND: Could we say that sometimes we don't understand what
             people do and maybe we should think about it?
CHILDREN: Yes.

It is interesting to notice Mrs. Bond's technique in using this
picture:

1. She made sure the picture communicated the central idea to all
the children.
2. She asked carefully planned questions to keep the children thinking
and to keep the discussion going.
3. She did not moralize or force her opinions on the children. She *did*
reflect their feelings and helped them to rephrase their statements of
values.
4. She helped to draw together the greatest value of all when the children
brought it out.
5. She did not preach about the concepts learned. She left them for the
children to think about.

The second picture was used by a fourth-grade teacher whose
children were "razzing" each other for buying valentines. Although

this teacher considered such "razzing" to be normal behavior, she felt she could make it easier for the boys to exchange valentines with the girls if she developed some understandings about love and giving. The children studied the picture and then discussed the reasons why the boy was looking so shy and hesitant. Many responses were given, all of which the teacher accepted. The teacher then led the discussion to an explanation of why we exchange valentines and to the differences between "like" and "love." The children explored the feelings of the receiver of a valentine—and those of a giver. They concluded it was as much fun to give as to receive. After the discussion the teacher noticed that the children made valentines for each other, and there was much less tension and more enjoyment in the Valentine Day festivities. She felt she had helped these children develop some important social values.

A book by Thelma Kier Reen and Thomas J. Darell, *Basic Social Studies Discussion Pictures* (Evanston, Illinois: Row-Peterson and Company, 1958), contains pictures especially drawn for the purpose of developing social understandings in children. The teacher guide book which accompanies this book is a rich source of discussion suggestions which help develop concepts.

Bibliotherapy

Bibliotherapy is a technique that can best be used to help individuals adjust socially, although some teachers have had a great deal of success using this technique with groups of children. The teacher chooses a book for a child to read wherein the main characters have the same social or emotional problems as the reader. The theory is that the child will identify so closely with the main character of the story that he will live successfully through the solution of his problem. A series of books dealing with the same or similar problems eventually help the child to see that his own problem is not insurmountable.

One example of the use of such a book is the case of a fourth-grade teacher who used Eleanor Estes' *The Hundred Dresses* to help a child who was rejected by her peer group. A second-grade teacher used *I Saw It On Mulberry Street,* by Dr. Seuss, for a child who had a vivid imagination that was not accepted at home. This was followed by Louis Slabodkin's *Magic Michael* and other such stories. A third-grade teacher who had an especially troublesome class read such stories to them as *Bad Trouble in Miss Alcorn's Class* to give them a more objective look at their behavior.

Filmstrip Situations

Some commercial filmstrips provide open-ended picture stories for helping children develop values, understandings, and appreciations. These filmstrips are accompanied by a recording. They present a series of pictures that illustrate a social or ethical problem. Then the recording is stopped, while the children discuss a solution to the problem. The filmed ending may then be shown if children and teacher care to see how the problem really worked out. This ending can, of course, lead to further discussion.[7]

Film Problems

The National Film Board of Canada has produced a series of films that provide problem situations useful in the upper grades for discussion purposes. This series is called "What Do You Think" (distributed by McGraw-Hill). Other films often lead into problems that are excellent in helping children develop values. Some of them are "The House I Live In," "Boundary Lines," "Brotherhood of Man," and "The Toymaker."

Activities

Certain activities used in unit teaching promote sound attitudes and values among children. But before we discuss them, a word must be said about activities in the elementary-school program.

A few years ago, a great deal of energy was expended on the so-called activity program of the elementary school. The activity movement made great contributions to education. However, activity for

---

[7] A. M. Films, *What Do You Think Series* (Hollywood: Q U E Recording Co.: four filmstrips—"Martha's Discovery," "Timmy's Choice," "Mark's Present" and "Sara's Surprise").

activity's sake is no more valuable than knowledge for knowledge's sake. And some schools not only went activity-mad, they also incorporated into their programs activities that approached the ridiculous.

Behind the use of every activity should lie a clear-cut objective. Drummond sets some general criteria for the selection of activities in the classroom. Activities and projects have significance and worth when they:

1. Have content of social importance.
2. Provide opportunities for children to gain deeper and more accurate understandings of the community in which they live.
3. Build sound attitudes toward people in differing groups.
4. Help boys and girls develop increased understanding of democratic values and traditions.
5. Provide opportunities for children to learn how to solve problems through critical thinking.
6. Provide opportunities for children to develop and retain social interests.
7. Help children learn to accept the fact that the world in which we live is changing rapidly and that change can be directed and controlled as intelligent people work together cooperatively.
8. Help children learn essential social studies skills, such as interpreting maps and globes and developing a sense of time and chronology.[8]

Here is an excerpt from a teacher's report showing some samples of worthwhile activities used in connection with a unit on Spain.

Spanish Fiesta—Grade 6

The children decided to study a unit on Spain because three children in the class had relatives in Spain with whom they were corresponding, and one child had a grandmother living in Spain.

The youngsters listed many questions of things they wanted to know about Spain. These questions were then organized. Books were secured from the library, travel booklets from the travel agency in town. We secured slides, films, and pictures. Magazines and periodicals were examined for information. One child even found a woman in town who had come from Spain recently, and she came to talk to us.

The boys and girls worked in groups as committees and planned their research activities. They decided to work in various areas. The areas of study were: history of the people, religion, language, government, music, art, climatic conditions, education, products, industries, important cities, literature, entertainment, costumes, food, occupations, and the life of the people.

[8] Harold D. Drummond, "Projects and Activities in the Primary Grades," *Social Education*, XXI (February 1957), pp. 59–62.

The children expressed a desire to learn Spanish; therefore, some books in beginning Spanish were secured. They learned to read and speak Spanish to a limited degree. I found that my poorest readers were reading the Spanish readers as well as my best reading pupils. The challenge of beginning on an equal basis spurred them on.

One boy was greatly interested in the bullfights. He drew pictures and wanted to make a model arena. He found out that there was more than he had thought in the technique of bullfighting.

In all the activities that the children pursued, they came in with more and more materials. They began writing reports from their notes and outlines. They worked in one group or another, changing or bringing in something that another group could use.

We learned songs in Spanish, and our orchestra learned to play some Spanish numbers. We had a products map, we counted in Spanish. Spanish money was brought in, and we played store using the exchange value in arithmetic. One group wrote a simple play about farm life in Spain.

A Spanish exchange student came in costume and talked to the class, and she later returned when we had our Fiesta. We had film strips, movies, and visited the Cleveland Art Museum. All the work was to be culminated in the big event, "A Spanish Fiesta." As time passed we planned the program and our invitations, and decided to have an exhibit in a display room.

The children wrote simple invitations in Spanish to their parents. They wanted to write English on the back, but I told them that they could translate it to their parents. You can imagine what a thrill it was for them to be able to tell their parents something that the parents didn't know. We invited the Superintendent, Supervisors, Principal, and the other sixth grade.

We decided we must have some Spanish food. The menu consisted of Spanish chicken and rice, olives, citrus fruit, homemade bread rolls (baked by three mothers assisted by pupils) and grape juice. The children chose what they wanted to contribute such as rice, onions, tomatoes, etc. The school bought the chickens, explaining that was their part in the Fiesta. The children helped in preparing the chickens. Each child brought two oranges and two grapefruit. They scrubbed their hands and proceeded to peel their fruit, after which a girl and boy cut the sections, placing them in a large bowl from the kitchen. This was all done the morning of the Fiesta.

Another group arranged the display room with all the articles that we had collected pertaining to Spain. The large room was beautiful with Spanish shawls, large baskets, dolls, shoes, clothing, jewelry, pottery, even a cage with a large artificial parrot that someone had brought back from Spain. All around the room were murals, posters made by the children. Large posters advertising the bullfights in Madrid were donated by a person who had recently returned from Spain. A large products map had authentic products brought from Spain. One girl's aunt was traveling in Europe and sent many samples, such as salt, spices, etc., with Spanish wrappers on them. All articles on display were marked or identified as to history and owner's name.

The Fiesta was held in the afternoon and was attended by parents, friends, and the other sixth grade. The latter had been asked to participate but due to another project were unable to do so. The display room had been opened to the school for exhibition from 10 A.M. to 2 P.M.

The program was presented by a pupil announcer as follows:

1. Selections by orchestra.
2. Group reports given by students concerning their areas of interest. These reports were made in booklet form with attractive covers.
3. Exchange student from Spain—brief talk.
4. Spanish songs
5. Spanish Club from the high school presented a play, musical numbers, dances, accompanied by guitars. All were in costume.

Refreshments were served from a gaily decorated Fiesta cloth-covered table, which carried out the traditional Spanish pottery theme. Gourds and wooden bowls were also used.

The students were all in Spanish costume—as was I, the teacher. The boys had brought black hats that Zorro had made popular. Black boots and bolero jackets had been made. The girls brought everything from lace curtains for mantillas to bright-colored shoes with high heels that belonged to their mothers. Some had beautiful fans.

The boys and girls served their parents and were in full charge of arrangements at the buffet style table. We had previously talked over the serving of refreshments, and the boys and girls both wanted to wait upon their parents. Therefore, several volunteered to work at the big table.

After the Fiesta we had our committees for the cleanup at the close of school—kitchen committee, sweeping committee, props committee, and historical committee. The latter were in charge of seeing that all the display materials were returned to their owners.

The Spanish Fiesta Unit carried over into five weeks, from the very beginning to the final stages. Actual work on the various activities consumed four weeks.

The response of every one of the thirty-three pupils was wonderful. Everyone had not only a part but several parts in making the project a success. Each felt that he was important. Motivation was provided from the beginning by new discoveries each day in the areas of interest, which kept the pupils on their toes. The school and city libraries were very helpful. People in the community who heard of the project sent in things and asked if they could attend the Fiesta. We had several historical items that were later sent to the Smithsonian Institute in Washington, D.C. Persons attending who had traveled in Europe remarked that our open market and display transported them back to Spain.

Surely such a project or unit is one of the most gratifying in results for all concerned—pupils, teacher, parents, and community.[9]

The attitudes, skills, values, knowledges, abilities, appreciations, characteristics, and traits to be developed in each child as an effective

---

[9] The author is indebted to Mrs. Helen Cleveland, a teacher in the Alliance, Ohio, public schools for this account of her Spanish Fiesta.

citizen for a democratic society were developed in this unit. Also the opportunity was there to promote good public relations as well as sound human relations.

Summary

The fields of psychology, sociology, anthropology, and education have contributed a great deal of information through research to an understanding of human behavior. We should expend our energies and our monies toward building healthy human beings, both physically and mentally. Rightfully the skills of living together should be taught in the schools. Many teachers are doing it through the use of the above techniques or other forms of sociodynamics. In the years immediately ahead all teachers must try.

TO THE COLLEGE STUDENT

1. Try a structured dramatization in class which will help you gain a better understanding of children. A good one for this purpose is "Random Target" (Human Relations Aids, 419 Park Avenue South, New York, New York. An American Theatre Wing Community Play by Nina Ridenour, 1954). After you have given this social drama, discuss these questions:
   a. Where did the play get its name?
   b. What do you think would happen if the mother and father in the play followed Mrs. Knox's advice?
   c. What do you think might happen when the Stewarts reached home if they were convinced that their form of punishment was better than that proposed by Mrs. Knox?
   d. Dramatize a second act to this play, using situation b above. Then dramatize it using situation c above.
   e. Make a list of understandings, values, or new knowledges you learned from this dramatization and the subsequent discussion.

2. Here is a situation that occurred on one college campus. The girls in a large dormitory met to make plans to serve as hostesses for their parents at a Parent Week-end breakfast, which was to be held on Sunday morning. The girls agreed they would decorate the tables in the dining-hall with flowers and they would all rise early and wear

dress-up frocks for breakfast. Instead of a cafeteria style breakfast, as was the usual custom, they agreed to serve their parents at the tables.

On the morning of the breakfast everything went as planned. However, shortly after all had been seated, the doors of the dining-hall swung open to admit a group of coeds who were dressed in dungarees and sweat shirts and some of whom were wearing curlers. They were laughing and joking boisterously. These girls had been present when the plans for the breakfast were made. Their parents had not come to Parents Week-end. Many of the coeds at the breakfast were embarrassed and shocked. A meeting was called by the house mother for Monday night to discuss the matter.

Role play this meeting. Assign five girls to the part of the offenders. Have the rest of the class be the other coeds in the dorm. Can you develop a creative way to handle the situation in your sociodrama?

3. Start to collect stories and plays that you may use in your classroom to build values, understandings, and appreciations.

4. A tape-recording by Laura Zirbes will stimulate discussion in your class. (*Resource:* The Teaching Aids Laboratory, The Ohio State University, Columbus, Ohio.) This includes:

No. Z-16   (*Moral and Spiritual Values in Education*) 15 min.
No. Z-30   (*Developing the Creative Potentialities of Children*) Two Parts, 56 min.
No. Z-38   (*The Value Approach*) 16 min.
No.   5   (*Conditions That Threaten Values We Hold*) 11 min.

TO THE CLASSROOM TEACHER

1. The next time an appropriate social problem or a behavior problem arises in class, think of ways you can use it to develop a creative learning situation rather than trying to settle it at once by yourself.

2. Try some of the ideas in this chapter with your children.

3. Use an open-ended story dealing with some ethical problem and try to evaluate the values of the children in your classroom.

4. Ask a group of students to write a play of some problem recently experienced in school. Have them present it before the rest

of the class. If you teach a primary grade, have them dramatize it without a script.

TO THE COLLEGE STUDENT
AND THE CLASSROOM TEACHER

1. Write to the address below for a catalogue of other social dramas. Also write to the National Education Association, Washington, D.C., for their list of social dramas. Put on one of these dramas for a P.T.A. meeting or for a college class, and conduct a discussion about it. (*Address:* Human Relations Aids, 1790 Broadway, New York 19, N.Y.)

2. Make a collection of pictures that might be used to develop creative solutions to social or ethical problems.

3. Psychodrama is another use of a projective technique for helping individuals with personal problems. Find out what a psychodrama is. Perhaps someone from the psychology department will come to class and demonstrate the psychodrama.

4. Look up the topic "Projective Techniques" and discuss ways techniques other than those mentioned in this chapter can be used creatively to help children solve problems.

5. Here is a film you will enjoy: *Role-Playing in Guidance,* 14 min., black and white, University of Southern California, Department of Visual Instruction.

SELECTED BIBLIOGRAPHY

ARGYRIS, CHRIS. *Role Playing in Action.* Ithaca, New York: New York State School of Industrial and Labor Relations, 1951.

ASSOCIATION FOR CHILDHOOD EDUCATION INTERNATIONAL. *Helping Children Solve Their Problems.* Washington, D.C.: The Association, 1950.

————. *Learning About Role Playing for Children and Teachers.* Washington, D.C.: The Association, 1960.

CITIZENSHIP EDUCATION PROJECT. *Caring for Public Property.* New York: Teachers College, Columbia University, 1956.

————. *Taking Responsibility.* New York: Teachers College, Columbia University, 1956.

————. *Choosing Good Leaders.* New York: Teachers College, Columbia University, 1956.

GRAMBS, JEAN D. *Group Processes in Intergroup Education.* New York: The National Conference of Christians and Jews.

HAAS, ROBERT B. (ed.). *Psychodrama and Sociodrama in American Education.* Beacon, New York: Beacon House, 1949.

HELLEN, J. *A Two-Hour Introduction to Value Analysis.* Washington, D.C.: Value Engineering Weekly, 1963.

HOCK, LOUISE G. *Using Committees in the Classroom.* New York: Rinehart and Company, 1958.

ILG, FRANCES L., LOUISE BATES AMES, EVELYN W. GOODENOUGH, and IRENE B. ANDERSEN. *The Gesell Institute Party Book.* New York: Harper and Brothers, 1956.

JENNINGS, HELEN H. *Sociometry in Group Relations.* Washington, D.C.: American Council on Education, 1948.

————. "Sociodrama Teaches Democratic Living," *Journal of Home Economics,* XLIV (April 1952), 260–262.

LANE, HOWARD and MARY BEAUCHAMP. *Human Relations in Teaching.* Englewood Cliffs, N.J.: Prentice-Hall, Inc., 1955.

LINDBERG, LUCILE. *The Democratic Classroom.* New York: Bureau of Publications, Teachers College, Columbia University, 1954.

LIPPIT, R. and R. K. WHITE. "The Social Climate of Children's Groups," in *Child Behavior and Development,* ed. by R. Barker, J. Kounin, and B. Wright. New York: McGraw-Hill, Inc., 1943, 484–408.

MARTINSON, RUTH and HARRY SMALLENBURG. *Guidance in Elementary Schools.* Englewood Cliffs, N.J.: Prentice-Hall, Inc., 1958, Chapter V.

NICHOLS, HILDRED. "Role-Playing in Primary Grades," *Group Psychotherapy,* VII (December 1954), 238–241.

SARASON, SEYMOUR B., KENNETH S. DAVIDSON, FREDERICK F. LIGHTHALL, RICHARD R. WAITE, and BRITTON K. RUEBUSH. *Anxiety in Elementary School Children.* New York: John Wiley and Sons, 1960.

SHELLHAMMER, LOIS B. "Solving Personal Problems Through Sociodrama," *English Journal,* XXXVIII (November 1949), 503–505.

STIRLING, NORA. *Family Life Plays.* New York: Association Press, 1961.

WOOD, GERTRUDE. "Demonstrations and Discussion of Sociodrama," *Occupations,* XXX (May 1952), 647–648.

ZIRBES, LAURA. *Focus on Values in Elementary Education.* New York: G. P. Putnam's Sons, 1960.

The Creative Teaching of Study Skills

Creativity is rarely a single flash of intuition: it usually requires sustained analysis of a great many observations to separate out the significant factors from the adventitious. A keen observer once said of Einstein that part of his genius was his inability to understand the obvious. Rejection of superficial explanations of one's own as well as of others is prerequisite to understanding. To reach a correct solution efficiently also requires unconcern for all except the truth. Science practiced to bolster a faulty hypothesis rather than to test it objectively is often worse than useless.[1]

HENRY EYRING

TO THE READER

How well can you read a road map? a weather chart? a table of statistics? Think back over your own school experience to the point where you remember being taught these skills. Were you ever taught or did you just pick them up? One suggestion for using this chapter would be to break your class into four committees, one for each of the following headings: study skills, research skills, using original sources, and map skills. Have each group meet and read together some of the concepts and illustrations presented here and then demonstrate each in some creative way before the class.

Introduction

An important part of a sound social studies program is teaching the skills needed to live effectively in a democratic community. When the teachers of Freeport (Chapter II of this book) met together to outline their objectives for teaching social studies, they listed the following skills as necessary for social living and individual growth in each child:

1. Skills in problem-solving.
2. Skills in critical and creative thinking.
3. Communication skills.

[1] Henry Eyring, "Scientific Creativity," in *Creativity and Its Cultivation*, ed. Harold H. Anderson (New York: Harper and Brothers, 1959), p. 3.

4. Study skills—
   a. the ability to do research;
   b. the ability to use original sources;
   c. the ability to outline;
   d. the ability to summarize;
   e. the ability to record data;
   f. the ability to take notes;
   g. the ability to select main ideas;
   h. the ability to read for details;
   i. the ability to make oral and written reports;
   j. the ability to plan;
   k. the ability to read and use maps;
   l. the ability to read and use charts, graphs, and cartoons.
5. Group dynamics skills—
   a. the ability to listen;
   b. the ability to discuss issues;
   c. the ability to debate issues;
   d. the ability to take turns in discussion, to share viewpoints, to react intellectually rather than emotionally.
6. Evaluation skills—
   a. group evaluation;
   b. self-evaluation.

The teaching and learning of these skills can be a creative process accomplished largely by the method used in teaching. Conditions can be set for teaching them if a few basic principles for developing creativity are applied to the teaching act:

1. The experiences children have in developing these skills should be open-ended rather than fact-centered. Each skill learned or discovered should be applied at once to problem-solving.
2. Teachers can use techniques that are devised to evoke original behavior, discovery, and unusual responses as well as the necessary common ones.
3. New skills should be utilized in new situations so children can apply them to solve many problems; functional fixedness should not destroy their multipurpose use.
4. Skills are necessary to all functions of living and are learned to enable children to solve certain problems. They must become as automatic as possible and learned as quickly as possible.
5. A full account of complete creative-artistic performance involves evaluative abilities and abilities that are not primarily creative. The learning of these abilities makes possible creation of other sorts. In setting conditions for creative teaching of skills, the teacher must provide for ways these skills may be creatively applied, even though, in themselves, they are not creative acts.
6. The development of skills may contribute to the development of many intellectual factors: cognition, production, and evaluation.
7. The motivation of children to learning falls into two categories:

children may be motivated by *content* or by *method* of teaching. When the material being studied is of high interest value, children often are eager to learn it, and almost no other motivation is necessary. This is generally true of material about the Space Age or dinosaurs. When the material being studied is not of such high interest value, yet is of importance to the children, motivation may be built through the use of an interesting technique or method for motivation. A film or filmstrip, a puppet show, a stimulating question, a dramatization, a picture, a flannel-board presentation, a model, a diorama —all these create immediate involvement on the part of the children, and, when children become involved, learning can take place.

8. Skills development helps develop creativity in many ways. Learning skills of research and note-taking, for instance, leads a child toward independence in his learning and independence is a quality of creative people. Learning skills of map-, chart-, graph-, and cartoon-reading enables children to initiate their own learnings. Creative children are able to initiate their own learnings.

9. The unit method of teaching calls for the learning of the above-mentioned skills in a normal and logical way. If the unit method is not used, the skills must be taught in lessons. It is essential that they be taught as tools and utilized by the child.

10. The learning of study skills gives children techniques to verify opinions and evaluate discussions, to synthesize, summarize, draw conclusions, and help in passing judgment and making decisions—all of which are affiliated characteristics of creativity.

11. Skills learning is as important as learning content or developing creativity. It is often necessary to take time out (see page 84) to learn skills so that content learning can move forward.

With a rapidly changing society and our knowledge explosion, we cannot expect children to acquire all of the knowledge they will need in order to live effectively in the Space Age. But we can teach them the skills they need to help them acquire knowledge and find solutions to problems after they leave school. Such skills should be identified and incorporated into the instructional program in the social studies.

On the following pages are some examples of ways the principles of creative teaching can be applied to the development of study skills.

Developing Study Skills

It is extremely important that children realize that there are many *ways* to study. Robinson[2] has reported the research that designates

[2] Frances P. Robinson, *Effective Study* (New York: Harper and Brothers, 1946).

best ways to study. But the manner in which study skills are taught can contribute to creative development or destroy it.

Too often children are exposed to *one* way of attacking a problem. Day after day they approach social studies lessons by the *same* method of study. Motivation for study can be greatly enhanced when each unit of work (or at least parts of units of work) is approached through a variety of study techniques. Use of the same approach to problem-solving or application of a skill to *one* use may result in a fixedness in the use of that technique or skill which will prevent the learner from using it in other creative ways.[3]

Textbooks *can* make a contribution here by suggesting to children ways to approach the units of work set up between their covers. Some textbooks are beginning to do this. In the introduction to each chapter, they *set conditions* for developing effective study habits and applying these new learnings in creative ways. But if the textbook does not do this for the teacher, it is imperative that the teacher expose the children to as many ways of study as possible.

The material on the following pages shows a variety of creative ways to develop study skills as teachers and children approach new units of work. These techniques were developed by the author; some have been utilized in a recent textbook series.[4]

Primary Grades

In the preceding chapters we have discussed ways of helping primary children to study. Most of these have been centered around the following skills:

1. Helping children plan.
2. Helping children learn by experience.
3. Developing concepts by moving from concrete to abstract experiences.
4. Helping children to organize and schedule periods within a day as well as the entire day.
5. Building values, attitudes, and appreciations about study.
6. Setting the best environment possible to stimulate good study skills.[5]

[3] R. E. Adamson, "Functional Fixedness as Related to Problem Solving, A Repetition of Three Experiments," *Journal of Experimental Psychology,* XLIV (1952), pp. 288–291.

[4] The author is indebted to the L. W. Singer Company, Inc. of Syracuse, New York, for permission to use material in this chapter from The Singer Social Studies, published in 1963.

[5] James A. Smith, *Creative Teaching of the Language Arts in the Elementary School* (Boston: Allyn and Bacon, Inc., 1967), Chapter VIII.

7. Learning skills of discussion, recitation, drawing, handcraft and reading[6] (see Books II, III, and IV of this series).
8. Learning how to tackle problems.
9. Learning democratic procedures of operation and democratic ways of living together.

Although several textbooks in the social studies are now available at the primary level, the formal use of the textbook in many schools is often delayed until the fourth grade. At this point an introduction to study skills is made. This formal approach means that teachers try to develop within the children a study consciousness—a knowledge of the value of study, an understanding that there are many ways to study and an appreciation of studying different materials in various ways.

Following are examples of suggested approaches to developing study skills. They have been selected from textbooks or observed in classrooms.

1. Studying through anticipation.
2. Studying by finding facts to be applied to critical thinking.
3. Using subheadings as an aid to studying.
4. Using pictures as an aid to studying.
5. Using an outline as a way to study.
6. Developing group skills for studying.
7. Studying through use of activities.
8. Studying through audience-type motivation and group processes.
9. Studying by use of supplementary materials.
10. Studying by use of map skills.
11. Studying through reading and discussion.
12. Studying through the use of dramatization.
13. Learning to study by pooling known experiences.

The Intermediate Grades

The most common method of study is when the teacher and children use the textbook for a question-and-answer lesson. This is mainly a reading lesson in comprehension.

Using the textbook in a variety of ways for studying has been discussed previously in this book (see pages 125–127). The use of unit teaching as a more dynamic and flexible method for developing study skills has also been discussed (see page 80). The use of socio-

[6] *Ibid.,* Chapter VIII.

dynamics for exploring social problems has also been explored (see page 159). To these techniques we can add others, designed specifically to motivate children to learn a variety of ways to approach the *act* of studying. A creative teacher will use all these techniques (and more of her own) to motivate children.

Studying Through Anticipation

Following is an excerpt from a fourth-grade workbook:

A Way To Study

On the following pages are four stories about Indian boys and girls. They live in four different places: the Great Plains, the Southwest, the Northeast, and the Southeast. Make a list of things you would like to know about all four tribes. Then read each story to find the answers to your questions.

Other textbooks suggest ways to study; here is an excerpt from a sixth-grade textbook:

A Way To Study

After you have read this chapter about Egypt and China, you will want to know more about these strange lands far across the sea.

One way to study is to think up questions and then find the answers. After you have read this chapter think of all the things you still want to know about Egypt and China. Make a list of them. Then make a list of all the places you can go to get information. Get some of these materials at your library and look for the answers. There is a list of books that will help you at the end of this chapter.

One way to save time would be to have different people look for the answers to different questions and report to the class.

This is always a good way to study because you are looking for something definite.

Studying by Finding Facts To Be Applied to Critical Thinking

One way to study is to look for answers to questions already set up. This is practical, but not particularly creative, because children should be supplied with supplementary questions, which require that they apply this new knowledge to thought-provoking situations. They will use convergent thinking for divergent processes.

Notice how Miss Parker provided for creative thinking by using newly learned material in the situation that follows. The children read about the Fall of Pompeii to answer "fact" questions of this nature:

1. How many days did it take to destroy Pompeii?
2. How long was Pompeii a city?
3. What unusual thing happened on August 24, 79 A.D.?
4. Why did the people die suddenly?
5. What caused Pompeii to disappear so suddenly?
6. How did the burying of Pompeii help us today?
7. How long did Pompeii remain buried and forgotten?
8. What were some of the things men learned about Pompeii after the stones and ashes were cleared away?
9. Why was the forum important in Roman cities?
10. About how large was the city of Pompeii?
11. What were houses like in Pompeii?
12. How were people able to discover what plants and flowers grow in Pompeii?
13. What did the people of Pompeii do for entertainment?
14. Did the people of Pompeii know how to read and write? How do we know?

At the end of the reading of the chapter in the textbook, Miss Parker and the children discussed the questions, reread material for specific answers, and then discussed these questions:

1. Why do you suppose Pompeii was never rebuilt?
2. If men had understood about "dead" volcanoes in those days, do you think Pompeii would have been buried?
3. Make a list of all the things you can find in this chapter that the Pompeiians had learned to do.

Now answer these questions:

1. Did the people of Pompeii know as much about their world as the Egyptians? Would you say they had as great a civilization as the Mayas? How many of the things they did are we still doing today?
2. Did the people of Pompeii take advantage of their geography and their wonderful climate? Did they really understand their geography?
3. Pompeii is sometimes called "The City of Frozen History." Why do you think it is called this?
4. Is there still danger of Mt. Vesuvius erupting? If so, why has the city of Naples been built on the Bay of Naples near Mt. Vesuvius?

Using Subheadings as an Aid to Study

In another fourth grade the teacher divided the chapter on the Vikings into subheadings. Some textbooks are designed in this manner and can be used easily this way. The teacher put this material on the board as a suggested way for her children to gather material:

A Way To Study: The Vikings

Sometimes people can get ideas about what they are going to read by looking at the titles or names of the sections they are to read. Below are the titles of the sections in this chapter. Can you tell by reading them what this chapter is about? Can you also tell the order in which the chapter is going to be written?

Titles to sections:
1. The Boat Mound
2. Graves Again
3. Who Were the Vikings?
4. The Sea-Warriors
5. Iceland Is Settled
6. Eric the Red
7. Leif Ericson
8. Vikings in America
9. The Sagas
10. The Ships

Using Pictures as an Aid to Study

For another chapter in the textbook, the teacher developed the skill of using pictures as an aid to studying.

A Way To Study: Leonardo da Vinci

Another way to study and learn about new places is to study pictures. You have had many pictures to study in this book. Up to now you have looked at them as you read the book. In reading this chapter, try this: Look at all the pictures first. Read the captions. Think about what each picture is telling you. Do they make you want to know more? Do they give you a clue as to what this chapter is about? Now read the chapter and fill in all the things that the pictures do not tell you about.

Using An Outline as a Way to Study

Children can be helped to study when they are taught to follow an outline:

A Way To Study: (a sample)

This chapter is a long one but a very exciting one. One way to study long chapters is to see it in smaller parts. A chapter is sometimes written in "units." This means that an author writes about one idea and then goes on to another. All the ideas in this chapter are written about using energy but the different ways to use energy are put into units. Read these units and you will know what is coming. Units arranged like this are called an outline. After you read this chapter come back to the outline and see if it doesn't help you to remember all you have read.

Outline—Chapter 15

Unit I: The Secret of Man's Growth
  A. Man learns
  B. Man thinks
  C. Man has muscles and mind
Unit II. Early Man Makes Energy
  A. Energy through tools
  B. Energy from wood
  C. Energy from inventions and animals
  D. Energy from wind and water
Unit III: Man and Water Invent Energy with Steam
  A. Steam power
  B. Early uses of steam
  C. Steam power starts to work
  D. Thomas Newcomen invents a steam engine
  E. James Watt improves the steam engine
  F. The power of steam changes man's life
 (etc.)

A similar sixth-grade study situation would be as follows:

One way that people often use to study is to try to organize their ideas under main topics and then read to fill in the topics. Below is an outline of this chapter with the main topics and the subtopics. Read this chapter and then see if you can fill in all the details. You might do it alone or as a class.

  I. Introduction
    A. The meaning of democracy
    B. The origins of democracy in Greece
    C. Children in a democracy
    D. A controversial issue
 II. Characteristics of Democracies
    A. Government of the people
    B. Majority vote but minority rights
    C. Direct or representative participation
    D. Republican government
    E. Constitution
 (etc.)

An extension of this idea is found here:

A Way To Study

In this chapter you will study about a great country that is now fighting for its freedom. That country is Africa. Before you read this chapter, make an outline of important headings on the chalk board. Use the chapters about other countries for your ideas. Then, as you read, fill in your outline together. When you are through you will have a good summary, which you can use in your notebooks on Africa.

Developing Group Skills for Studying

Textbooks could make children aware of the skills they will need to study and live together effectively, if they were designed as follows:

Chapter XX
Earth's Last Frontier, the Sea

A Way To Study

In Chapter IV you learned some ways of working together. You learned that people who live together must learn:
1. To respect each other's rights.
2. To share things.
3. To cooperate.
4. To listen to each other's ideas.
5. To be polite and courteous.
6. To find answers to problems.
7. To look for information.
8. To discuss problems.
9. To plan carefully.

In this chapter you will read about a new frontier: the sea. In the future men will have to depend a great deal on the sea. They will need to explore the sea as they are now exploring the air.

As you read this chapter read it with the ideas above in mind. Sometimes we study by looking for answers. Sometimes we study by thinking of problems. As we read this chapter, think of all the problems of living together that nations and peoples will need to solve as men explore and use the sea. List some at the end of each unit of study.

A follow-up of this chapter might help children build certain skills in this manner:

Some Problems To Think About

Take time to list problems you thought of as you read this chapter. Add them to the ones below. Take time to discuss ways you think they might be solved.

1. *To respect each other's rights*
   Problems:
   a. How will the nations work out ways to share the products of the sea?
   b. How will they get the gold and other minerals in the sea?
   c. What are some of the rules that people have already made up regarding rights at sea? What happens to an abandoned ship? Where is the sea open to the ships of all nations and where does it belong

to the country which it touches? Are there traffic rules about speed at sea? How do ships avoid crashing into each other at sea?

2. *To share things*
   a. How will the nations be sure that each has its share of the sea's treasures?
   b. How will men learn to avoid the dangers of the sea?
   c. How will men *share* the gold from the sea?

3. *To cooperate*
   a. What are the best ways of taking treasures from the sea?
   b. Who will decide what are the best ways?
   c. How will poorer nations be able to get their share of the sea's treasures?
   d. What will Israel probably do with the method of freezing sea water to make it fresh if this method works?

4. *To listen to each other's ideas*
   a. What laws will need to be made about sharing the sea's treasures?

5. *To plan carefully*
   When we talk about the frontier of the sea we have to learn a whole new language. Here are some of the new words you learned in this chapter. They are strange and wonderful. Try them out on your friends. See if they know what they mean.

fossil	sea serpent	nylon nets
Charybdis	snorkel	bromine
skin divers	helmet	Scylla
bathysphere	electro-fishing	Atlantis
Loch Ness Monster	Maho	aqua-lung
echo sounder	whirlpool	squid
diving barrel	Maelstrom	soundings
aluminat	pressure	diving bell
albatross	atomic submarine	bathyscape
Odyssey	coelacanth	plankton
tribolite	flippers	magnesium
decompression chamber	diving suit	

Studying Through Use of Activities

Here is a chance for your class to cooperate by working in groups and then to share ideas. Have your class divide into three groups. Let each group do one of the following assignments, then report to the whole class:

A Way To Study (a sample idea)

Group 1: Dramatize the story of Ab.
Group 2: Make a chart of all the animals you can find that lived in the time of the caveman.
Group 3: Make a report on the Great Glacier. Read about it in books and tell the class what you have found.

Studying Through Audience-type Motivation and the Use of Group Processes

Another way to study is by the audience-type reading situation. This technique is most effective when children are highly motivated to a topic and are eager for information. One such topic is outer space.

The study method suggested below not only helps children to gather information; it also develops values, appreciations, attitudes, and social skills previously discussed in other chapters.

A Way To Study: Man Explores Space

This chapter tells much of what man knows now about outer space. These topics are discussed:

1. The History of Space.
2. Man's Dreams of Space Travel.
3. Dreams Begin to Come True.
4. Dr. Robert Goddard: A Pioneer in Space.
5. How a Rocket Works.
6. Rockets Today and Tomorrow.

This chapter is very important to you because in your life man will explore outer space and find out many things he does not know at present.

It would be a good idea for you to read this chapter together. Discuss what you read. Then you will want to make a list of other questions you have about outer space. Group your questions under topics such as these:

1. The Astronauts: How They Were Selected and Trained.
2. The Satellites and What Happened to Them.
3. The Space Program for the Next Twenty Years.
4. Space Platforms: How They Will Work.
5. The Moon: What Life Is Like There.
6. What Makes a Satellite Stay in Orbit.

Then allow every member of the class to sign up for a problem he would like to work on. All the boys and girls whose names appear under one topic will be a committee.

Each committee will meet and do these things:

1. Choose a chairman.
2. Choose a secretary.
3. The chairman will read the questions under the topic.
4. The committee will add more questions to the topic.
5. The committee will decide on ways to find answers to the questions.
6. Each committee member will be given a job—something to look up or something to do.
7. The committee will look for the answers to their questions.

8. They will discuss what they have found.
9. They will decide how to tell the rest of the class what they have found.
10. They will make an interesting report to the rest of the class.
    Some ideas:
    a. give a puppet show.
    b. make a play of the report.
    c. make a roll movie.
    d. have a panel discussion.
    e. have a quiz, TV, or radio show.
    f. make charts or use bulletin boards.
    g. have an exhibit.
    h. use shadow scenes.

Working on committees is one way to see how well *you* have learned to work together, to share ideas, to listen to other people, and to co-operate.

Studying by Use of Supplementary Materials

Following is a suggestion that one teacher used effectively with supplementary material of interest to the children:

A Way To Study

1. Read the first part of the chapter together through the map study.
2. Then divide your class into five committees. One committee will work on each of the following topics:
   a. Pacific Islands
   b. The Mainland (Indo-China, Thailand, Burma, and Malaya)
   c. The Philippine Islands
   d. Australia
   e. New Zealand
3. Each committee will meet around tables in the room, one in each corner and one in the middle. They will appoint a chairman and will study one part of the book together.
4. Each committee will plan a report to give to the whole class. Use maps, globes, pictures, dramatizations, shadow plays, or any other clever way of giving your reports.
5. Each committee should then plan a test for the rest of the class to see if everyone understood the report. There should be a discussion of all the items missed on the test.
6. Have each committee meet again for a story time over a period of days. Get these books from the library and have someone in each group who reads well read to the rest of the committee, or take turns reading to each other.

Committee 1: Pacific Islands
Far Into the Night, by Clare and George Louden (Island of Bali)
Guadalcanal Diary (Landmark Books), by Richard Tregaskis

We Were There at the Battle of Bataan, by Appel (We Were There Series—Grosset)

Committee 2: The Mainland
(Indo-China, Thailand, Burma, Malaya)
Burma Boy, by Willis Lindquist
Anna and the King of Siam, by Landon (Globe Readable Classics)
Getting to Know Malaya, by Jim Breetweld

Committee 3: The Philippine Islands
The Picture Story of the Philippines, by Hester O'Neill

Committee 4: Australia
Australia, by Rafello Busoni
Australia, by Ferrine Moti and Nell Reppy

Committee 5: New Zealand
Down Under, by Mario James

Studying by Use of Map Skills

Still another approach to study through the use of maps follows:

A Way To Study: (a sample idea)

In this chapter of your book you will have a chance to see how well you have learned some of the things you have been studying. You will be able to see how much you have learned about world geography and how well you can read maps. You will have a chance to see how well you think critically and share ideas. You will have a chance to see how well you can put certain facts you have learned to work for you.

To help you to learn about Europe today, that continent has been divided into sections in this chapter. The authors chose these sections because their climate is similar, the geography is similar, and the industries are similar. Each section may have more than one country in it.

To see how well you can use what you have learned, there are four maps about each section which will tell you many things about each country as it is today. The first map is always one that shows you the way the land looks from an airplane. From studying this map you will be able to see whether this section has plains, hills, or mountains. You will see what great rivers there are and the direction in which they flow. You will see whether there are winds that blow over this land and change the climate. You will be able to see how near the equator each section is.

All this will help you in telling about the climate, the things the people do for a living, and the natural harbors where they will build seaports. It will tell you about the coastline and whether or not each nation is industrial or agricultural.

By using a scale of miles, you can see how far apart places are from each other.

Maps like these, which show the natural features of a country, are called *physical maps.*

Questions for you to study:

1. What are the names of all the countries of Europe?
2. Which is the largest country of Europe? The smallest?
3. Where are the mountains of Europe? The plains? The hills? The plateaus?
4. What bodies of water are around Europe?
5. Name the large rivers of Europe. In what direction does each flow?
6. What is the capital city of each country?
7. On a globe or world map find the equator. Notice how far above the equator New York City is located. What cities in Europe are on the same degree of latitude?
8. What will the climate be like in Lisbon and Madrid? Will it be like New York or are there ocean currents which will make it different? Will the mountains make any difference in the climate?
9. Find how far above sea level New York City is. Then find out how far above sea level Madrid is. Will this make any difference in the climate?
10. Last year you studied Canada. If Paris, Amsterdam, and London are above the 50 degree latitude as Canada is, can you tell what summers might be like in Paris? Winters?
11. How many miles is it by plane from Paris to Berlin? From Milan to Madrid? From Rome to London?
12. If we take a boat from LeHavre in France to go to London, what bodies of water will we sail through?
13. To go by train from Barcelona to Vienna means we will go through four countries. What are they?
14. If we sail from New York to Athens, what bodies of water will we travel?
15. Why do the people of the Netherlands have dairying as one of their chief industries?

The second map on each section will tell you about the man-made features of each section. A map like this is called a *political map*. From it you can learn about the great seaports, the riverports, and the inland cities. The star by each city indicates the capital city.

You will also learn what the boundaries of each country are, whether they touch seas or other countries. You will be able to tell the size of each country compared to the other countries in that section. You will also be able to see, in some cases, why certain cities have become the center of great battles or the envy of other countries.

By the time you get to the third map in each section you will already know many of the things that people do for a living. You will know this because the geography and the climate of a country influence what people will do. This map will help you to check to see if you are right.

For instance, in countries where there is a rugged seacoast, we often find many seaports, and fishing is an important industry. In countries that are low and fertile there are generally good farms and rich grass growing, so farming and dairying are important industries. Often in rugged, mountainous countries we find excellent water power and minerals, so mining and manufacturing are great industries. After reading Map 1 you can guess at the industries of each country and the products that come from these industries. By looking at Map 3 you will be able to check your work. You will also be able to tell *exactly* what products come from the farms and the mills of each country. We will call this a *product and industry map.*

The last map on each section will tell you some new things. It is a map that will tell you some of the things this country does to help the rest of the world. It will tell you, too, how the rest of the world helps it.

You will want to know when you read Map 3, whether or not each country makes enough of anything to sell some to other countries. Goods that are sent out of a country are called "exports." The prefix "ex" means "from"—so this is easy to remember. Exports are goods going out from a port to other lands.

The prefix "im" means "not"—such as *not* produced. Imports are goods that come into a country. These are the goods a country does not raise and has to buy to feed its people or to help them live comfortably.

Also, on the fourth map of the sections of Europe, you will often find a small inset map, which will show you other countries controlled by the countries in Europe. You will be able to tell how powerful each country is in the world today. We will call this a "world relations" map.

A good way to study this chapter will be for you to do it together, or in small groups. You will then be able to read the questions together and share ideas about the answers. You, with your teacher to help you, can share many ideas in answering the questions. And if you are in doubt about the answers or want to learn more than you find in the book, many references are given. You can turn back to the pages mentioned in the book and review what you already know about each country. Also you can find the books mentioned in the text and read many stories by yourself about each country. You will find lists of good books and films about each country in the pages at the end of the chapter. This is a good chance for you to see how well you can think, study, and share ideas.

Studying Through Reading and Discussion

In a classroom of good readers the following is a good way to study:

This is a short chapter that will show you how people rose up against the kings, who were power-hungry, and secured more freedoms.

Because there are many new words and new ideas in this chapter, it is a good one to read together as a class. You could read each section silently with the idea that you will ask questions about it of your teacher and your classmates. After everyone has read each section, hold a discussion and allow all students to ask their questions.

Perhaps you can find pictures, books or films which show some of the events mentioned in this chapter.

Often the textbook can be used as a springboard for studying more specific areas as the following technique demonstrates.

A Way To Study

This part of man's great adventure is sad in many ways; many of the freedoms accomplished by man were lost. However, it is very exciting too. It was a very adventurous time. It was the age of knights and outlaws, of fairs and tournaments. It was the age of kings and romance.

There is so much written about this time that only a small part can be put in this book. This has been put in story form, which will make it easy for you to read together. Then you can look up material in other books and report to each other about these exciting times. Here are some things you will enjoy reading about in other books:

1. Who was Sir Lancelot? A great poet named Tennyson wrote about him in a book called *Idylls of the King*. It is a book of poems about knights.
2. Read about King Arthur and the Knights of the Round Table.
3. What was the Holy Grail? Read about it.
4. How did a boy in a castle become a knight?
5. What went on at a tournament?
6. Who was Little John? Read *The Adventures of Robin Hood* and find out.
7. What weapons were used in the Middle Ages? How were castles stormed?
8. How were castles built in the Middle Ages? Were slaves used? Did they pile the stones like they did in ancient Egypt?
9. Choirs began in the Middle Ages. Can you find out how?
10. How was food preserved at that time?

Keep a list of all the other questions that come to mind as you read this chapter. It is true that learning about one thing often makes us want to know about other things. After you read this chapter you can look up the answers to your new questions. Use textbooks and encyclopedias.

Studying Through the Use of Dramatization

Some study skills and other skills can be developed around an activity, as this textbook suggests.

A Way To Study

By now you have learned to work well on committees. You may feel you want to learn new ways of working together. Talk about this and decide *how* you want to study about the Romans. You might want to read about the Romans together and then give a television play in your classroom. You could use a large mattress box and cut out a hole for a TV screen. You could have committees work on writing the scenes for your play. Perhaps you would like to make up a story about Marcus, a Roman boy, or Lenya, a Roman girl, as we did about Seneb, the Egyptian boy, and Dario, the Greek boy. Then you would need committees to work to find out about the kind of clothes the Romans wore, the kinds of food they ate, and what their houses were like. You could make scenery and show how the people lived. If you do not have much room in your classroom, you may want to make a puppet show or a marionette show instead. This will give you a chance to practice sharing ideas and working together.

Learning To Study by Pooling Known Experiences

Good study skills can be developed when we begin with the knowledges and experiences the children already have.

A Way To Study

Here are some things to do that will help you to understand this unit:

1. Make lists of the changes you remember that have been made in clothing, transportation, communication, education, etc. Go as far back as you can remember, and then go back even farther by asking your grandfather and grandmother about these changes.
2. Collect pictures to show the changes that have taken place in your town or city. Also collect pictures that show changes in tools, in ways of traveling, and in ways of communicating. Use your family picture albums if you are allowed to do so.
3. Collect newspaper articles that tell about the problems men have always had (food, clothing, shelter, communication, transportation, protection, government, education, etc.). For example, one problem about education used to be to give everyone a chance to learn to read and write. Now our problems are different. We worry about teacher shortages and having enough buildings so that all boys and girls can go to school in a comfortable place.
4. Ask your teacher to tell you what is different in your schoolroom from the schoolroom she or he went to as a girl or boy.

This unit will help you to realize how much and how fast things change. You will enjoy studying it by working alone some of the time and by working with other class members part of the time.

Other Ways To Do Research

The *ways* children study can be varied, creative and highly motivating. When they are subjected to new ways of studying, and many variations of the old ways, they soon learn to select ways to study which are appropriate to the situation.

It is important to realize that all of these skills do not necessarily require the skill of perfected reading as a prerequisite. Slow-learning children need not be deprived of a good social studies program because of their reading disability. Information can be obtained in many ways besides the textbook. It is important to notice that the skills of research, for instance, are stated as *reading, looking,* and *listening* for details. The concept of research with elementary-school children is to be considered broadly and must include many techniques for assembling and utilizing material (see p. 131). All children can participate in many kinds of research regardless of intelligence or abilities.

The following list of suggested activities illustrates the variety of ways in which research can be developed and information obtained:

1. Make a list of all the things you would like to know if you were to visit a lumber camp. Now look at the filmstrip, *Life in a Lumber Camp,* and answer the questions you listed. (Grade 4)
2. Collect all the pictures you can find on life in Alaska and tell what you learned from studying these pictures carefully. (Grade 4)
3. Ask your grandmother and grandfather to tell you about the mail and how it was delivered when they were your age. (Grade 4)
4. Make a collection of all the things you can find that were made in Japan. (Grade 4)
5. Visit an ice cream factory and learn how ice cream is made. (Grade 4)
6. Study a model of an airplane and list the parts of the plane. (Grade 4)
7. Make a list of all the materials used in building a house. (Grade 4)
8. Make a chart of all the ways nature spreads seeds. (Grade 4)
9. If you like Greek myths, make up a myth and talk it into a tape recorder. Play it for the rest of the children. (Grade 4)
10. Demonstrate how the use of a pulley makes men's work easier for them. (Grade 4)
11. Using the outline you made as you studied this chapter together, start a notebook on Africa. Find pictures, stories, maps, and clippings to go with your outline. (Grade 6)
12. Many Americans now are allowed behind the Iron Curtain. If you have anyone in your community who has been in Russia, invite him to speak to your class. Find out from him what freedoms children have in Russia. (Grade 6)
13. Look about your own town and see if you can find any churches or other buildings built in Gothic style. Do they have beautiful stained-glass windows? Ask someone to tell you how these windows were made. From where did they come? (Grade 5)

One group of sixth-graders made some startling discoveries about their community. They found the population was diminishing each year and set out to find the reasons why this was so. This led to a study of many things; among them were the lumber industry, soil erosion, local tax plans, financing, mortgaging, job opportunities, and local history. This group made a film of their findings and gave a Parents Night exhibit which helped stir the community to the point where a revival took place. School children, themselves, took on the project of replacing seedlings on the depleted hillsides.

Discovery is a part of the creative act—it may be the discovery of a problem or the discovery of a solution to a problem. It should be a part of all planned learning experiences.

New materials have been designed which will help many children develop certain research *and* study skills independently. These materials can be of great assistance to the teacher and children when properly used. Children can often be made aware of more advanced kinds of research than simply "looking up material" and gathering facts to arrive at solutions to a problem.

Mr. Arnes, a fifth-grade teacher, heard his children grumbling when he asked them to write their spelling words ten times. After a discussion of the reasons for doing this, some children commented that they didn't think it helped them much to write the words. Mr. Arnes suggested they find out. By asking probing questions the children were helped to set up the scientific method. The class was split into two groups of fifteen each. Half the class wrote their words for two months, and half did not. Mr. Arnes had controlled the structure of the groups so they were equal in ability. At the end of each month all the children took a review test, and the results were compared. Interestingly enough, in this instance the group who did not write their words ten times came out as well on the review exams as those who did. The value of the experience lay in the fact that the children learned that there were ways to solve problems through the application of the scientific method. Later in the year, *they* proposed studies they might carry out.

With scientific research methods being applied in many schools these days, children can be made aware of the research project if it is feasible, and can understand that they are taking a part in it.

Teachers, too, can take part in research, especially action research where they work with controlled and experimental groups in the classroom. Active participation in research projects helps an entire school, including the children, to understand and develop research study techniques.

Using Original Sources

Often children can have many creative experiences when they are taught how to use original sources in doing research. While studying the Civil War, Mr. Jones took a group of children to a neighboring university library where they brought home eye-witness accounts of some of the battles and events which the children had discovered in the library archives. These accounts were compared with more recent ones and great disparities were discovered. Excellent creative thinking as to why the accounts differed came out of the discussion. The children discovered that history tends to be embellished and sometimes distorted in the retelling.

Mr. Jones found a painting of the Battle of Gettysburg done shortly after the close of the war by an eyewitness. He then found an impression of the same battle painted by an artist twenty years later. He also found one that had been painted by a contemporary artist. The scenes were very different in many respects. In trying to decide why they were different, the children learned a great deal about accurate reporting and artistic license. The creative and critical thinking resulting from this experience were excellent.

A fourth-grade group discovered a great deal about their community when they decided to make a motion picture about it. Their study took them to places they had not known existed. One very exciting discovery was made when they surveyed a field outside of town to discover the geographical center of their state. They painted a pole, and, with the farmer's permission, planted it on the spot. On the top of the pole they hung a flag that said, "This is the geographical center of Alabama. It was discovered by the fourth grade." Each child then signed his name to the flag in crayon. This experience later took on additional significance when state surveyors, planning for a new highway to be built through the state, informed the children by letter that they had discovered their flag and that their measurements were only off by two feet!

Discovery can play a great part in developing research skills in children when the local resources of a community are used—parks, town records, an industrial plant, a survey of occupations, a visit to a farm or dairy, a study of local watershed and geography, an art museum, or an old graveyard.

Lacking material to interest his children in local history, Mr. Smith took them to an old graveyard that adjoined the school property. Children became interested in the inscriptions on the gravestones and eventually copied every one to bring back to school. They tried to trace local families by the names on the gravestones and to reconstruct local history. One very interesting discovery was made by a boy who noticed that many children had died at one specific period of time. Further research disclosed this to be the year when a great typhoid epidemic hit the community.

In promoting this type of research, the teacher plays a new kind of role. Instead of answering questions she poses them: she sets problems in the children's way and then provides means for them to solve them. Many problems can be solved by experimentation and the scientific method—the creative way to problem-solving.

Other Study Skills

Many of the skills outlined on page 195 have already been developed in other books in this series. They are:

The ability to outline: (this skill has been developed in Book II,[5] Chapter VIII).

The ability to summarize: (see Book II,[6] Chapter VIII).

The ability to record data: (see Book II,[7] Chapter VIII).

The ability to take notes: (see Book II,[8] Chapter VIII).

The ability to select main ideas: (see Book III,[9] Chapter VI).

The ability to read for details: (see Book III,[10] Chapter VI).

The ability to make oral and written reports: (see Book II, Chapters V and VIII).[11]

The ability to plan: (see Chapter V of this book).

Summary

Study skills taught in meaningful context and applied to problem-solving situations help children to function independently and to

[5] James A. Smith, *Creative Teaching of the Language Arts in the Elementary School* (Boston: Allyn and Bacon, Inc., 1967).

[6] *Ibid.*

[7] *Ibid.*

[8] *Ibid.*

[9] James A. Smith, *Creative Teaching of Reading and Literature in the Elementary School* (Boston: Allyn and Bacon, Inc., 1967).

[10] *Ibid.* Chapter VI.

[11] James A. Smith, *Creative Teaching of the Language Arts in the Elementary School* (Boston: Allyn and Bacon, Inc., 1967).

develop their creative powers. The degree to which this is accomplished is determined by the creative techniques utilized by the teacher in presenting these skills and providing practice for their mastery.

The component skills of creative development, such as problem-solving, critical thinking, organizational skills, the ability to perceive and synthesize, keen audio and visual perception, the ability to evaluate, the ability to verify opinions, the ability to pass judgments and make decisions, the ability to identify and define problems, flexibility of thinking, the ability to redefine and rearrange and to self-initiate learning are developed in the creative teaching of study skills. Good study habits can lead a child to independence in his learning, a valuable asset.

TO THE COLLEGE STUDENT

1. Now that you have read this chapter, discuss it in terms of the shortcomings of your own training in study skills.

2. Stop at a gas station and pick up a road map. Look at it and ask yourself if you really can read all of it intelligently. Very few schools teach the use of road maps. With the increase in our thruway, turnpike, and freeway systems, how important is a road map? How could you find ways to read the ones you brought to class?

3. Invite a geographer to class and ask him to bring samples of the maps that he uses in his work.

4. Think of ways the suggestions for "Ways to Study" could be applied to your college classroom. Try some of them. Were they more motivating than regular textbook assignment-recite study techniques?

5. Brainstorming is a technique often used to promote critical thinking. Suppose you were a manufacturer presented with the problem of having one million hula hoops left in your warehouse after the hula hoop craze had subsided. Brainstorm the uses to which you might put these hula hoops so you will get back your investment.

6. Make a list of all the ways you see in which Telstar will promote communication. Now discuss all the creative ways you could use to develop these concepts with children.

TO THE CLASSROOM TEACHER

1. Try using the different ways of studying with your students as they are suggested in this chapter. To these suggestions, try creating other ways of studying such as:
   a. Studying through the use of a moving picture.
   b. Studying through the use of a filmstrip.
   c. Learning to study by use of a television.

2. Concepts are developed by giving children many experiences over a period of time so generalizations may develop. In what ways could you develop the following concepts in children?
   a. The first man who will put foot on the moon has already been born.
   b. The coldest place in the world is not in the Arctic Zone; it is in the Temperate Zone.
   c. The hottest place in the world is not on the equator but in the Temperate Zone.
   d. Hawaii is actually the peak of a huge mountain range.
   e. The Eskimos have no science because they adjust to their environment rather then try to change their environment to suit them.

3. Think of all the ways you can teach children about maps by using modern materials (mock-ups, films, army air maps, road maps, plastic maps, etc.) that will cut down on the time you usually spend on maps but which will, at the same time, do a more efficient job of teaching.

4. Have the children collect all the different *kinds* of maps and charts they can find. Then study them to see how well they can read them.

TO THE COLLEGE STUDENT AND THE
CLASSROOM TEACHER

1. In light of the discussions of this book, determine the place of each of the following organizational plans of various modern schools. Which ones are sound in principle and fulfill the functions of a good social studies program?

   a. The ungraded school.
   b. The multigraded school.
   c. Team teaching.
   d. The self-contained classroom.
   e. The Joplin Plan.
   f. Track teaching.
   g. Departmentalized teaching in the primary grades.

2. Make a collection of graphs and charts from newspapers and magazines which can be used with children.

SELECTED BIBLIOGRAPHY

AMMONS, MARGARET P. and John I. Goodlad. "Time, Space and the Developing Child," *Childhood Education* (April 1956), 374–379.

BROWN, JAMES W., RICHARD B. LEWIS, and FRED F. HARCLEROAD. "Using Graphics," *A.V. Instruction: Materials and Methods.* New York: McGraw-Hill, 1959. Chap. 16.

BROWNELL, W. A. and G. HENDRICKSON. "How Children Learn Information, Concepts and Generalizations," *Learning and Instruction.* Forty-ninth Yearbook, Part I, National Society for the Study of Education. Chicago: University of Chicago Press, 1950.

CANNELL, L. D. "The Inseparability of Geography and Visual Aids," *Educational Screen,* XXIV, No. 4 (April, 1945), 141–142.

CROW, LESTER D., ALICE CROW, and WALTER MURRAY. *Teaching in the Elementary School: Readings.* New York: Longmans, Green and Co., 1961.

DALE, EDGAR. *Audio-Visual Methods in Teaching,* rev. ed. New York: Henry Holt & Co., 1954, pp. 323–33 and Chap. 18.

EAST, MARJORIE. *Display for Learning: Making and Using Visuals.* New York: Dryden Press, 1952.

FORSYTH, ELAINE. "Map Reading," *Journal of Geography,* 42:249–257, October 1943; November, 1943; 327–332, December, 1943; 43:13–17, January 1944; 71–75, February, 1944; 92–96, March, 1944; 140–144, April, 1944; 168–176, May 1944.

GLENN, WILLIAM H. and DONOVAN A. JOHNSON, *Adventures in Graphing.* St. Lewis: Webster Publishing Co., 1961.

GREENWOOD, DAVID. *Down to Earth: Map Making for Everyone.* New York: Holiday House, 1951.

HOLUB, K. A. "Introducing Maps in the Fourth Grade," *Journal of Geography,* LII, No. 9 (December, 1953); 374–377.

JAROLIMEK, JOHN. "Helping Children Interpret Graphs, Charts and Cartoons," *Social Studies in Elementary Education.* New York: The Macmillan Co., 1963. Chap. 9.

MERRITT, EDITH. "Making Maps, Charts and Graphs," *Working With Children in the Social Studies*. Belmont, Calif.: Wadsworth Publishing Co., Inc., 1961. Chap. 10.

MICHAELIS, JOHN U. "Graphic Materials," *Social Studies For Children in a Democracy*. Englewood Cliffs, N.J.: Prentice-Hall, Inc., 1963. Chap. 12.

RAISZ, ERWIN. *Principles of Cartography*. New York: McGraw-Hill, 1962.

SABAROFF, ROSE. "Map Making in the Primary Grades," *Social Education*, Jan. 1960, 19–20.

THOMAS, R. MURRAY and SHERWIN G. SWARTOUT. *Integrated Teaching Materials*. New York: Longmans, Green and Co., Inc., 1960.

WESLEY, EDGAR B. and MARY A. ADAMS. *Teaching Social Studies in the Elementary School*, rev. ed. Boston: D. C. Heath & Co., 1952, 301–306.

WHITTEMORE, KATHERYNE T. "Maps," *Geographic Approaches to Education*. Nineteenth Yearbook, National Council for the Social Studies. Washington, D.C.: National Education Ass'n., 1948, 117–229.

WITTICH, WALTER A. and CHARLES F. SCHULER. "Graphics," *Audio-Visual Materials: Their Nature and Use*. New York: Harper & Row, 1962. Chap. 5.

Using Audio-visual Materials To Develop Creativity

. . . Every teacher wishes to be an excellent one. But each falls somewhat short of his aspirations. This is true of the entire range, from the finest who may miss the goal only occasionally to the poorest who are constant and depressing failures.

There are varied reasons for this gap between a teacher's desired excellence and actual performance. In some cases the gap is caused by an inability to understand how students think. In others it is a result of a poor knowledge of subject matter or of an inability to maintain order in class. But often poor teaching is due to *a lack of skill in selecting and using teaching methods and materials!*[1]

THOMAS AND SWARTOUT

TO THE READER
Make a list of all the audio-visual aids you can think of. Then skim the preceding chapters of this book to find illustrations of the various ways teachers have used the aids on your list in the classroom. If some are not mentioned, this chapter will give you references to other books in this series, which show how audio-visual aids may be used, not only to develop good teaching, but to develop creativity in children as well.

Introduction

The most commonly accepted uses to which audio-visual materials have been put are: (1) as *aids* to teaching; (2) as dispensers of information; and (3) as vicarious experiences when direct experience is impossible or impractical. To these concepts a new one must be added: Audio-visual aids can serve as a means to develop creativity in children.

Thomas and Swartout[2] list three experience levels: direct real-life experiences; substitute or vicarious experiences (more than words); and words alone, spoken or written. Most audio-visual experiences in the classroom fall in the second category.

[1] R. Murray Thomas and Sherwin G. Swartout, *Integrated Learning Materials* (New York: Longmans, Green and Company, Inc., 1960).

[2] *Ibid.,* p. 1.

In teaching a unit on a foreign country, the best experience a group of children could have would be to visit the country and live there for a period of time. Since this is impossible, the next best experience is a *vicarious one, as nearly like the actual experience as possible!* The experiences most like the real one which are currently available to children are colored sound-films or colored television programs where the camera selects sample experiences from a culture, reproducing them as they actually occur. Next are colored pictures with a narrator or accompanying tape. Then would come a colored picture, next a black and white picture and least effective of all are words. In Book II of this series,[3] a rather detailed exposition was given on the ineffectiveness of words alone, as well as other kinds of symbols in the communication process.

Audio-visual aids have not always been used to the best advantage, nor have they been used to any extent to develop creativity in children. Sometimes courses in the use of audio-visual materials set such rigid concepts about their application that teachers have been limited by the principle of predetermined use. A good example of this is shown by a dittoed sheet given to the students enrolled in an audio-visual course at a university. The sheet contained this information:

HOW TO USE A MOVING-PICTURE FILM IN THE CLASSROOM

I. Prepare Yourself
   A. Preview the film.
   B. Take notes on the information it gives.
   C. Check to see if it helps to accomplish your objectives.
   D. Make up leading questions for the students.
   E. Make note of points you especially want them to observe.
   F. Prepare your materials.

II. Prepare the Students
   A. Get them ready for viewing. Make sure chairs, projector, and screen are ready. Be sure film is threaded.
   B. Present guide questions.
   C. Mention special aspects of the film you especially want them to see.
   D. Indicate the objectives you are trying to meet.

III. Show the Film
   A. Be sure the film is in focus.
   B. In some instances it may be wise to stop the film or rewind a part for reshowing to stress the importance of a particular segment.

[3] James A. Smith, *Creative Teaching of the Language Arts in the Elementary School* (Boston: Allyn and Bacon, Inc., 1967).

IV. Follow-Up
  A. Get a general reaction to the film.
  B. Discuss main idea of film.
  C. Review specific questions given at beginning of film.
  D. Discussion on conflicting points of view.
  E. Summarize learnings from film.

Now this may be a sensible procedure in some instances, and certainly is much better than using moving pictures alone as an entertainment medium, but it overlooks the fact that the moving picture can be put to many uses.

Miss Crane used a film as motivation for a unit. Her second-grade children in a large metropolitan area had never seen the farm animals with which most rural children are familiar. In order to introduce a unit on animals of all kinds, Miss Crane used the films *A Trip to the Dairy Farm* and *The Circus* so the children would learn to identify domestic and wild animals and develop a nomenclature that would have meaning for them. Her preparation of the students was not at all like the one suggested on the university guide sheet.

Mr. Jones used a film in his sixth grade as a *source of information*. The children were studying the national government, and Mr. Jones felt that the film, *How a Bill Becomes a Law,* explained more clearly than the textbook this particular function of the government. His preparation for viewing and follow-up was not like that of the university guide.

Miss Ellis used a film to develop *aesthetic appreciation.* The children in her fourth grade were studying all phases of communication, especially creative expression, and they examined some films because of their ability to communicate with a variety of techniques. They were enthralled by *The Loon's Necklace, The Face of Lincoln,* and *The Brotherhood of Man.*

Mr. Andrews used films such as *How To Make Lantern Slides* as a *source of instruction.* He often encouraged a group of children to view these films in the rear of the room behind a screen while he worked with another group at the front of the room.

Miss Farnsworth used films as a *motivator for creative writing.* She often showed short cartoons without the sound track and encouraged the children to write their own scripts. She also showed an art film of flowing colors and asked children how it made them feel, or encouraged them to write poetry about unusual shots.

Miss Dempsey used films for *appreciation of good literature.* Such films as *The Red Balloon* and *Make Way For Ducklings* added depth to her literature program.

Mr. Grimes often used a film as an *evaluation* of a piece of work. After the children in his fifth grade had done research on questions pertaining to their units, he would say, "I have a film today which will help us. Watch it with this in mind: How well did we research our questions?" A film on Switzerland then served as an evaluation device and added enrichment to the verbal reports the children had given.

Mr. Carnes used films in a similar manner as a *summary to a unit*. After the children in his sixth grade had done extensive research with a variety of materials, he would show a film that would pull together all the material and information they had found.

Miss Martin used films as a *vicarious experience* when a real experience could not be taken. Like Miss Crane in the first illustration above, she helped children establish a working vocabulary and some basic concepts for lessons that would follow.

Many teachers use films simply for *enjoyment or entertainment value*. Such films as *Fiddle Dee Dee* and *Treasure Island* are worth viewing simply for their aesthetic and enjoyment value.

Mr. Kent used films as a *readiness technique*. Many films such as *What Is Four?* provided a kind of readiness for work that was to follow in mathematics.

Miss Fellows used films as *supplementary material*. After her sixth grade had studied Africa, she showed the art film, *Masks of Africa,* to add depth of meaning and enrichment to the facts they had studied.

Mr. Marcin, a physical education teacher, often used films as a *problem-solving technique*. He helped children diagnose their own problems in the art of skiing, for instance, and then showed the film *How To Ski Well* so each child could look for the answers to his own particular problem in the film.

Mr. Roberts used films as a *testing device*. He found a film that presented many concepts, such as *How Television Works*. The children were given a list of questions previous to the film, which centered around their studies, the answers to which were reviewed in the film. After viewing the film, children wrote the answers to the questions.

Miss Pella used films as a *study of techniques*. Her class wanted to present the landing of the Pilgrims on a small stage. She made a list of questions, such as: How can we give the impression of large groups of people in a small area? How can sound help us to give the illusions we want to give our audience? How can a war with the Indians be staged in a small space? How can we show the passing of time in our play? She then showed *A Tale of Two Cities,* and the children studied the techniques of production while they enjoyed the film.

Here are many illustrations of the use of a film, all of which require different preparation, a different purpose, and a different follow-up than that mentioned in the university outline.

The setting of stringent regulations for the use of audio-visual materials has limited their use. Lack of understanding of the purpose has often caused misuse. It is a common experience to see teachers use a moving-picture film as a means of summarizing a unit when actually it could serve many more purposes, as demonstrated above. Just as a field trip serves to give children the needed new vocabulary and concepts to *begin* the study of a new topic, so can a moving picture substitute for the *real* experience and provide children with labels for the new things about which they will learn. If the stages of language development as outlined in Book II of this series[4] (listening, speaking, reading, and then writing) are followed, it is much more sensible to show a film at the onset of the unit than at the end of it. Children, in viewing a good, colored talking film on Mexico, not only hear the music, language, and sounds of the country, they see a serape, a sombrero, a fiesta, a siesta, a tortilla, a burro, and a piñata. Once the words are spoken they can be printed and read. New vocabulary introduced in this manner is easy to master because it rises from experience, in context with meaning, and is a sound way to introduce new concepts. Reading is greatly enhanced when children learn new words in this manner.

Creative Uses of Audio-visual Materials

Audio-visual aids, however, can be used directly to develop creativity in children. Our concern here is with the utilization approach to creative development. Throughout this series instances have been cited where teachers used audio-visual materials to develop divergent thinking processes and to encourage the development of traits and characteristics needed for creativity.

In Books II[5] and III[6] of this series, for instance, examples were

[4] *Ibid.,* Chapter III.
[5] *Ibid.,* Chapter V.
[6] James A. Smith, *Creative Teaching of Reading and Literature in the Elementary School* (Boston: Allyn and Bacon, Inc., 1967), Chapter I.

given of Mr. Smith using the fluorescent chalk and the black light to develop creative writing and creative reading. In Chapter XI of this book an example was given of children making their own moving-picture film to learn about the history of their community. This project not only involved the planning of the scenes, shooting the scenes, and creating a sound track to go with the film, but also involved costume and scenery-making, sponsoring a world premiere, making posters and a float to advertise the film, collecting and creating props, and writing letters, poems and stories.

In Book III[7] of this series Miss Wilson used a slide projector to teach a reading and literature unit on *The Elephant's Child*. She had the children explore all the materials that would project color on a screen when applied to glass, and then each child made a slide to represent a part of the story. The slides were put in logical sequence, the story was read on a tape, and the completed project was shown to other children in a Book Week assembly program.

In Book III[8] of this series, excellent examples were given of the use of dioramas and peep shows to tell stories to children. Both the diorama and the telling of the stories were creative.

In Book II of this series,[9] Chapter VII, an illustration is given of the creative use of the opaque projector in the teaching of handwriting. In Book IV[10] an excellent example is given of the use of motion-picture leader film to develop a new, creative experience for children in experimenting with the fluidness of color on a screen and using the tape recorder to make a sound track of verbal impressions to accompany the colored film.

In Chapter IX of this volume excellent examples were given of the use of pictures, puppets, films, records, and tapes to help children develop values, appreciations, and character in a creative manner.

Throughout Book II of this series[11] there are illustrations of ways charts may be used to develop creative thinking and creative writing. Book VI[12] has verbal and pictoral illustrations of the uses of

[7] *Ibid.*, Chapter VII.

[8] *Ibid.*, Chapter III.

[9] James A. Smith, *Creative Teaching of the Language Arts in the Elementary School* (Boston: Allyn and Bacon, Inc., 1967), Chapter VII.

[10] James A. Smith, *Creative Teaching of the Creative Arts in the Elementary School* (Boston: Allyn and Bacon, Inc., 1967), Chapter IV.

[11] James A. Smith, *Creative Teaching of the Language Arts in the Elementary School* (Boston: Allyn and Bacon, Inc., 1967), Chapters IV, VII.

[12] Alvin M. Westcott and James A. Smith, *Creative Teaching of Mathematics in the Elementary School* (Boston: Allyn and Bacon, Inc., 1967).

charts, blocks, flannel boards, games, and homemade devices for the creative teaching of mathematics. The use of the flannel board as a tension-builder for creative problem-solving is illustrated frequently in Books II, III and V of this series.

Even common household equipment such as flowers, air spray, candy, and phonograph records can be used effectively as audio-visual materials to develop creativity. A referral to Mr. Smith's lesson in Book III of this series[13] will illustrate the use of these materials for this purpose.

Realia, of course, can be invaluable as a teaching aid. In Book III of the series[14], it was suggested that five unrelated objects be placed in a bag and that children create a dramatization using all five objects. In Book II, it was suggested that one piece of realia be placed on a table and children write how they felt from looking at it. The poems in Book II about the candle are evidence of the effectiveness of this technique.[15] Realia can develop creativity when it is subjected to the "new uses" criterion. It can also be used to force children into creative thinking when subjected to Parnes and Osborne's creative ideation criteria: minimizing, elaborating, new uses, etc. An excellent example of this kind of creative teaching was given in Chapter I, Book II of this series[16] when Mrs. Wilson stimulated the children into creative writing through the use of the brandy snifter of fruit.

In using audio-visual materials for creative development it is wise to teach the children the use of the various machines and make them responsible for their care. Once children are comfortable with the materials, they can put them to use in solving their problems. Old experiences put to new uses can be creative ones.

One of the characteristics of creative children is that they have keener auditory and visual perception than noncreative children. And teachers can improve creative output by helping them to develop sharper auditory and visual perception.

[13] James A. Smith, *Creative Teaching of Reading and Literature in the Elementary School* (Boston: Allyn and Bacon, Inc., 1967), Chapter V.

[14] *Ibid.*, Chapter VII.

[15] James A. Smith, *Creative Teaching of the Language Arts in the Elementary School* (Boston: Allyn and Bacon, Inc., 1967), Chapter V.

[16] *Ibid.*

Summary

Audio-visual materials are not only effective teaching devices; they serve as motivators and developers of creative power as well. The possibilities for creative development through the use of these materials is limitless.

TO THE COLLEGE STUDENT

1. Sometimes vicarious experiences can be better than a direct experience. For instance, the Army used mock-up models and slow-motion pictures to explain the functioning of the M-1 rifle to its trainees. A picture of a bicycle accident is better for teaching safety than a real bicycle accident. Make a list of all the instances you can think of where vicarious experiences excel first-hand experiences in an instructional program.

2. Think of the college classes you attend which are dull or difficult. Think of all the ways you can to employ audio-visual aids to make these classes more interesting.

3. Have you ever had a visual experience that you felt was especially creative, such as the clever use of color and lines on the screen during the overture of the moving picture *West Side Story?* Keep a record of such visual stimuli during the next few weeks. Also try collecting examples of creative audio stimuli, such as the unusual use of sound effects in *Boundary Lines.*

4. How creative are you? Take this problem and see what you can do with it: demonstrate color in motion.

5. Brainstorm this idea: How many ways can I use a tape recorder in the classroom?

TO THE CLASSROOM TEACHER

1. Examine your audio-visual program and check it against the following:

    a. Do I use audio-visual materials simply to impart information?
    b. To what other uses do I put them?
    c. How many times have I used the following aids in my class-
       room in the past week?

          realia
          moving picture film
          the tape recorder
          a new bulletin board
          a diorama
          a film strip
          a mock-up
          slides
          charts
          textbooks
          workbooks
          an exhibit
          maps
          globes
          science equipment

    d. Is there an overbalance? Should there be?
    e. How many different ways did you use these materials?

    2. Odds and ends can be utilized to make excellent audio-visual aids and to develop creative potential. Collect a box of odds and ends—call it "beautiful junk"—and challenge your children to use what they can to make an unusual time-line, a map, a chart, or a meaningful bulletin board.

    3. Have your children brainstorm this idea: how many things can we use a moving picture for? Check their list against the one in this chapter.

    4. Have your children write themes on this idea: what would happen if all movie film in the world should suddenly melt?

TO THE COLLEGE STUDENT
AND THE CLASSROOM TEACHER

    1. Have the children with whom you work brainstorm this problem: how would we spread the news if all newspapers and magazines were suddenly destroyed?

2. Creative use can be made of all materials. Open your desk drawer and take the first object you see. Then ask yourself: how many ways could I use this object as an aid in teaching the social studies?

3. Make a list of all the uses to which a film strip can be put similar to the uses of the film described in this chapter.

4. Do the same for a diorama, a view-master, a bulletin board. How can each be used to develop creativity?

5. How creative are you? Try this: how could you have your students create a musical poem called "The City" without using musical instruments?

6. Here are some materials that will help you in the use of audio-visual materials.

Bring the World to the Classroom. Wayne University, 1952, black and white filmstrip.
How To Teach With Films. Cathedral Films, 1946, sound, black and white.
Using the Classroom Film. Encyclopedia Britanica, 1945, 21 min., sound, black and white.

SELECTED BIBLIOGRAPHY

DALE, EDGAR. *Audio-Visual Methods in Teaching.* New York: Dryden Press, 1954.

DEBERNARDIS, AMO. *The Use of Instructional Materials.* New York: Appleton-Century-Crofts, Inc., 1960.

GUGGENHEIM, RICHARD. *Creative Vision for Art and for Life.* New York: Harper & Row, 1960.

KINDER, JAMES S. *Audio-Visual Materials and Techniques,* 2nd ed. New York: American Book Company, 1959.

LINDERMAN, E. W. and D. W. HEBERHOLZ. *Developing Artistic and Perceptual Awareness.* Dubuque, Iowa: William C. Brown Co., 1964.

SANDS, LESTER B. *Audio-Visual Procedures in Teaching.* New York: Ronald Press, 1956.

THOMAS, R. MURRAY and SHERWIN G. SWARTOUT. *Integrated Teaching Materials.* New York: Longmans, Green and Company, Inc., 1960.

WITTICH, WALTER A. and CHARLES F. SCHULLER. *Audio-Visual Materials.* New York: Harper and Brothers, 1957.

WITTICH, WALTER A. and JOHN G. FOWLKES, *Audio-Visual Paths to Learning.* New York: Harper and Brothers, 1946.

The Skills
of Group
Living

. . . Perception is much more than imprinting. It is a creative process in itself. The perceiver creates the field from which his percepts, signs and symbols emerge.[1]

HAROLD RUGG

TO THE READER

Review the effect of the socialization process on creative development in Chapter III. What behavior and which qualities may we have to accept in children in order to develop creativity and still maintain individual and democratic rights for other people? Try to recall any classes or conferences which you attended where you felt free to speak and where you felt some good creative thinking resulted. What conditions were set to bring this about? In this chapter the author attempts to show how practice in group living can be developed creatively in children. Try some of these techniques in your classes.

Introduction

Membership in a democratic society demands of each individual certain skills for living in harmony with his fellowmen. Therefore, in teaching for social living much stress is placed on social processes—the techniques for conducting group work that make it possible to live effectively together. Certain values must be developed in children for them to become effective, stable group members. A good social program develops these values by providing life situations in the classroom where use of these values becomes a common occurrence.

From an early age it is essential that children recognize *variance of opinion* so that they later will accept a *conflict of ideas.* All through life it will be necessary for them to *make choices,* and they must learn to *evaluate effectively and critically* in order to do this. In a democracy it will be necessary for them to *identify common goals*

[1] Harold Rugg, *Imagination: An Inquiry Into the Sources and Conditions That Stimulate Creativity* (New York: Harper & Row, Publishers, 1963), p. 82.

with their coworkers and yet maintain a degree of *flexibility*. Children will need practice so that they may learn to *discover and define problems,* and so that they will know when and how to *find facts* to solve these problems.

They will need to learn how to consider opinions, to be scientific in making decisions, to be able to communicate their own ideas; they will find it necessary to *assume leadership* or *followership* as the situation demands, and to *plan intelligent action.* In times of crisis they must know the value of morals. They will need to know how to *delegate or accept authority.* They will need to know how to inspire fellowmen to *work on a common cause* and how to help *reach consensus* in community-school affairs. They will need to understand, above all other skills, that *creative thought is valuable,* and they will need to learn how to accept creative thought which differs from their own. They will also have to *defend their own ideas* when they know they are right and be unwilling to conform to group pressures. All of these and many more techniques must be developed for cohesive group living.

The children will also need to understand when to think *intelligently* and when to think *emotionally;* when to *conform* and when they may be *individual.* Much creative behavior, for instance, calls emotional factors into play. This is especially true of that phase of the creative process in which insight or a break-through begins; ideas emerge, thoughts bubble to the surface. Afterwards, the ideas must be tested in the light of the intellectual; they must meet certain criteria and stand the test of logic. But the ideas could not have been attained through reasoning—creative thinking was required.

Emotional reaction may often have a decided effect on the decision-making mentioned in the paragraph above and on the behavior of the individual, especially if he is reluctant to surrender his own ideas for better or more appropriate ones. Sometimes emotional reaction may interfere with sound decisions. In the classroom, children should be provided with experiences that will help them see how emotional behavior can be used as a constructive or as a disruptive force. One factor that indicates a creative child is that he is neither compulsively conforming nor compulsively nonconforming, neither emotionally controlled nor intellectually controlled; he has the freedom to decide when he will be either and bases his decision on the appropriateness of the situation.

Much attention has been devoted to techniques for bringing this about in recent years, and many techniques for fostering group dynamics have been developed. There is a place for all of them in the elementary classroom, though some are more effective at certain times and under certain circumstances than others.

What does research have to say about group work as it relates to creativity and conformity? Various studies of group dynamics have led to some interesting discoveries. For instance, group dynamics as they relate to creativity have been studied at the Foundation for Research on Human Behavior at Ann Arbor, Michigan.

Some of these studies bear educational implications for the teacher who is trying to preserve creativity in children. The results show that group pressures can inhibit originality. Groups discourage deviate opinions; they exert pressure on members to conform, and these pressures tend to reduce the amount of originality of which the group is capable.

The studies also show that original people *do* succumb to group pressures but that they tend to conform less than unoriginal people when they receive even a small amount of support.

Much of the research at the institute is significant for all group work. Following is a list of stated observations which the teacher may well keep in mind while employing group processes.

1. People conform more when their actions affect other people than when they themselves are the only ones affected.
2. People conform more when they consider the task of the group is important and relevant to the group's goals.
3. People who feel rejected by the group conform more than people who feel accepted.
4. Status differences within a group increase conformity, discourage deviate opinions, and reduce the effectiveness of group work.
5. Participation in decision-making can change the direction of group goals and conformity pressures.
6. The introduction of expert opinion to support an opinion tends to increase the amount of conformity to that position.[2]

Groups tend to prefer the security of the status quo and may therefore interfere with the divergent thinking of their creative thinkers. Even in school, children who deviate from group standards may be punished and the conformers may be rewarded. By establishing such a set of values, the teacher is often setting up blocks to creative thinking and originality.

[2] Foundation for Research on Human Behavior, *Creativity and Conformity,* ed. Carol Lundington (Ann Arbor, Michigan: Edwards Brothers, Inc., 1958), pp. 1–2.

Group processes can increase creativity, especially when creativeness is a goal for the group. Divergent thinking can be rewarded; the teacher can set values on originality, and the conditions will be such that creative ideas will come more frequently. Conformity within a group by any one individual is determined by the meaning of the situation to him, the strength of his conviction, his need for group acceptance, and his own past experiences.

In studies of conformity made with young adults, the following observations evolved:

1. Women appeared to conform more than men.
2. Some people conform more than others. The passive conformer generally is a person with inadequate self-perception; he has a great deal of doubt and anxiety in his personality. He feels inferior. He is unable to cope with stress. He rationalizes his answers. The expedient conformer knows the right answer but adopts the group's opinion anyway. He is high on measures of authoritarianism.
3. Nonconformity correlates negatively with intelligence, ego-strength, dominance, ascendancy, masculinity. Nonconformers achieve high scores on tests of social acuity, or the ability to understand other people.[3]

Although these studies were performed with adults, they indicate possible observations and cautions to be exercised by the classroom teacher. She will utilize group processes in her classroom with new understandings. This knowledge gives her ideas for studying her children and suggestions for conducting group discussions.

Conformity is not a bad thing. If there were no conformity, schools could not run, traffic would not move, production lines would not function, and jobs would not be completed. The teacher's job is to teach when conformity is necessary and when it is not. More specifically, it is to be certain that in every instance where creativity can be developed the proper *creative* rather than *conforming* conditions are set for it.

The Class Discussion

Discussion can contribute to creative development. It can also be used to help children understand those instances where conformity is necessary in order to develop democratic processes.

[3] *Ibid.,* pp. 13–16.

Premature structuring of the class discussion may act as a deterrent to creativity.[4] The teacher will remember that when discussion is used for creative purposes it should not be too heavily structured. It is also important for her to remember that the process is as important as the product when originality is being encouraged into reality. The teacher will also keep in mind that the part she plays in the discussion will close or open the flow of ideas. Her comments will help children to clarify what they have said or will reflect their feelings, but will not close issues. Her questions will be open-ended in that they suggest new ideas rather than one set solution. The teacher will look for the uncommon response, the remote or unusual ideas, and the cleverness of responses to give her cues for leading the discussion forward toward creative production.

In creative discussion children are able to make use of a question: they examine it, think it through, and create answers of their own rather than coming up with a preconceived one.

The teacher will need to be aware that some research on group processes in its relation to creativity shows that groups have tremendous influence on individuals and individuals often conform to the opinion of group majority—even when they are right.[5] Ability to be independent seems to be less possible under social pressures.[6] Yet independence in human beings is essential for creative production. Part of the teacher's job will be to help individuals who have unusual or different beliefs to stand their ground until proven incorrect. On the other hand, the teacher will help all group members to be tolerant of any one person's ideas until they are proven to be impractical for the situation.

Research also shows that we may expect greater descriptive social stress when classroom groups are divided heterogeneously than when they are divided homogeneously. Creative thinking is stimulated by social stress. It would seem then that heterogeneous grouping in a classroom might be more productive than homogeneous grouping.[7]

In Chapter IV of this book some attention was given to the fact

[4] Barbara Biber, "Premature Structuring as a Deterrent to Creativity," *American Journal of Orthopsychiatry*, XXIX (1959), pp. 280–290.

[5] S. E. Asch, "Studies of Independence and Conformity: 1. A Minority of One Against a Unanimous Majority," *Psychological Monographs*, LXX, No. 416 (1956).

[6] G. Moeller and M. J. Applezeig, "A Motivational Factor in Conformity," *Journal Abnormal Psychology*, LV (1957), pp. 114–120.

[7] E. Paul Torrance, "Can Grouping Control Social Stress in Creative Activities?" *Elementary School Journal*, LXII (December, 1961), pp. 139–145.

that some "positive" tension is necessary as a condition to stimulate creativity. On the other hand, research has shown that excess stress may disrupt thinking and diminish productivity. This was referred to as "negative" tension earlier in this volume. Torrance has concluded that social stress may be controlled in the classroom to some degree by using various patterns of grouping.

Class discussions can serve other purposes. They may help children learn when to conform. Many class discussions may be directed toward convergent thinking or used as a problem-solving device. These discussions will differ from those directed toward divergent thinking or creativity.

The fetish for getting everyone to participate in a discussion can be overdone. Also, the fetish of discussion for discussion's sake is pointless.

How can a teacher control or evaluate problem-solving class discussion so it is worthwhile? In some classrooms children have learned to talk and talk—but they don't talk about much!

First of all, a class discussion must have a purpose—*and every child should be aware of that purpose!* In a classroom where chart-making is encouraged, one chart might be entitled, "What Makes a Good Discussion" and may be used as a guide for the class. A review of this chart before each class discussion will focus the purpose of the discussion and the techniques for discussion more clearly. In a fifth or sixth grade such a chart might read as follows:

DISCUSSIONS

1. What is the purpose of our discussion?
    A. Are we trying to settle an issue?
    B. Solve a problem?
    C. Make a judgment?
    D. Build an attitude?
    E. Share ideas?
2. How shall we go about our discussion?
    A. Who will act as chairman?
    B. Do we need a recorder?
    C. Do we need an observer?
    D. Will we need follow-up committees?
    E. Consultants?
3. How will we conduct our discussion?
    A. Give everyone a chance to present his views.
    B. Stick to the problem at hand.
    C. Seek for facts when they are needed.
    D. Avoid arguments if possible.
    E. Do not interrupt. Be courteous.

4. Evaluation
   A. Was discussion well conducted?
   B. Did we accomplish our purpose?
   C. What are our next steps?

After each discussion is over, a quick check of the chart will serve as an evaluation device.

The teacher's role in a class discussion is that of guidance, the degree of which will vary with the topic under discussion and the types of children involved. In working toward a solution to a problem, the teacher may plan questions that are thought-provoking and which will keep the group from wandering off on a tangent. With her wide background of experiences, she will be able to make suggestions and offer pertinent factual material. At times she will be chairman or leader according to the nature of the discussion. Much of her skill will be determined by her ability to ask pertinent questions as discussed on page 180.

In discussions whose goal is to develop creative solutions or invent some original idea, the teacher will take a less active part and will listen carefully to the contribution of each child, recognizing and lauding the original contributions all the children make.

Different kinds of questions for different kinds of guidance are necessary. A question such as, "What do we already know about such rules that will help us?" invites recall and previous knowledge. A question such as, "How would you feel if this was done to you?" invites emotional response and the power of empathy. And a question such as, "It seems that no one to this time has ever had this problem before, so what can we suggest as a solution?" calls for creative response.

There will be many discussions much more informal and unplanned than these imply. Nevertheless, the teacher functions in the same capacity. She keeps the discussion directed to a purpose; she reflects individual and group feelings and clarifies the progress of the group by helping them verbalize clearly what they are thinking; she facilitates communication.

In the lower grades, the informal discussion is more common than the more formal planned discussion, though, even at this level, there will be times when class discussions will be planned and group decisions made.

A teacher who has not conducted group discussions may be easily discouraged. She must remember it is difficult for the children until they practice, too. She can assure herself of greater success if she structures her first discussions rather heavily. Later the class will take over gradually. She can preplan with a committee and delegate responsibility. One child can act as secretary and recorder to write down the important points. One can serve as an observer; he watches the group for participation, checking for arguments, for domination by one person, and other shortcomings. Many teachers are acquainted with group processes now popular in adult groups and their applicability, with alterations, to various class levels.

It is well to have some check to be sure all children who want to are participating. The use of a flo-graph is helpful here, since it shows the teacher how the conversation is going. To insure worthwhile discussion, the environment is most important. Democratic discussions are encouraged when children and adults sit in an informal circle or at least see each other. The teacher or chairman presents the topic. Teachers may structure the first discussion by stating the job of the recorder, the observers, and the chairman, and by designating each member of the group as a contributor. Leadership fluctuates with the flow of the contributions.

On a piece of paper, the teacher has a series of circles to represent each student. As they speak she writes a name in the circle and then draws a line from it to the next person speaking, and so on. A supply of such sheets duplicated previously and kept handy makes the flo-graph comparatively easy to use. This graph clearly shows the number of people who have participated and the flow of the conversation. It does not attempt to record what was said—it is a measure of the dynamics of the group.

A flo-graph may be coded to give a teacher a more accurate picture of the *kinds* of participation within the group. Sometimes the child who talks a great deal *appears* to be taking a very active part in discussion and may seem to have a well-developed concept of group dynamics. A closer examination of his contribution may reveal it to be merely questions or repetition of other members' contributions.

A suggested code is as follows:

> C—contribution
> RR—repeats what someone else has said
> Q—asks a question
> R—makes a response to a question

Using this code, a flo-graph was designed which looked like the one in Figure 12–1.

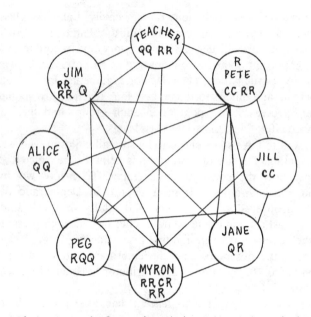

FIGURE 12–1. *A simple flo-graph will show the teacher whether a group discussion is dominated by one person (top), or whether it is a cooperative sharing of ideas (bottom).*

This graph reveals the following facts:

1. The part that each person played in the discussion is easily diagnosed.
2. The teacher asked two questions and gave two responses.
3. Jim asked two questions and repeated what someone else had said twice.
4. Alice asked two questions.
5. Peg asked two questions and answered one question.
6. Myron made a contribution and answered three questions.
7. Jane asked a question and answered one.
8. Jill made two contributions.
9. Pete made two contributions and gave one answer to a question.
10. All members participated in the discussion, which moved from one person to the other very freely.

We now see, however, that some people ask questions or repeat what others say. If this pattern continues repeatedly, the teacher knows which children need help in developing discussion skills.

Some teachers use "participation charts" for recording the dynamics of the discussion. A supply of duplicated sheets is kept

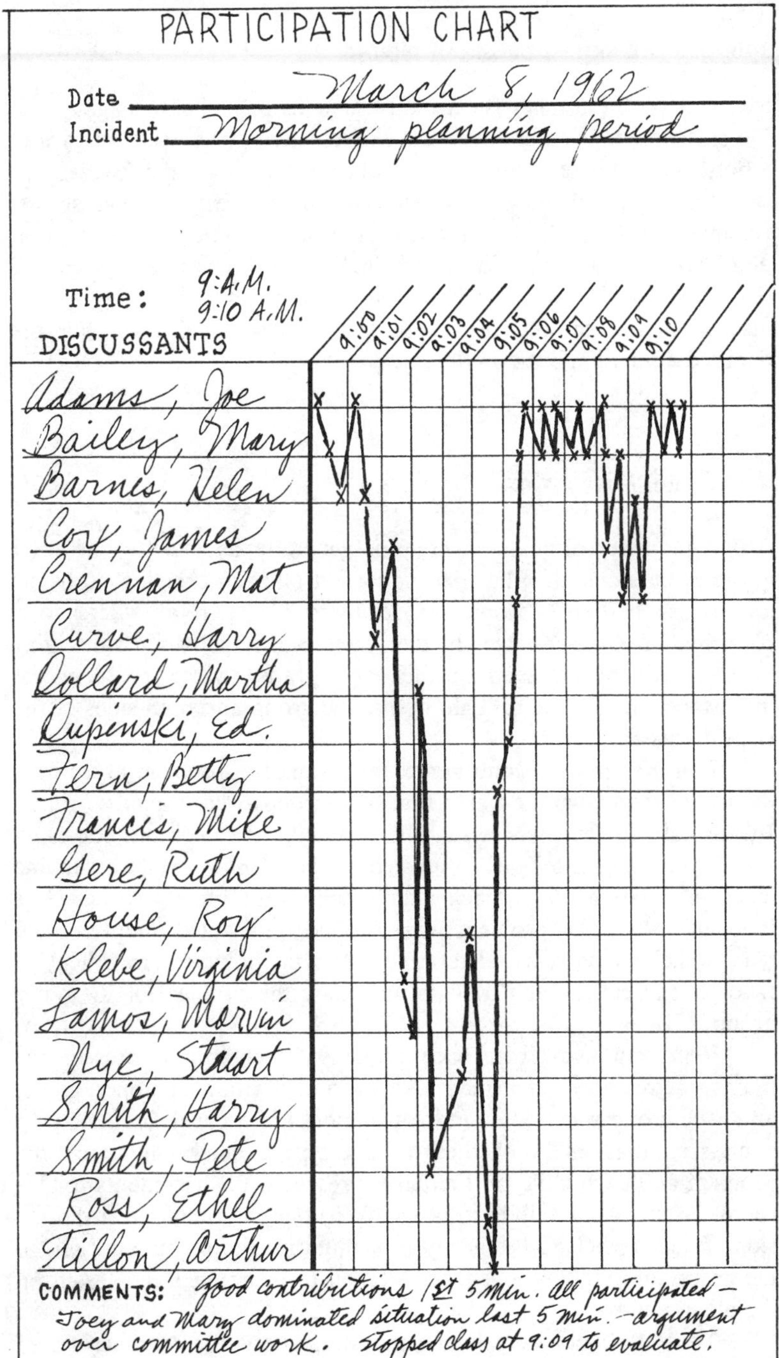

FIGURE 12–2. A sample participation chart will help teachers and children follow the trend of discussion and will help to avoid deadlocks.

available by the teacher for instant use. This helps her see again who the participants were and how the conversation progressed. In case of a bottleneck, where two people get into an argument, the teacher can stop the class and show the chart. The chart in Figure 12–2 shows, for instance, that in a fifth-grade class discussion between 9:05 A.M. and 9:10 A.M. Joe and Helen dominated the discussion. The rest of the class was bored and discourteous. So the teacher stopped the discussion and showed the chart, and a hasty evaluation put the derailed discussion back on the track.

The Panel Discussion

Although panel discussions are not generally as effective as total group discussions, they have an important place in bringing problems and issues before a group—especially a large group where total participation is impossible. In the classroom, panel discussions may be used effectively, even in the early grades, when problems of importance need to be brought before the group and both sides of the issue discussed.

In a first and a second grade, for instance, a problem arose over the use of the playground area that both groups were forced to share. In this case the teachers wisely did not make the decisions for using the playground. Instead, they utilized the *problem* to create a genuine learning situation. Each teacher discussed the problem with her class independently. The problem was clarified and stated simply. Each teacher helped her class determine the main points of argument in favor of the class. Each tried to anticipate the problem of the other group.

Representatives from each group were chosen to present the main arguments. A chairman was appointed from an upper grade, and each group was briefed in the techniques of a panel discussion. In a classroom assembly of the two grades the chairman stated the problem and each child on the panel presented the arguments for his room. After all the children had spoken, the chairman led a discussion. Teachers helped the group to summarize the points and guided the group into making a general decision to be applied and tested on the playground.

These teachers were laying the foundations for effective use of panel discussions in upper grades. A panel discussion contributes some unique factors which a general discussion does not. It can be more carefully planned and thought through as groups anticipate the trend of discussion. It gives training in critical thinking since it calls for "projection" into the other fellow's mind in order to see his point of view. It gives each person (or side) a chance to state the problem and to present points before the general discussion takes place, thus economizing on time. And, hopefully, a panel discussion results in some creative solutions to problems.

Teachers using panel discussions for the first time should point out their value to the children to be sure that they understand the purpose of using this as a particular technique at this specific time. The children will need to learn the techniques for conducting a panel, which is equally as important as the subject-matter. At first the panel may be crude and faltering, but an evaluation of the technique, as well as the material covered, will help refine the process for later use.

There is much value in the meeting of people to express conflicting ideas and to make points relative to these ideas. In this instance, a group of people meets before an audience and each presents his case—generally about one topic. Individual preparation has gone into this situation, but there has been little group preparation. The motivation is present because the topic is generally one of current interest. This is more commonly known as a "symposium" than as a panel discussion. The panel discussion is better used by groups as a technique for arriving at a consensus about their own problems.

Also, it often lays the basis for debating, which is another effective group process even for intermediate-grade pupils.

Buzz Groups

"Buzz" groups are extremely valuable in instances where the class is too large to be handled effectively in a general discussion. They are also effective for smaller groups. In the classroom they can help the teacher who has a large number of children to find instances for using democratic procedures without losing control of the group.

Buzz groups can be used in many ways. A teacher beginning a unit may be overwhelmed by numbers of children who wish to put questions on the board. She is conscious of the value of independent contributions and of the dangers of crushing some children who do not often participate, yet physical limits often make it impossible for her to respond fully to the demands of her conscience. She can control the situation by dividing the class into buzz groups, where children just turn around and face each other in small groups and discuss the question at hand. In this instance she may structure the buzz group by telling each group to choose a leader and then for the group to think of a list of ten questions they would like to have put on the board. At the end of ten or fifteen minutes, each leader reads his questions, which are put on the board. Duplications are checked to indicate the strongest interests of the class as a whole. In this manner, each child has had the opportunity to contribute, and a true opinion of the class interest is observed.

Teachers who do not have immediate success with buzz groups will perhaps need to structure them more carefully at first. They may meet with a committee of "leaders" and set up some criteria for conducting a group.

It is important in this instance that the leaders change frequently. It is also wise to discuss buzz groups and their purpose before using them with the entire group. As the mechanics are understood, the teacher will find children using buzz sessions fluently.

Teachers may use buzz groups in various ways. It is an effective method for getting issues before the class; it may be used for obtaining divergent ideas about a class problem; it may be a technique to use in discussing a report, an assembly program, or a sociodrama.

Brainstorming

One technique that has been used to promote creative ideation in industry, and which some teachers have used effectively in the classroom, is brainstorming.

There are some basic ground rules about brainstorming which must be followed in order for it to be successful. First, the problem that needs a creative solution must be carefully defined. The scope of the problem must be limited, and everyone must understand it completely.

Second, a noncritical, informal, nonjudicial atmosphere must be established in the classroom. The teacher makes it clear that no negative comments or criticisms are to be accepted, and judgment will be deferred. No one is to consider anyone else's idea as useless or silly. To do so may cut off the flow of creative ideas. In fact, unusual, bizarre ideas are to be encouraged. Sometimes such ideas spark others that are more practical. But this decision is made only after all the ideas are expressed.

The problem is posed, and each person raises his hand if he has an idea. The objective is to obtain a large quantity of ideas in a short period of time. Through a tape recorder, or a stenographer, or by writing on the chalkboard as quickly as possible, every idea is recorded. Should an idea from one person give another one an idea along the same line, the second person snaps his fingers to show the two ideas fit together. This is often called a "hitchhiking" idea, and writing them together serves the purpose of grouping similar ideas on the chalkboard. The teacher's objective is to urge responses from the children in a short period of time. She may even say, "Let's see how many ideas we can get on the chalkboard in the next five minutes." At the end of the five minutes (if ideas still seem to be coming) she may say, "Good—we have fifteen ideas in five minutes, let's see if we can get five more in the next three minutes!"

After the ideas are all on the chalkboard, criteria are applied to each, and those which cannot possibly be used because they fall outside the criteria are erased. Each of the other ideas is considered (each for its own merit) until the one that seems most appropriate for the situation is chosen. Sometimes the total list of ideas may be turned over to a small committee who meet later with the teacher to evaluate it. This meeting should be held as soon after the initial brainstorming session as possible.

In a fourth-grade class at the end of the year, $20 remained in the class treasury. The children had raised money for their contribution to a school TV set by giving a country fair as a culminating activity to a travel agency unit. The affair had been so successful that they had netted the $20 after their contribution was made and their expenses paid. They held a brainstorming session to determine ways they might use the $20. Among the ideas suggested were:

1. Have a theater party.
2. Support the community chest.
3. Have a class picnic.
4. Buy a gift for the school—
   a. a TV rolling stand (hitchhiking idea),
   b. some film strips (hitchhiking idea),
   c. a trophy case (hitchhiking idea).
5. Buy something for the old people's home.
6. Buy materials for the classroom.
7. Give it to the teacher.

8. Split it up among themselves.
9. Have a class party.
10. Hire a bus for a field trip (several places were suggested).
11. Buy candy.
12. Have a dance and invite the fifth grade.
13. Buy a transistor radio, etc.

A committee went through a list of some forty different ideas and recommended the class picnic. They decided to make it the most unusual picnic they had ever attended. This led to other brainstorming sessions, which resulted in a "kookie" picnic. It was held in the morning. They ate breakfast out of doors. One committee invented a kind of "kookie" pancake, and they made honey syrup to put on it. In addition, the menu consisted of Egyptian eye egg sandwiches, bacon strips, fruit juice, "kookie" cookies, and jam and toast.

They played "kook" games, one group put on a skit, they made up a "kookie" song, and designed "kookie" paper plates and napkins from which to eat. In this instance, the brainstorming technique resulted in unusual creative thinking and production.

Developing Evaluation Skills

Guilford has said that thinking factors fall into three general groups. There is a group of *cognition* factors, a group of *production* factors, and a group of *evaluation* factors. We become aware of a problem with which we are confronted, we produce something of our own because of this awareness, and we evaluate the product of our thought. He states that a total creative act involves all three aspects mentioned above.[8]

Evaluation is a part of the creative learning process. It contributes to the development of creativity in that it keeps learnings from closing in and becoming complete. It provides the open-endedness to learning which is so essential to divergent thinking. By using evaluation, the teacher helps the group assess its acquired skills and learnings but immediately applies this assessment to new and more complex learnings.

Evaluation is wide in scope and may be applied to the individual, to the group, to the process, or to the total program; and since none of these can be considered in isolation, evaluation must be concerned with all of the involved interrelationships.

[8] J. P. Guilford, "Creative Abilities in the Arts," *Psychological Review,* LIV (1957), pp. 110–118.

Because evaluation is a part of the creative learning process, the teacher should help each child to evaluate himself. The student may be evaluated in terms of any or all of the following: readiness, intelligence, achievement, social and emotional development, physical and mental health, creativeness, and special talents and abilities. Evaluation must also be concerned with the interrelationships of these factors.

Self-Evaluation

Self-evaluation can be achieved in many ways. Children evaluate when they first come to the kindergarten. When a five-year-old says, "That is good," or "I like that story," he is, in essence, evaluating. When the teacher asks primary children to tell what they think about Jimmy's picture and asks Jimmy if he had fun doing it, she is asking them to evaluate.

Some instances where self-evaluation may be employed have been described in this book. The spelling record mentioned in Book II in this series can be used effectively if children learn to study it for what it is worth. Children in all classrooms should have their own folders arranged in an easily accessible file drawer. In these folders they can place samples of their creative writing, as mentioned in Book II. They can also keep samples of their handwriting, their arithmetic papers, and their teacher-made tests to study their own progress from time to time.

The techniques for self-evaluation are numerous. Children must be taught the value of all of them. Some methods which can be used effectively with children are given below.

Observation. Children must be helped to be keen observers. Acute observation is the base of both the creative process and the scientific process. Sensitive observation may be applied to self-evaluation in the following way:

1. Did I do the job as well as I can?
2. Does the paper look as well or better than the others I have done?
3. Did I omit any parts of the exam?
4. Did I leave out any capitalization and punctuation?
5. Have I put away all my materials?
6. Did I omit any main parts of the outline?
7. What sort of impression did I make on the class?
8. Did I do the job assigned to me?
9. Have I found all the information necessary to make a complete report?

10. Am I able to read maps correctly?
11. Do I understand charts and graphs?
12. Do I get the point of this cartoon?
13. Do I get the main idea from this picture?
14. Does the filmstrip mean something to me?
15. Am I able to find the parts from a film for which the class is looking?
16. Does the diorama or exhibit tell me something?
17. Am I able to see the purpose in the bulletin board?
18. Was I able to get the right sequence of events in the television show?
19. To how many new uses can I put this information?
20. For what can I use this material?
21. How could I make that color with tempera paint?

A teacher must realize that observations by children (indeed, by many adults) is often accompanied by inaccuracy or emotion. Often children, like adults, see only what they *want* to see. Self-deception and distorted perception are common partners of faulty observation. The teacher's goal will be to continually refine accuracy in observation and reporting. She will also guide the children to improve the accuracy of observations made in relation to their predictions. This aspect is illustrated in Book VII of this series, *Creative Teaching of Science in the Elementary School.*

Listening. Listening can be used by children as an evaluation skill in situations such as the following:

1. Did I follow all directions carefully?
2. Did I hear all the main ideas?
3. Did I hear the plans for this period so that I know exactly what to do?
4. Did I understand the ideas Bill was trying to get across in his report?
5. Was I attentive when the announcement was made so that I know exactly what I am to bring and what my part is in the program?
6. Did I get the idea of the joke?
7. Was the musical background of the television show appropriate?
8. Did the consultant really tell us what we wanted to know about Alaska?
9. Was I able to fill in my notes from what the teacher told me?
10. Do these words end with the same sound?
11. Do I sound well on the telephone?

Skills for the teaching of listening can be found in Book II of this series. Children can evaluate many of their own activities by using listening as an evaluation skill.

Conferences. Conferences may be held for evaluation purposes frequently. Self-evaluation on the part of the child may play a very important part in these conferences.

In Miss Stillman's fifth grade, the children helped to evaluate their own progress every five weeks through the conference technique. Two afternoons were set aside during the week when Miss Stillman scheduled a conference with each child. On these two days, Miss Stillman planned the daily program with her group very carefully so that all children were gainfully occupied during the conference periods. Usually each child planned his entire afternoon around assignments made by Miss Stillman, his own unfinished work, and work with special teachers and consultants.

Miss Stillman placed a conference table in the rear of the room where she could be somewhat removed from the class but where she could see all the children while she worked with one child at a time. As each child took a seat by Miss Stillman she opened his folder and read to him the last report letter which had been sent home. After reading the letter, Miss Stillman asked such questions as these:

MISS STILLMAN: In your last report letter it said that you weren't doing as well as you could do in arithmetic, Johnny. I know mother has been helping you at home. How do you feel about your arithmetic now?

JOHNNY: I know I'm doing better, Miss Stillman. I've had better papers.

MISS STILLMAN: Yes, you have. Let's look at your folder. My, these *are* good papers. I'm real proud of your progress, Johnny. I guess I'll have to say we've just about got this problem solved when I talk to mother next time or when I send home your next report. Don't you think so?

JOHNNY: Yes.

MISS STILLMAN: John, there is one other thing mentioned here on which we were going to work. Last time we agreed we would try to help you to do a better job in group discussion. You interrupted all the time and did not wait your turn. How do you feel about that?

JOHNNY: I think I'm better. I've been trying hard.

MISS STILLMAN: Yes, I've noticed that. One thing that has helped is that you are stopping to think about what you plan to say and as a result you say more when it is your turn. I'm glad you have learned to organize. I'm proud of the way you have worked on that problem, too, Johnny. Now, tell me how you feel about the rest of your school work.

JOHNNY: Well, I think I'm doing okay in everything else. I like school.

MISS STILLMAN: I'm glad about that. How do you feel about your reading? Do you read much outside of school?

JOHNNY: No, I don't read much outside but I guess I'm doing okay in reading. I like to read.

MISS STILLMAN: I'm glad you like to read. That is the most important thing. But I am a little concerned about your reading. Johnny, do you remember some tests we took just about the time we had our play about Robin Hood? Well, I want to tell you why I gave you those tests. They showed me how well you *can* do. Now the tests you took in reading last week also told me something. They told me you are not doing as well as you can do. I'd like to suggest that you start taking books home to read. Days are getting shorter now and you won't be able to play outdoors as long and perhaps you can find some time to read each evening after dinner. I think that will help you.

JOHNNY: Okay.

MISS STILLMAN: How do you feel you are getting along with the other children?

JOHNNY: Fine.

MISS STILLMAN: Let's talk about your study skills. I've watched you work and I have a few notes here that I'd like to share with you. First of all I'd like to say I think you are a good worker. Your work is always done on time, and you work very well independently (*etc.*).

After these conferences Miss Stillman wrote summary reports of the children's progress to go home to the parents. Each child's letter was read to him before it was typed so that he and the teacher could discuss any points he did not understand. When the letter went home, each child was able to discuss it with his parents. Miss Stillman used these letters as a basis of her conferences with the parents.

Conferences of this sort help the child to develop self-understanding and self-awareness. Self-awareness is a characteristic that must be exploited to develop creative people—self-awareness leads to self-realization. Roe has said, "You cannot be easily manipulated if you know more about yourself than your would-be manipulator does."[9] Self-awareness suggests an ability to look at one's self objectively.

In one school system, simplified conferences of this nature were held with kindergarten children. The conference was based on the checking of a series of stick-figure cartoons. One showed a child sharing with other children. The teacher asked the child, "Do you think you share well?" If the child said "Yes," and the teacher agreed, a check was placed in a little box drawn under the left side of

[9] Anne Roe, "Man's Forgotten Weapon," *American Psychologist,* XIV (1959), p. 263.

HOW WELL DO I STUDY ?

Name _____

Grade _____ Date _____

STUDY SKILLS	I DO THIS VERY WELL	I DO THIS WELL	I DO THIS FAIRLY WELL	I DO THIS POORLY
1. I FIND OUT WHAT I HAVE TO DO				
2. I GET MY MATERIALS READY				
3. I GO TO WORK AT ONCE				
4. I REMOVE ALL DISTRACTIONS				
5. I GET HELP WHEN I NEED IT				
6. I FINISH MY WORK ON TIME				
7. I PLAN FOR EXTRA TIME WHEN I NEED IT				
REPORTS—CONTENT				
1. I READ MY ASSIGNMENT CAREFULLY				
2. I DO ALL PARTS OF THE ASSIGNMENT				
3. I USE MATERIALS WELL				
4. I PLAN MY REPORT WELL				
5. I GIVE MY REPORTS WELL				
6. I AM ABLE TO HOLD THE INTEREST OF THE CLASS				

FIGURE 12–3. *A primary rating scale.*

FIGURE 12–4. *A self-rating scale.*

the picture. If the teacher and child talked it over and felt he needed to work on this, a check was made in a box on the right side of the picture.

Conferences with children can be held for each subject. Through a series of questions the teacher helps the child evaluate himself. These conferences need not always be formally arranged as in the case of Miss Stillman. They may well be the casual, informal type that takes place when a child hands in an assignment or when the teacher sits in a chair beside him.

Rating Scales. Children can be taught to use self-evaluating rating scales. The kindergarten picture-card mentioned above is really a simplified rating scale. Any device that puts judgments on a continuum may be classified as a rating scale, which may be used for group evaluation as well as for individual evaluation.

In a sixth grade where Mr. Salem was trying to develop good study skills among his boys and girls, they listed together what they considered to be good study habits. Once a month they rated them-

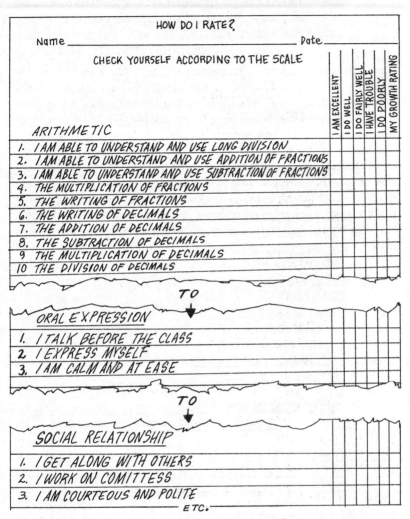

HOW DO I RATE?					
Name _____ Date _____					
CHECK YOURSELF ACCORDING TO THE SCALE	I AM EXCELLENT	I DO WELL	I DO FAIRLY WELL	I HAVE TROUBLE	I DO POORLY	MY GROWTH RATING
ARITHMETIC						
1. I AM ABLE TO UNDERSTAND AND USE LONG DIVISION						
2. I AM ABLE TO UNDERSTAND AND USE ADDITION OF FRACTIONS						
3. I AM ABLE TO UNDERSTAND AND USE SUBTRACTION OF FRACTIONS						
4. THE MULTIPLICATION OF FRACTIONS						
5. THE WRITING OF FRACTIONS						
6. THE WRITING OF DECIMALS						
7. THE ADDITION OF DECIMALS						
8. THE SUBTRACTION OF DECIMALS						
9 THE MULTIPLICATION OF DECIMALS						
10 THE DIVISION OF DECIMALS						
TO						
ORAL EXPRESSION						
1. I TALK BEFORE THE CLASS						
2. I EXPRESS MYSELF						
3. I AM CALM AND AT EASE						
TO						
SOCIAL RELATIONSHIP						
1. I GET ALONG WITH OTHERS						
2. I WORK ON COMITTESS						
3. I AM COURTEOUS AND POLITE						
ETC.						

FIGURE 12–5. *A self-rating scale.*

selves according to a scale they set up. Figure 12–5 shows Mr. Salem's rating scale.

In Miss Andrews' third grade, children evaluated themselves by using a rating scale which Miss Andrews drew and ran off on a ditto machine. She used simple stick drawings which the children checked, as shown in Figure 12–3. Another class used the rating scale shown in Figure 12–6 to evaluate each person's work habits. Such rating scales can be used in a variety of ways to help children assess their own progress.

Teacher-made Tests. Teacher-made tests serve two basic purposes: they tell the teacher how much the child has learned and how well she has taught. When tests are handed in, corrected, and the grades recorded, they do not really serve as an evaluation device. But if the teacher uses the test for further teaching or as a diagnostic instrument to help the individual child, it serves an evaluative purpose.

Teacher-made tests may help children evaluate their own progress when they are carefully corrected, when personal notes are written along the margins, and when they are used for individual conferences. They may also serve as a springboard for keeping personal charts and profiles from which each child can see his own growth.

	ALWAYS	USUALLY	SOMETIMES	NEVER	NOT SURE
I TAKE PART IN ACTIVITIES					
I LIKE TO TRY OUT NEW IDEAS					
I VOLUNTEER FOR COMMITTEE WORK					
I WORK WELL WITH OTHERS					
I WORK WELL ALONE					
I SHARE MY IDEAS					
I LISTEN TO THE OTHER FELLOW'S IDEAS					
I AM COURTEOUS WHEN I WORK WITH OTHERS					
I STAY WITH THE JOB UNTIL IT IS FINISHED					
I KEEP MY TEMPER WHEN PEOPLE DO NOT AGREE WITH ME					

Name _____ Grade _____ Date _____

HOW WELL DO I WORK WITH OTHERS?

FIGURE 12–6 *Checklist for self-evaluation of ability to work with others.*

Pupil-made Tests. In evaluating knowledge and some skills, pupil-made tests are appropriate for classroom use. They can serve as an evaluation device for the teacher as well as self-evaluation for the child. They also afford an opportunity for creative development.

In the intermediate grades children reveal what they are learning as much by the questions they ask as by the answers they give. It is on this premise that pupil-made tests are valuable.

In a fifth grade, Mr. Herring finished teaching a unit on the Middle Ages. He felt his students had learned a great deal. He talked with them about the things they had learned and asked if they knew of ways he could find out exactly what each person had learned. They suggested a test. Mr. Herring felt this was the opportunity for which he had been waiting to use pupil-made tests.

Mr. Herring set aside a period to teach the children about test-making. He discussed first with them the reasons behind testing; these were listed on the board. Then he asked the children to think of all the tests they had ever taken and asked them to think specifically about the kinds of questions they had answered. The following list resulted:

1. True and false.
2. Making choices.
3. Filling in blanks.
4. Matching.
5. Ending sentences.
6. Writing about a question (essay).
7. Choosing correct answers.

Using each type of question, the class proceeded to make up some samples from their Middle Ages unit. Mr. Herring then asked them if they felt they could make up a good test about the Middle Ages. The children were eager to try.

It was decided that all the people who had worked on various committees would meet together. They would review their reports for the class and then proceed to make up the following:

5 true-false questions
5 matching questions
5 filling-in-blanks questions
5 sentences to be completed
5 multiple-choice questions
5 selection questions
1 creative application question

These were to be handed to Mr. Herring. He was to edit them, delete duplications, and make a composite of the remaining items.

Mr. Herring was well able to tell how much his group had learned by the questions that were submitted. Nevertheless, the test was dittoed, and each child took it. From it he was able to evaluate himself in these ways:

1. Facts he had learned from the unit.
2. How well he had listened to reports.
3. How much he had learned from the unit as compared with other members of the class.
4. How well he had observed the exhibits, bulletin boards, etc.
5. How well he had studied.
6. How well he was able to select what the classroom committees felt were the main ideas.

Pupil-made tests may be constructed in a variety of ways and for a variety of purposes. They serve both teacher and children to good purpose in the evaluation process.

Standardized Tests. Standardized test results can be useful to children if they are used discreetly and with a great deal of interpretation. If the rapport in a school is such that children can have the test interpreted in relation to their ability, these tests are very valuable in helping children evaluate their own progress from year to year. Profile charts of individual scores can be made yearly, using a different colored pencil from year to year on the same chart so that the child can see his growth in the same area.

The danger in using achievement test scores with children is that grade-levels are used more than subject-age or growth-age. A child with an I.Q. of 90 cannot do a complete year's work in a year. A nine-month gain each year is normal for this child. Half of any class will be below grade level if the group is a normal one. Therefore, in using achievement test profiles teachers should explain to the child that a certain line on the chart shows what he is capable of doing and the colored pencil shows what he *is* doing. When these lines are far apart they indicate a problem, which teaching and learning may correct. When the lines are fairly congruent (whether the child is up to grade level or not), it means he is performing normally according to his intelligence (even though he may be two years below grade level).

Standardized tests often serve as an individual diagnostic device as well as a measuring device for pupils.

Graphs and Charts. Research shows that slow-learning and

average children learn best in cooperative environments, and that bright children tend to thrive under some competition. In all cases, self-competition is a stronger motivation than peer competition. Charts, graphs, and profile charts provide an excellent way for children to keep their own grades and scores and to have a long-term pictorial record of their progress. Continued encouragement and help from the teacher will keep the child striving to do better each week.

Self-evaluating Stories. In the section on creative writing (Book II of this series, Chapter V) a device was suggested which can well be used as an evaluation technique. Children were encouraged to write stories about themselves and their feelings. These topics were suggested:

> How I Feel About Tests.
> How I Feel About School.
> The Person I Like Most.
> (To these the following might be added:)
> What Am I Like?
> What Kind of Person Am I?
> How Good Am I in School?
> Me as a Speaker.
> My Self-Portrait.
> My Feeling About Arithmetic (or Spelling, Social Studies, etc.).
> What I Think About My Teacher.
> Things That Make Me Angry.
> People I Like in School.
> What I Thought About John's Report.
> My Book Report.

Simply by organizing his thoughts to write about such topics, a child must evaluate himself. The value of writing in this fashion is enhanced if the child is not required to put his name on papers, where he might feel threatened if he expressed himself freely. The act of writing itself serves as a catharsis for the child, and the material he writes can be of great importance to the teacher.

Autobiographies, Logs, etc. Autobiographies, logs, and other types of records help children to keep records of their activities from day to day and can be of great help in evaluation when reread at some later date. How often a child in the spring, reading what he did in September, says, "I did that! Gee whiz! Was I a dope!" Self-evaluation of personal growth!

Pupil Files. Pupil files have been mentioned as a means of keeping records for comparison of work from month to month. They can serve as a cache for keeping graphs, test records, profile charts, and other evaluative material.

One other use of the pupil file is that it serves as an informal method of communication from teacher to pupil. It is a simple matter for a teacher to write a note to a child when she examines some of his work after school, either to praise him or to offer suggestions to him. These notes can be dropped in his file. If children are encouraged to look in their file folders each day, this can become an effective way of pupil-teacher evaluation on an individual basis. Teachers can often leave work sheets made by them or torn from a workbook with a note clipped on it for a child who needs extra help. If the teacher also has a file folder in the drawer, children can be encouraged to drop finished material and informal notes into the teacher's file. This means a more orderly accumulation of materials for the teacher than having the material dropped all over her desk.

As teachers work with children and give them increasing responsibility and independence, together they will discover many ways for pupils to evaluate themselves. It is important to remember that the techniques must be chosen in terms of the goals to be evaluated, but that they must also be viewed in terms of numerous other criteria. Evaluation should serve as a steppingstone toward planning the next course of action. Objectivity aids in decreasing the degree of error in evaluation, so children should be made aware of objectiveness in their evaluation experiences. The technique must always be tested in terms of reliability—does it measure consistently what it purports to measure? Is it valid and is it practical? Can the children understand the directions and purpose for using it?

Group Evaluation

To establish a working rapport and to bring a group spirit into play, continual group evaluation is as necessary as continual individual evaluation. Consciousness on the part of the members as to their contribution to group progress is essential if group living is to be realized in a classroom.

Throughout this text, reference has been made to the evaluation procedures necessary to promote group growth. This evaluation is an integral part of the instructional program. Evaluation is the summarizing of evidence at a given point which gives proof of group growth and a remustering of forces into a new plan to move ahead.

Group evaluation is of necessity a cooperative process. The

group sets an objective; it works toward that objective; and it evaluates in light of that objective. This may be done in terms of one period during the school day or for a semester or a year's work, depending on the objective or purpose being evaluated.

A second grade plans to attend its first assembly program in the auditorium. The teacher prepares the children so that they may meet this new experience securely. The trip is planned and each child understands: (1) the purpose of the trip and (2) his responsibility to his group on the trip. After the trip is over, the group evaluates in terms of its purposes.

Likewise, in launching a unit the group establishes long-term purposes and as the unit progresses they are evaluated to determine whether or not the purposes are being achieved. In this manner children learn to face their obligations to the class and, later, to the community.

The teacher may have objectives for the group which are not the objectives the group has for itself. She may, for example, have as one of her objectives helping each member of the group grow in ability to assume responsibility toward group procedure. In this case, she provides opportunities for individuals to assume responsibility in group situations.

The teacher must evaluate the outcome of her planning. After her goals and objectives are clear, she must try to envision behavior patterns in the work of the children which show her purposes are being developed. She sees each member of the class assuming leadership at one time, offering suggestions at one time, bringing in material for group work, and speaking freely before the group. As these behavior patterns occur in her classroom, she is reassured that her methods are working effectively and that her goals are being accomplished. Anecdotal records are important for recording evidence such as this, as well as other evidence of group behavior, so that she may later study and interpret this evidence. From these interpretations the teacher is able to plan the next step in meeting her goals or establishing new group goals.

It is important whether it be the group's evaluation of itself or the teacher's evaluation of the group, that the evidence be gathered from many situations. The teacher will need to use many devices, and the group itself can use some individual and group techniques.

Cumulative Records. Each school should have a confidential folder for each child which will be passed from teacher to teacher. This folder should reveal a series of cards containing pertinent information on the child at home, at school, and as an individual. Samples of his report letter and summaries of parent conferences should be included. His health record, valuable and important information from agencies, and other important information will help the teacher to know the child even before he arrives in a particular classroom.

Cumulative records may also contain comments on the creative endeavor of the child as he proceeds through the school program. They help each succeeding teacher and all members of school personnel to understand each child's strengths, weaknesses, problems, and abilities. They also provide a record of what has been done to help each child with his specific problems. They help in planning a continuous remediation or corrective program. The records can reduce discontinuity of creative development in the school program and thus serve the same purpose as the parent-teacher conference does when it decreases discontinuity between the home and the school.

Summary Reports. Some school systems have their teachers write detailed summaries of the experiences children have in each grade, including the grouping arrangement, changes made in groups, etc. A copy of this is sent along with the cumulative records to each teacher. In this way the new teacher learns about the child's school life in the preceding year and about the groups and people with whom he worked.

Sociometric Techniques

Each teacher should frequently make a sociogram of her group. Sociograms provide clues for grouping. When children do not seem to group themselves effectively, a teacher may discover her isolates, "rejects," leaders and cliques. She may find clues for grouping; ideas for putting shy children on committees with children they like; ideas for helping isolates make friends in small groups. Later on, another sociogram will help her to see if her group structure has improved, and how the children are growing socially.

Personality tests also will assist the teacher in finding social and emotional areas where she can help her children.

Natural or Interest Grouping

Plenty of opportunity should be afforded children to work on committees and in groups of their own choice. At some time during the school day a child needs to feel comfortable with his friends. Oppor-

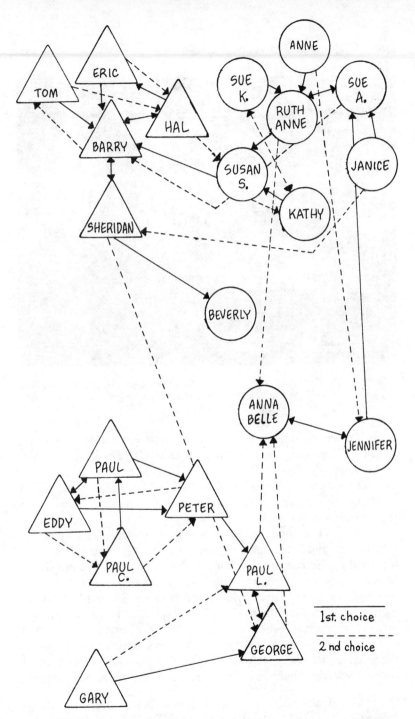

FIGURE 12–7. *A sociogram constructed for a ten-, eleven-, and twelve-year-old group readily shows the influence of the "gang" age and the "cliques" of the sexes.*

FIGURE 12–8. *Grouping meets interests: a first-grade teacher utilizes a trip to the television station to build good social relationships and a fund of knowledge.*

tunity for such grouping often presents itself in choosing teams for games, in unit work, and in sitting together for lunch or for other common interests.

The groups a child chooses naturally can provide the teacher with clues concerning his likes and dislikes and will help in discovering the child's problems.

These ideas point up the numerous ways teachers may gather evidence to make decisions concerning their classroom groups and the small groups operating within the classroom group. No one device is more important than any other. Each is used to measure some phase of the group's work. *All* should be used if needed. After the required evidence is gathered it must be organized in useful form and interpreted in terms of the children's level of development.

Michaelis[10] says evaluation involves such steps as (a) formulating goals as behaviors, (b) securing evidence on the achievement of goals in selected situations, (c) summarizing and recording evidence,

[10] John U. Michaelis, *Social Studies for Children in Democracy* (Englewood Cliffs, N.J.: Prentice-Hall, Inc., 1956), p. 395.

(d) interpreting evidence, (e) using interpretation to improve children's learnings.

Reporting to Parents

Teachers must not only teach group processes to children through classroom experiences, but must use group processes in the act of educating the parents of the children. "Reporting to parents" might be more accurately phrased "conferring with parents," for if the school situation is a good one, parents know what is going on. They meet with the teacher frequently to evaluate their child's growth process, but this is no more a report for parent than it is for teacher. It is a sharing of ideas and a formulation of plans for the child's formal education. That plan should include as many ideas and suggestions for work at home as it does work at school. To be truly creative with each child, the teacher must know all about him.

Too many schools still send home outmoded and uninformative report cards wherein a child is given a symbolic grade in the subject-matter areas and in various overt acts supposedly indicative of worthy character or personality traits. What this report hopes to do is of great doubt in the minds of many parents and many teachers. Evaluation is a part of instruction itself. Why this one small part of any evaluation program should be given such stress is difficult to imagine. To segment a child's life and to evaluate him at the end of each segment becomes absurd when we know the complexities of the growth process, how learning takes place, and the function of the school. Schools that carry on a reporting system of this kind generally consider the "report" an end-product of a teacher's evaluation of a year's work. Actually it is really the beginning. If the report is to be of any value at all, it acts as a springboard for group processes between parent and teacher for mapping out a plan of action for a child. Evaluation is in a sense diagnosis.

No teacher alone can teach a child. He needs to know how the child acts at home, his interests and hobbies, his attitudes, his experiences, his home environment. Teachers, because of their indirect acquaintance with family problems, can bring an objective point of view to the study of the child. But parents, more emotionally related to the child, will bring the more subjective points of view which are necessary if teachers are to determine causes of behavior and help the child with his problems.

On the other hand, few parents today are capable of teaching their children all they need to know without professional assistance. Parents and teachers want the same things for every child—the best education for him. Often they travel parallel roads in achieving this goal with the child running confusedly back and forth between them. It is easier and more effective to join hands—child, parent, and teacher—and travel the main road together.

There are many problems and situations that will concern every parent. The teacher will want to discuss these problems with the parents. This need not be an additional burden on the teacher, for a room-mother and father will generally do the phoning and prepare some refreshments for the meeting. The teacher will not dominate the situation; this destroys the feeling that all are going to learn together. Rather, she will act as guide and help the parents state the problems they want to discuss during the year or the activities they want to undertake. She will suggest ideas and offer necessary information, but must make sure that it is the parents' meeting and that the parents *feel* it is their meeting.

Actually, the whole process is similar to that of starting a unit with children. As a result of a first planning meeting, a committee organizes the ideas into a program for the year. The teacher introduces the parents to group processes in a way similar to working with the children. In this way, a group functions and grows along with the teacher and the educational policies of the school, the educational objectives of the classroom, and the teacher's goals. Parents and teacher work and learn together. If the meetings are structured around their problems, the interest will grow and attendance will improve. If a teacher is realistic, however, she will understand that not all parents will be able to attend these general sessions. In order to keep the absentee group informed, the recorder's minutes can be duplicated and sent home to each parent. In this way a communication line is kept open.

For problems concerning the specific child, a parent-teacher or a parent-teacher-child conference will need to be held. A record should be kept of this conference. Some teachers make out a form which they check with parents and on which they write comments as the conference progresses. One such form is included as a sample. Each school will need to work out a form best suited to its needs.

The teacher slips a carbon under one form and clips another form under the carbon. In this way the parent has a copy to take home. This is an effective way of reporting.

No evaluation session is complete unless the next step for

HILLSBORO CENTRAL SCHOOL

Parent-Teacher Conference

Donnelley, Jim   Grade 5

Name, Last   First

Date of Conference June 8, 1966   Age 10

SKILL AREA	STRONG AREA	DOES VERY WELL	DOES WELL	FAIR WORK	DOES POORLY	WEAK AREA - NEEDS HELP	COMMENTS ON PERSONALITY ADJUSTMENT, WORK HABITS, STUDY SKILLS, EMOTIONAL, SOCIAL AND PHYSICAL GROWTH:
Creative Arts	X						We discussed Jim's academic work. He is above average as a student. Mrs. Donnelley was concerned about Jim's sudden aggressiveness. He is becoming defiant at home. No signs of this in school however. We talked about the possibility of his behavior changes being a characteristic of his age—the need for peer approval as against parental approval. His striving for independence (see next page)
Language Arts							
Reading			X				
Writing				X			
Spelling				X			
Grammar				X			
Oral Expression		X					
Written Expression			X				
Social Studies	X						
Science	X						
Arithmetic Skills		X					

COMMENTS ON SKILL AREAS	SUGGESTED WAYS TO HELP AT HOME
Jim loves art work - his language arts are only fair due to his rapid physical growth, in part, which makes him clumsy at writing. He needs motivation for reading. I am going to let him chair a science committee which he likes very much	Mrs. Donnelley took home the booklet, "How Children Develop." We thought we might change Jim's home chores - his lack of responsibility may be due in part to boredom. He will tend the furnace instead of making his own bed for awhile - also help his father in the

USE ADDITIONAL SHEETS FOR COMMENTS. CARBON OF REPORT GOES
HOME WITH PARENT, ORIGINAL IS PLACED IN CUMULATIVE RECORD FILE

FIGURE 12-9. *A report form used with parents.*

progress is planned in terms of decisions reached. On the conference sheet, or on a separate form, a plan for the child should be mapped out so that parents will not negate the work of the school nor will the school confuse the child by making demands on him that are different from those of his home.

Healthy home-school cooperation is essential if the modern school is to accomplish its objectives. Blocks, such as uncommunicative "report cards," must be removed to facilitate the learning process. Parents have a right to a part in their children's education. This must not be interpreted as meaning teachers should teach what parents think they should teach. It means, rather, that the job of education is that of teaching everyone, and parents can gain security and confidence in the school only when they have an opportunity to discover, understand, and participate in what the school is doing. The teacher can provide the opportunity for the parents to learn.

When step-by-step growth is evaluated regularly, promotion issues diminish in importance. When a school system has set up artificial goals that can be evaluated only in terms of achievement, schools become concerned with promotion from grade to grade. In situations where parents and teachers work together and where a school is still administered by a graded system, parents and teachers evaluate the growth of children and *jointly* decide whether or not he should "pass." This decision to hold a child back in a grade, thus causing him to adjust to a new group and a repetition (in many cases) of material is a serious one. Research has shown this can do as much harm as good. Such a decision should be made only when the teacher and parent feel assured it is for the good of the child. A modern school is concerned more with development and learning than with promoting. A creative teacher cannot exist without knowing her pupils, their home problems, and their living conditions at home. With home understanding and home cooperation, the teacher has set one of the best conditions for creative teaching.

Deferred Evaluation

Mention must be made here of one phase of evaluation peculiarly unique to creative development: *deferred judgment*. It has been mentioned often in this book and in others of the series. Research shows that creative development is enhanced when criticism or judgment is deferred until all ideas or products are before the group.

Criticism or evaluation offered too suddenly may act as a block to further creative development and may impede the creative process. It is well for teachers to remember this when using the techniques of group dynamics suggested in this chapter.

Creative Evaluation

Since creative development is the main topic of this series of books, a word must be said about its evaluation. Until recently, most creative growth in children was recognized and evaluated through the observation of the teacher and other adults who worked with children.

Since the intelligence test does not evaluate creative giftedness, many researchers are currently engaged in developing tests that *do* measure creativity. While many of these tests have not as yet been validated or checked for reliability, some are currently available for use[11] and have been effective up to this point. Teachers can add to

[11] The following sources are listed as sample tests on various aspects of creativity:

Raymond M. Berger and J. P. Guilford, *Match Problems* [divergent production] (Beverly Hills, Calif.: Sheridan Supply Company).

Raymond Berger, Arthur Gershon, J. P. Guilford, and Philip R. Merrifield, *Tests of Fluency, Flexibility and Elaboration with Figural Content* (Beverly Hills, Calif.: Sheridan Supply Company).

Paul R. Christensen and J. P. Guilford, *Word Fluency Tests, Ideational Fluency Tests, Associational Fluency Tests, Expressional Fluency Tests* (Beverly Hills, Calif.: Sheridan Supply Company).

Paul R. Christensen, P. R. Merrifield and J. P. Guilford, *Consequences* (Beverly Hills, Calif.: Sheridan Supply Company).

Paul R. Christensen, J. P. Guilford, P. R. Merrifield and Robert C. Wilson, *Alternate Uses Test* (Beverly Hills, Calif.: Sheridan Supply Company).

Sheldon Gardner, Arthur Gershon, Philip R. Merrifield, and J. P. Guilford, *Decorations* [test elaboration ability] (Beverly Hills, Calif.: Sheridan Supply Company).

Sheldon Gardner, Arthur Gershon, Philip R. Merrifield, and J. P. Guilford, *Making Objects* [tests divergent thinking] (Beverly Hills, Calif.: Sheridan Supply Company).

Arthur Gershon and J. P. Guilford, *Possible Jobs* [elaboration ability] (Beverly Hills, Calif.: Sheridan Supply Company).

Jacob W. Getzels and Philip W. Jackson, *Creativity and Intelligence* [test items published in text and in appendix] (New York: John Wiley & Sons, Inc., 1962).

Industrial Relations Center, *AC Test of Creative Ability* (Chicago: University of Chicago Press, 1959).

E. Paul Torrance, *Torrance Tests of Creative Thinking* (Princeton, N.J.: Personnel Press, Inc., 1966).

Kaoru Yamamoto, *Revised Scoring Manual for Tests of Creative Thinking* (Form VA and NVA) (Buffalo: Creative Research Foundation [mimeographed]).

the knowledge being gathered about these tests by using them with their classes and reporting their work to the authors of the test. Some have fairly high reliability and may be used to help teachers detect creative potential as well as the results of their creative teaching with children.

Summary

Group dynamics can be an agent for the developing of creativity among individuals and for building the necessary attitudes for accepting creative people and creative ideas. Many techniques for using group dynamics creatively have been discussed in this chapter. Among them is evaluation.

Evaluation is a very essential and integral part of the learning process. It is wide in scope and may be applied to the individual, the group, the process, or the program. It is that part of the learning process which lets us know where to start and to what degree we have been successful. It is recognized that while present-day techniques and methods of evaluation may be in keeping with today's knowledge regarding these matters, there is still opportunity for the improvement and refinement of both. And in the meantime, the existing evaluative practices with their admitted shortcomings are far superior to human judgment alone.

TO THE COLLEGE STUDENT

1. Make up evaluation check lists or self-evaluation sheets to use in your college class.

2. Think of all the ways you can where a sociogram would be of advantage to use in a college class (a flo-graph, a participation chart). Try some out in your class discussions and analyze the functions of each member of the class.

3. With your instructor, plan a series of classes using his topics but employing each of the techniques suggested in this chapter for developing social competence: the discussion, buzz groups, a panel discussion, and other democratic processes. Evaluate each class session in relation to its value as against the lecture system. List advantages and disadvantages of each type of class.

4. Brainstorm the following topics:
   a. Ways I Can Make History Interesting to My Fifth and Sixth Grade Students.
   b. Ideas I Can Use to Develop Creativity in a Unit on Canada.
   c. Field Trips I Can Take in My Town to Build Necessary Concepts in the Second Grade of Man's Interdependence.

5. Make a collection of report cards from many school systems —perhaps you can each bring a sample report card back to college from your home town when you go on vacation. Compare them. What does each really tell a parent? Do they have any consistency? Any great differences?

TO THE CLASSROOM TEACHER

1. Try using some of the evaluation devices suggested in this chapter, especially that of encouraging your students to help you make up a test as suggested on page 253. Think of ways you can evaluate children other than those mentioned here.

2. Examine your program and note what devices you are using each day to: (1) help your pupils evaluate themselves and (2) to help you evaluate your instructional program. Are they adequate? If not, determine which of the techniques discussed in this chapter you could begin to use.

3. Set up some evaluation criteria against which you can rate yourself as a teacher. Use it from time to time. Does an awareness of the objectives of good teaching as you have spelled them out on the evaluation sheet tend to improve your teaching?

4. In Book I of this series an evaluation sheet against which teachers may check themselves in terms of creative teaching is given on pages 196–198. Use it to check your own effectiveness as a creative teacher.

5. In what way does the nongraded school enhance creative development and the development of group skills? See if you can adapt some of the principals of nongradedness to your classroom if you are not in a nongraded school.

TO THE COLLEGE STUDENT
AND THE CLASSROOM TEACHER

1. Take half of a class of children and demonstrate the use of a funnel to them by using colored water, a pitcher, a funnel, and a can with a narrow opening. After the experiment, place the objects on a table before the group. Have the other half of the class return to the room, and ask *all* the children to write as many uses as they can think of for the objects on the table. Give them three minutes. Then compare the responses by *number* of items, *unusual uses* of responses and *variety* of items. If the group that did not see the demonstration has more responses and has come up with more ways to use them, you will have demonstrated the principle of functional fixedness.

2. New tests have been designed which predict creativity. Send for some and administer them to your class. Before you score them make lists of the children who you feel are most creative in your classroom. Then check your judgment against the test scores. How well can you identify creative children through observation?

3. Are there differences in the following terms? Discuss them or use the dictionary to observe what each means:

> evaluation   marking
> appraisal   reporting to parents
> testing   judgment
>   measuring

4. Set up a good rating scale for a student-teacher cooperating-teacher situation. Decide how you could use it most effectively.

SELECTED BIBLIOGRAPHY

AHMANN, J. STANLEY and MARVIN D. GLOCK. *Evaluating Pupil Growth.* Boston: Allyn and Bacon, Inc., 1959.

AMBROSE, EDNA and ALICE MIEL. *Children's Social Learning.* Washington, D.C.: Association for Supervision and Curriculum Development of the National Education Association, 1958.

ARMSTRONG, F. A. *Idea-Tracking.* New York: Criterion Books, 1960.

BARON, DENNIS and HAROLD W. BERNHARD. *Evaluation Techniques for Classroom Teachers.* New York: McGraw-Hill Book Company, 1958.

BIBER, B. "Premature Structuring as a Deterrent to Creativity," *American Journal of Orthopsychiatry,* 1959, *29,* 280–290.

BOTTRELL, HAROLD. *Teaching Tools.* Pittsburgh, Pennsylvania: The Boxwood Press, 1957.

BROWNELL, W. A. and G. HENDRICKSON. "How Children Learn Information, Concepts and Generalizations," *Learning and Instruction.* Forty-ninth Yearbook, Part I, National Society for the Study of Education. Chicago: University of Chicago Press, 1950.

CHORNESS, M. H. "Increasing Creativity in Problem-Solving Groups," *Journal of Communication,* 1958, *8,* 16–23.

CLARK, C. H. *Brainstorming.* Garden City, New York: Doubleday, 1958.

CRAWFORD, R. P. *How To Get Ideas.* Lincoln, Nebraska: University Associates, 1950.

CROW, LESTER D., ALICE CROW, and WALTER MURRAY. *Teaching in the Elementary School: Readings.* New York: Longmans, Green and Company, 1961.

DEPARTMENT OF SUPERVISION AND CURRICULUM DEVELOPMENT. *Group Planning in Education, 1945 Yearbook.* Washington, D.C.: The National Education Association, 1945.

FIEDLER, F. E. "Leader Attitudes, Group Climate, and Group Creativity," *Journal of Abnormal Social Psychology,* 1962, *65,* 308–18.

GIBB, J. R. "The Effects of Group Size and of Threat Reduction Upon Creativity in a Problem-Solving Situation," *Amer. Psychol.,* 1951, *6,* 324.

HENDRICKSON, P. R. and E. PAUL TORRANCE. "School Discipline and the Creative Personality," *East. Art. Educ. Res. Bulletin,* 1961, *18,* 36–42.

HOFFMAN, L. R. and G. CLAGETT. "Some Factors Affecting the Behavior of Members of Problem-Solving Groups," *Sociometry,* 1960, *23,* 273–91.

HOFFMAN, L. R., E. HARBURG and N. R. F. MAIER, "Differences and Disagreement as Factors in Creative Group Problem-Solving," *J. Abnorm Soc. Psychol.,* 1962, *64,* 206–14.

HOFFMAN, L. R. and N. R. F. MAIER, "Quality and Acceptance of Problem Solutions by Members of Homogeneous and Heterogeneous Groups," *J. Abnorm. Soc. Psych.,* 1961, *62,* 401–7.

MAIER, N. R. F. and L. R. HOFFMAN, "Quality of First and Second Solutions in Group Problem-Solving," *J. App. Psychology,* 1960, *44,* 278–82.

MAIER, N. R. F. and L. R. HOFFMAN. "Organization and Creative Problem Solving," *J. App. Psychol.,* 1961, *45,* 277–80.

MEADOW, A. S., J. PARNES and H. REESE. "Influence of Brainstorming Instruction and Problem Sequence on a Creative Problem-Solving Test," *J. App. Psychol.,* 1959, *43,* 413–16.

MERRITT, EDITH. *Working With Children in Social Studies.* San Francisco: Wadsworth Publishing Company, Inc., 1961, Chapter X.

MIEL, ALICE. *Cooperative Procedures in Planning.* New York: Bureau of Publications, Teachers College, Columbia University, 1952.

NORTHWAY, M. L. and M. McROOKS. "Creativity and Sociometric Status in Children," *Sociometry*, 1956, *18*, 450–57.

PARNES, S. J. "The Deferment-of-Judgment Principles: A Clarification of the Literature," *Psychol. Rep.*, 1963, *12*, 521–22.

PRESCOTT, DANIEL. *The Child and the Educative Process.* New York: McGraw-Hill Book Co., 1957.

RAPP, M. A. "Brainstorming Attitude," *School Arts*, 1960, *59*, 5–8.

TAYLOR, D. W., P. C. BERRY, and C. H. BLOCK. "Does Group Participation When Using Brainstorming Facilitate or Inhibit Creative Thinking?" *Adminis. Science Quart.*, 1958, *3*, 23–47.

TORRANCE, E. PAUL. *Role of Evaluation in Creative Thinking.* University of Minnesota: Bureau of Educational Research, 1964.

WEISSKOPF-JOELSON, E. A. and T. S. ELISEO. "An Experimental Study of the Effectiveness of Brainstorming," *J. App. Psychol.*, 1961, *45*, 45–49.

WRIGHTSTONE, J. WAYNE et al., *Evaluation in Modern Education.* New York: American Book Co., 1956.

ZILLER, R. C. "Group Creativity Under Conditions of Success or Failure and Variations in Group Stability," *J. App. Psychology*, 1962, *46*, 43–49.

Conclusion

. . . To build any desired trait of character, the individual must *live* that trait: he must behave that way and in a setting which he feels properly calls for that behavior.[1]

WILLIAM HEARD KILPATRICK

Summary

The social studies concept in the American public school has never reached full fruition on a mass scale. The relationship between the product of the public school and the methodology and teaching in the public school cannot be denied.

The basic purpose of the social studies program is to develop the citizen for the democratic society. Too often this has been interpreted to mean the perpetuation of knowledge of the past and present. But this is not enough. No culture has ever survived which lacked a basic set of standards, values, morals, appreciations, and a certain character. If the elementary school is to continue to hold as one of its precious objectives that of providing a general education for all its young citizenry, it must teach the knowledges and truths of the past and present as well as those standards and values which serve to preserve the culture. To do this, a unique methodology is required. As Kilpatrick has pointed out in the quote that introduces this chapter, traits in individuals are developed when they are *lived*. Dewey's concept of the elementary school as a small society which prepares its young citizens to take their place in a larger society is still sound. Children will have to *live* their way of life as children before they can *live* a way of life as adults.

The most precious commodity of any society is its children. The child born into the American democratic society stands a greater chance of fulfilling his destiny than in any other place on earth—but only if he understands the world in which he lives through his knowledge and interpretation of it; only if he possesses the skills and techniques needed to take an active part in it; only if he covets certain attitudes, values, and appreciations toward it; and only if his mind

---

[1] William Heard Kilpatrick, *Philosophy of Education* (New York: The Macmillan Company, 1951), p. 366.

has been stimulated to its *fullest* development so that his knowledges, skills, values and appreciations can serve him to build a better life for himself and all of mankind.

To develop any mind to its fullest, as Guilford has pointed out, we must now direct our attention to the *creative potential* in each individual by considering the development of those *divergent* thinking processes that were so neglected in the past. If the creative potential of each individual could be released, what a dynamic force would be set free to cope with the problems of a troubled world!

Part of this can be done by a reassessment of the social studies program, the preservation of methods that now produce creative acts, and the implementation of new methods that will develop the potential and understanding for creative and aesthetic living together.

When the concept of creativity is applied to social studies teaching, individualism and individual worth in a democratic society take on a new dimension. And the teaching of the social studies, if it is to accomplish its goals, must take on new dimensions also.

Social studies programs throughout the country need to' be revamped in terms of our new understandings. The creative teachers of the nation will use the new concept and come up with ideas much more creative than those presented here. But these are all too few, and teacher-training institutions will also need to revamp methods courses in social studies so that new, young teachers can develop their own creativity and realize its fulfillment in their own teaching.

Creative teaching can be a dynamic force in developing the character of the nation. Creative teaching knows no limits in developing an exciting, stimulating approach to learning.

This book has only scratched the surface. But at least it *is* a start in the right direction.

SELECTED BIBLIOGRAPHY

COSNER, E. I. "What is Creativity in the Curriculum?" *Mid. Sch.*, 1960, 75, 22–23.

DUNKEL, H. B. "Creativity and Education." *Education Theory*, 1961, 11, 209–16.

FORSULAND, J. E. "Inquiry Into the Nature of Creative Teaching," *Journal of Education,* 1962, 143, 72–82.

FRENCH, R. L. "Research as a Basis for Creative Teaching." *Educational Horizons*, 1961, 40, 28–34.

GRUEN, W. "Utilization of Creative Potential in our Society." *J. Counsel. Psychol.*, 1962, 1, 79–83.

KNELLER, GEORGE F. *The Art and Science of Creativity*. New York: Holt, Rinehart and Winston, 1965.

LEVINGER, LEAH. "The Teacher's Role in Creativity Discussion," *American Journal of Orthopsychiatry*, 1959, *29*, 291–97.

MIEL, ALICE (ed.). *Creativity in Teaching*. Belmont, California: Wadsworth Publishing Co., 1961.

PARNES, S. J. "Education and Creativity," *Teachers Coll. Rec.*, 1963, *64*, 331–39.

REED, G. G. *Developing Creative Talent*. New York: Vantage Press, 1962.

RUBIN, L. J. "Creativity and the Curriculum," *Phi Delta Kappan*, 1962, *44*, 438–40.

RUGG, H. *Imagination*. New York: Harper & Row, 1963.

SCOTT, J. D. (ed.). *The Creative Process*. Ann Arbor: Bureau of Business Research, University of Michigan, 1957.

TAYLOR, C. W. and J. L. HOLLAND. "Development and Application of Tests of Creativity," *Rev. Ed. Res.*, 1962, *32*, 91–102.

TORRANCE, E. P. *Creativity: What Research Says to the Teacher*. Washington, D.C.: National Education Association of the United States, 1963.

————. *Education and the Creative Potential*. Minneapolis: University of Minnesota Press, 1963.

————. *Guiding Creative Talent*. Englewood Cliffs, N.J.: Prentice-Hall, Inc., 1962.

————. *Rewarding Creative Behavior Experiments in Classroom Creativity*. Englewood Cliffs, N.J.: Prentice-Hall, Inc., 1965.

WEISSKOPF-JOELSON, E. A. "Some Comments Concerning the Role of Education in the Creation of Creation," *Journal of Education Psychology*, 1951, *42*, 185–89.

WERTHEIMER, M. *Productive Thinking*. New York: Harper & Row, 1962.

ZIRBES, LAURA. *Spurs to Creative Teaching*. New York: G. P. Putnam's Sons, 1959.

Index

Activities:
  audio-visual aids, 220–227
  brainstorming, 242–244
  buzz groups, 241–242
  for concept development, inter-
    mediate grades, 135–138
  for critical thinking, 153–157
  culminating, samples of, 86–88
  for decision-making, 143–145
  to develop creative thinking,
    147–149
  evaluation, 244–264
  open-ended stories and, 176–178
  for passing judgment, 143–145
  for problem-solving, 145–147,
    186–190
  problem stories, 179–185
  to promote planning, sixth grade,
    75
  to promote research, 132–133
  puppets, 175
  putting knowledge to work, 130–
    131
  role-playing, 163–166
  role reversal, 163–166
  sample problem-solving, grade
    six, 186–190
  sociodrama, 166
  structured dramatization, 167–
    176
  study skills and, 204
  throughout unit, 91
Adamson, R. E.:
  cited, 197
Anticipation, study skills and, 198–
  199
Appreciations, as goals, 28
Asch, S. E.:
  cited, 234

Attitudes, as goals, 27
Audience type motivation, for study
  skills, 205
Audio-visual aids:
  creative teaching and, 220–227
  creative uses, 224–226
  uses, 222–224
Autobiographies, logs, 255

Barrows, Harlan H.:
  cited, 134
Biber, Barbara:
  cited, 234
Bibliotherapy, in problem-solving,
  185–186
Bloom, B. S.:
  cited, 16
Brainstorming, 242–244
Brogan, Peggy:
  quoted, 80
Buzz groups, in teaching unit, 85

Centers, room, 49–52
Character development, values and,
  159–191
Characteristics:
  of creative people, 34–35
  as goals, 28
Children, creative:
  characteristics, 37–40
  social-emotional nature, 34
Cleveland, Helen:
  cited, 187–189
Committees, in unit teaching, 85–
  87
Concepts, textbooks and, 135–138

Conditions:
for creative teaching, 47–57
intellectual, for creative teaching, 55–56
physical environment, appropriate, 48–52
as a principle, 12
psychological, for social growth, 54
social-emotional, 53–54
Conferences:
pupil-teacher evaluation, 246–250
report cards and, 261–264
Conformity, in groups, 232–233
Content, selecting in units, 103
Controversial issues, example, 144–145
Creative development through textbooks, 125–156
Creative evaluation, 265
Creative teaching:
through activities, sixth grade sample, 187–189
through audio-visual aids, 220–227
brainstorming and, 242–244
buzz groups, 241–242
of character development, 159–191
dramatization and, 160–163
example, second grade, 3–7
open-ended stories and, 176–178
principles basic to, 3–18
problem picture and, 180–185
with problem stories, 179–180
puppets and, 175
role-playing and, 163–166
role-reversal and, 163–166
for study skills, conditions, 195–196
of study skills, 194–216
of values, 159–191
Creative thinking, textbook concepts and, 135–138
Creativity:
audio-visual aids and, 220–227
basic principles, 16–17
definition, 8

grouping and, 36
individualism and, 108–120
intelligence and, 38–39
as method of teaching, 17–18
nurture in social studies, 45–72
parent attitude and, 38–39
social living and, 47–57
social studies and, 271–272
social-emotional nature, 34–40
textbooks and, 125–156, 147–149
as way of living, 63
Critical thinking:
as study skill, 198, 199–200
textbooks and, 149–155
Criticism, constructive, as a principle, 13–14
Culminating activities, unit on Mexico, 86–88
Cumulative records, 257–258

Decision-making, textbooks and, 138–145
Definitions:
social living, 23
social sciences, 23
social studies, 23
Democratic principles of living, 230–231
Democratic processes, as a principle, 14
Development, creative, contribution of unit teaching to, 103–104
Discussion:
for group living, 233
group processes and, 233–240
outline for, 235–236
and reading, as study skill, 209–210
Divergent thinking, as principle, 9–10
Donley, D. T.:
cited, 112
Dow, Allen:
quoted, 34

Dramatization:
  example of structured dramatization, 3–7
  examples of, 161–162
  situations for use, 163
  structured, for problem-solving, 167–176
  structured, sample in sixth grade, 167–175
  as study skill, 210–211
  value building with, 161–163
Drummond, Harold D.:
  cited, 187

Educational Policies Commission, goals for educated person, 25–26
Emotional-social conditions for teaching, 53–54
Environment, physical, for creative teaching, 48–52
Estes, Eleanor:
  cited, 185
Evaluation:
  autobiographies and logs, 255
  check list, 253
  creative, 265
  deferred, 265
  devices, 244–266
  chart for graphs and, 254–255
  group, 257–258
  listening skill in, 246–247
  observation in. 245–246
  as principle, 13–14
  pupil-made tests and, 253
  pupil-teacher conferences, 246–250
  rating scales, 249–254
  reporting to parents, 261–264
  self-evaluating stories, 255
  self-evaluation, 245–256
  skills, 244–264
  sociometric techniques, 258
  standardized tests, 254
  teacher-made tests and, 252
Experiences, study skill and, 211
Eyring, Henry:
  quoted, 194

Fifth grade, grouping plan, 112–120
Files, pupil, 254–256
Film problems, problem-solving with, 186
Filmstrips:
  problem-solving with, 186
  values and, 186
First grade, planning in, 66–72
Flo-graph, 237–240
Foundation of Research, Ann Arbor:
  cited, 232, 233
Fromm, Eric:
  quoted, 47

Getzels, Jacob W.:
  cited, 38
Gifted child, in heterogeneous grouping, 112–120
Goals, Educational Policies Commission, 25–26
Graphs and charts, 254–255
Group living:
  buzz groups and, 241–242
  discussion in, 223
  skills, 230–266
  sociometric techniques, 258
Group processes:
  brainstorming in, 242–244
  buzz groups in, 241–242
  discussion in, 233–240
  evaluation, 244–264
  study skills and, 205
Group skills, for studying, 203–204
Grouping:
  creativity and, 36
  example, fifth grade, 112–120
  fallacies in plans, 109–110
  individual development and, 112–120
  kinds of, 119
  natural and interest, 258–260
  skills in group living, 230–233
Guilford, J. P.:
  cited, 16, 244

Handlin, Oscar:
  cited, 126
Handwriting, place in elementary school, 201–204

Individual differences:
  meeting through organizational plans, 108–120
  in unit planning, 90
Individualism:
  creativity and, 108–120
  principle of, 12
  social studies and, 271–272
Information, sources for unit, grade five, 85
Intellectual conditions, for social living, 55–56
Intelligence and creativity, 38–39

Jackson, Philip W.:
  cited, 38
Judgment-passing, textbooks and, 138–145

Kilpatrick, William Heard:
  cited, 271
Kindergarten:
  planning in, 65–66
  sample units, 92–99
Knowledges:
  as goals, 28
  put to work in textbooks, 128–130

Learning, self-initiated, as a principle, 13
Levinger, Leah:
  cited, 159
Lorette, R. L.:
  cited, 112

Manipulation, as a principle, 14
Map skills, study for, 207–209

Marksberry, Mary Lee:
  cited, 12
May, Rollo:
  quoted, 3
Method, scientific, 100
Methods, unique for developing creativity, 14–15
Mexico, unit on, 82–92
Michaelis, John:
  quoted, 22
Moralizing, 9
Motivation:
  through audio-visual aids, 222
  tensions and creativity, 10
Moving-picture film, use of, 221–222

Nature of social studies, 1–43

Objectives:
  in kindergarten units, 92–93
  school example, 27–29
  skills, sample, 194–195
  social studies, 22–29
Open-ended story:
  in building values, 176–178
  samples, 176–178
Open-endedness, as a principle, 10
Organizational plans:
  grouping in, 108–120
  individualism and, 108–112
Organizational skills, 61–76
Original sources, developing study skills with, 214–215
Osborn, Alex F.:
  cited, 15
Outcomes:
  as a principle, 11
  unit teaching, 80–82
Outlines, as study skill, 201–203

Panel discussion, in group living, 241–242
Parent attitude, creativity and, 38–39

Parker, Edith Putnam:
cited, 134
Parnes, Sidney J.:
cited, 15
Pictures, as study aid, 201
Plan book, sample pages, grade
five, 89–92
Planning:
in first grade, 66–72
guides for first grade, 71–72
guides for kindergarten, 66
in kindergarten, 65–66
organization ideas, 64–65
pupil-teacher, 62–76
in sixth grade, 72–76
Plans, sample pages kindergarten
teachers unit, 92–99
Preconscious thinking, as a principle, 11
Principles:
basic to creative teaching, 3-18
creative teaching and social
studies, 8–16
of creativity, 16–17
Problem picture:
sample, fourth grade, 180–185
value building and, 180–185
Problem stories, problem-solving
with, 179–180
Problem-solving:
through activities, 186–190
bibliotherapy and, 185–186
dramatization and, 160–163
with filmstrips, 186
open-ended stories for, 176–178
problem stories and, 179–180
puppets and, 175
role-playing and, 163–166
sociodrama and, 166
as start of unit, 82–83
structured dramatization and,
167–176
textbooks and, 145–147
Problems in critical thinking, 150–
153
Process, creative, as a principle, 12
Processes, group:
discussion in, 233–240
observations for, 232

Product, creative, as a principle, 12
Psychological conditions, for creative social growth, 54
Pupil-made tests, evaluation and,
253
Pupil-teacher planning:
elementary school, 62–76
example, first grade, 66–72
example, kindergarten, 65–66
importance, 76
sixth-grade example, 27–76

Questions, critical thinking and,
150

Rating scales, sample, 249
Reading, as study skill, 209–210
Report cards, 261–264
Reporting to parents, 261–264
Research:
activities stimulated by textbook,
131–132
group conformity and, 232–233
kinds, 131–132
social-emotional characteristics,
34–40
ways to conduct, 211–213
Robinson, Frances P.:
cited, 196
Roe, Anne:
cited, 248
Role-playing:
creative teaching and, 163–166
examples of, 164–165
situations, intermediate grades,
165–166
situations, lower grades, 165
Role-reversal, character development and, 163–166
Rugg, Harold:
cited, 37
quoted, 61

Sanders, Norris M.:
cited, 16
Sargent, Dick:
picture by, 182

Scientific method, as creative social learning, 100
School objectives, sample, 27–29
Self-evaluating stories, 255
Self-evaluation:
    check list, 252
    social studies and, 245–256
Seuss, Dr.:
    cited, 185
Singer, L. W. Co.:
    cited, 197
Sixth grade, planning in, 72–76
Skills:
    buzz groups in problem-solving, 241–242
    creative conditions for teaching, 195–196
    of evaluation, 244–264
    as goals, 27
    of group living, 230–266
    organizational, 61–76
    pupil-teacher conferences, 246–250
    pupil-teacher planning, 61–76
Slobodkin, Louis:
    cited, 185
Slow-learner, in heterogeneous grouping, 112–120
Smith, James A.:
    cited, 7, 15, 47, 53, 54, 111, 112, 125, 128, 136, 197, 215, 224, 225, 226
Social-emotional:
    conditions for teaching, 53–54
    nature of creativity, 34–40
Social living:
    creative, 47–57
    definition, 23
    objectives, 25–29
Social sciences:
    definition, 23
Social studies:
    definition, 23
    definition extended, 29
    nature of, 1–43
    to nurture creativity, 45–72
    principles of creative teaching and, 8–16
    purposes, 271

purposes and objectives, 22–29
social-emotional creative nature, 34–40
unit teaching and, 80–104
Socialization process, creativity and, 34–40
Sociodrama, in social problems, 166
Sociometric techniques, 258
Sorenson, Clarence W.:
    cited, 134
Space Age, teaching, 23
Spoerl, Dorothy T.:
    cited, 176
Spyri, Johanna:
    cited, 135
Standardized tests, 254
Stoddard, George:
    quoted, 125, 127
Structured dramatization:
    example, 3–7
Study skills:
    activities and, 204
    anticipation and, 198–199
    audience-type motivation and, 205
    creative teaching of, 194–216
    critical thinking and, 198, 199–200
    discussion as, 209–210
    dramatizations and, 210–211
    experiences developed for, 211
    group processes and, 205
    group skills and, 203–204
    map reading, 207–209
    original sources as, 214–215
    pictures as aid, 201
    reading and, 209–210
    reference list, 215
    research and, 211–213
    subheadings as aid to, 200–201
    teaching in intermediate grades, 198–215
    teaching in primary grades, 197–198
    using outlining for, 201–203
    using supplementary materials, 206

Subheadings, as study skill, 200–201
Success, as a principle, 12–13
Supplementary materials:
  for study skills, 206
  textbook and, 133–135
Swartout, Sherwin G.:
  cited, 202

Teacher-made tests, 252
Textbooks:
  concept-building and, 135–138
  creative research activities and, 131–133
  creative thinking and, 147–149
  critical thinking and, 149–155
  decision-making and, 138–145
  making judgments and, 138–145
  problem-solving and, 145–147
  as resource material, 127–155
  supplementary material and, 133–135
  uses of, common, 128
  uses to develop creativity, 125–156
Thomas, R. Murray:
  cited, 202
Torrance, E. Paul:
  cited, 35, 36
  ideal child checklist, 39
  What Kind of Person Are You? 39
Traits, as goals, 29

Understandings, in unit teaching, 89–91

Unit:
  first steps, grade five, 90
  in kindergarten, 92–99
  steps in studying, 83
  teaching example, gradė five, 82–92
Unit teaching:
  character development and, 159–160
  content, selecting, 101–103
  contribution to creative development, 103–104
  criteria for content, 103
  social studies and, 80–104
  outcomes, 80–82
  values and, 159–160
Utz, Tom:
  picture by, 181

Values:
  bibliotherapy and, 185–186
  character development and, 159–191
  creative teaching of, 159–191
  dramatization for development, 160–163
  as goals, 27–28
  open-ended stories and, 176–178
  problem picture and, 180–185
  puppets and, 175
  sociodramas and, 166
VonFange, Eugene:
  quoted, 159

Westcott, Alvin M.:
  cited, 225